Technology Transfer to the USSR, 1928-1937 and 1966-1975

Westview Replica Editions

This book is a Westview Replica Edition. The concept of Replica Editions is a response to the crisis in academic and informational publishing. Library budgets for books have been severely curtailed; economic pressures on the university presses and the few private publishing companies primarily interested in scholarly manuscripts have severely limited the capacity of the industry to properly serve the academic and research communities. Many manuscripts dealing with important subjects, often representing the highest level of scholarship, are today not economically viable publishing projects. Or, if they are accepted for publication, they are often subject to lead times ranging from one to three years. Scholars are understandably frustrated when they realize that their first-class research cannot be published within a reasonable time frame, if at all.

Westview Replica Editions are our practical solution to the problem. The concept is simple. We accept a manuscript in camera-ready form and move it immediately into the production process. The responsibility for textual and copy editing lies with the author or sponsoring organization. If necessary we will advise the author on proper preparation of footnotes and bibliography. We prefer that the manuscript be typed according to our specifications, though it may be acceptable as typed for a dissertation or prepared in some other clearly organized and readable way. The end result is a book produced by lithography and bound in hard covers. Initial edition sizes range from 400 to 600 copies, and a number of recent Replicas are already in second printings. We include among Westview Replica Editions only works of outstanding scholarly quality or of great informational value, and we will continue to exercise our usual editorial standards and quality control.

Technology Transfer to the USSR, 1928-1937 and 1966-1975: The Role of Western Technology in Soviet Economic Development

George D. Holliday

This analysis of the basic Soviet orientation to the international economy in general, and to Western technology in particular, examines the Soviet experience in borrowing technology from the West during two periods, 1928-1937 and 1966-1975. It includes case studies of three major projects in the Soviet automotive industry.

Dr. Holliday studies the methods used by the Soviet Union to acquire foreign technology and evaluates the impact of Soviet attitudes, policies, and economic institutions on the technology transfer process. The evidence he presents--a new Soviet economic growth strategy that places emphasis on technological change, new attitudes among Soviet political leaders, and new institutional developments--suggests that Soviet policy is undergoing a gradual but definitive change away from the isolationist approach of the Stalinist period toward a policy of greater technological interdependence with the West.

George D. Holliday is an analyst in international trade and finance with the Congressional Research Service, Library of Congress.

Technology Transfer to the USSR, 1928-1937 and 1966-1975: The Role of Western Technology in Soviet Economic Development

George D. Holliday

Westview Press/Boulder, Colorado

A Westview Replica Edition

Published in 1979 in the United States of America by
    Westview Press, Inc.
    5500 Central Avenue
    Boulder, Colorado 80301
    Frederick A. Praeger, Publisher

Library of Congress Catalog Card Number: 79-4138
ISBN: 0-89158-189-8

Printed and bound in the United States of America

Contents

Tables

Acknowledgments

I wish to acknowledge the assistance of
Dr. Charles F. Elliott and Dr. John P. Hardt. Their
guidance, encouragement and gentle prodding contributed greatly to the completion of this research.

The Institute for Sino-Soviet Studies and the
Graduate Program in Science, Technology, and Public
Policy of the George Washington University gave
valuable financial assistance.

The final manuscript reflects the diligent
and expert typing assistance of Mary Helen Holliday
Seal.

I owe a special debt of gratitude to my wife,
Marsha, for her moral and intellectual support, for
her professional assistance in library matters and
for her forbearance. My daughter Lara, who at a
very early age learned the importance of silence
for scholarly research, also made an important
contribution.

Technology Transfer to the USSR, 1928-1937 and 1966-1975

1. Introduction

From the mid-1960s to the mid-1970s the Soviet
Union experienced a rapid increase in the scale of
its commercial relations with the industrial West.
An important component of these relations was the
transfer of modern industrial technologies from the
West to the Soviet Union. The Soviet experience
during this period contrasts with a much lower level
of commercial exchanges during the preceding three
decades, but is reminiscent of Soviet-Western commercial relations during the First Five-Year Plan
(1928-1932). During the First Five-Year Plan, as
during the 1960s and 1970s, Soviet industry was the
recipient of large-scale transfers of Western technologies which were critical to Soviet industrial
development plans. The resurgence of Soviet commercial relations with the West has generated considerable interest in Soviet policy making in this realm.
Western firms are studying this phenomenom in an
effort to determine if the Soviet Union is a profit-
able market for their products. Western governments
are interested not only in the prospective economic
benefits, but also in the political and national
security implications of wider commercial ties to
the Soviet Union.
Questions involving technology transfer command
a more general interest in the world today. This
interest has been sparked largely by a new awareness
of the central role of technology in economic growth.
The "technology gap" between advanced industrial
countries and the developing countries is widely
perceived to be a major cause of the uneven distribution of world production. The borrowing of technology from the more technologically advanced countries appears to be a key to economic development.
Technology transfer is also becoming an increasingly
important component of trade relations among the

1

advanced industrial nations. While Western-Soviet technological relations are in some ways unique, they appear to be largely an element of the world's growing technological interdependence.

PURPOSE

The purpose of this study is to examine the Soviet experience in borrowing technology from the West during two periods, 1928-1937 and 1966-1975. Specifically, this study analyzes the methods used by the Soviet Union to acquire foreign technology and evaluates the impact of Soviet attitudes, policies, and economic institutions on the technology transfer process. Central to the purpose of this study is an analysis of the basic Soviet orientation to the international economy in general and to Western technology in particular. A survey of the Western and Soviet literature on the subject reveals three basic hypotheses about the expansion of Soviet commercial and technological ties to the West since the mid-1960s.[1] The first hypothesis stresses the Soviet quest for autarky or economic self-sufficiency in its commercial relations with the West:

> HYPOTHESIS I: The recent upsurge in Soviet trade with the West is part of a cyclical pattern that is observable in the past, most recently during the First Five-Year Plan. Economic historians have pointed to similar periods in pre-Revolutionary Russia, such as the era of Peter the Great and 1890s and early 1900s. Soviet economic planners follow a strategy of importing as much Western technology as they need to modernize the economy and then cutting off or cutting back to a minimum economic ties with the West. Thus, they pursue a deliberate policy of autarky or economic self-sufficiency, interrupted by occasional expedient resorts to borrowing foreign technology in order to catch up with the West.[2]

The second hypothesis accepts this characterization for pre-World War II Soviet policy, but maintains that the basic Soviet orientation to the international economy has changed:

> HYPOTHESIS II: Soviet leaders have a fundamentally different orientation to the international economy today. Autarky or self-

2

sufficiency was the goal of Soviet foreign
economic policy during the 1930s (and during
certain Tsarist periods). However, the current
leadership has rejected this strategy in favor
of a policy of technological interdependence
or "interrelatedness" with the West. The new
policy portends continued and deeper commercial
and technological ties with the West.[3]

A third hypothesis, propounded by many Soviet observers and by some Western scholars, rejects both explanations. Its proponents maintain that a reduction of Soviet trade with the West in the 1930s was
necessitated by the need to protect the Soviet economy from hostile Western governments and by economic
factors beyond the control of Soviet policy makers.
They stress the continuity in the Soviet Government's
policy of promoting trade with the West:

> HYPOTHESIS III: The Soviet Union pursued a
> goal of economic and technological independence
> in the pre-War period in order to protect it-
> self against a "hostile capitalist encircle-
> ment." It has not followed a policy of autarky,
> but has consistently encouraged trade with all
> countries. Commercial relations with the West
> were poor in the 1930s and in the early post-
> War period because of trade restrictions and
> other hostile actions by Western governments
> and capitalist companies and bankers. Trade
> relations also worsened because of the inter-
> national economic situation. The recent up-
> surge in Soviet trade with the West is explained
> by a repudiation by current Western governments
> of their old policies.[4]

In this study, the validity of the three hypotheses
as explanations of Soviet foreign economic policy is
tested.
To put the central question of the basic Soviet
orientation to the international economy into perspective two related questions are examined. First,
how does the Soviet experience as a recipient of
foreign technology compare with the experiences of
other countries? Second, what has been the role of
Western technology in Soviet economic development?
(A variation of the second question is: How dependent is the Soviet Union on Western technology as a
source for technological change?) The answer to the
first question details what is unique and what is
commonplace in the Soviet approach and highlights

3

the impact of uniquely Soviet attitudes and institutions on the technology transfer process. The answer to the second question sheds light on the motivations of Soviet foreign economic policy and provides a basis for discussing the prospects for future Soviet commercial relations with the West.

A curious feature of Soviet technology borrowing is that many of the basic conditions (as identified in the Western literature) for successful technology transfers do not appear to be in place. For example, the movement of people across international boundaries is generally regarded as crucial to the effectiveness of international technology transfers. Yet, Soviet authorities have discouraged the free movement of people into and out of the Soviet Union. The official attitude toward foreigners visiting the Soviet Union has varied from outright hostility to suspicious tolerance. Likewise, while foreign direct investment has been a major mechanism for technology transfer to most countries, foreign ownership of the means of production in the Soviet Union is forbidden by Soviet law. Furthermore, Western export controls, restrictions on credit, and various other official barriers at times have complicated the transfer of technology to the Soviet Union.

In view of such barriers to technology transfer, has Western technology made a major contribution to Soviet industrial development? Western scholars tend to credit Soviet industry with achieving a considerable level of technology sophistication largely by importing Western technology. Abram Bergson, for example, finds that "in transforming its production methods under the five-year plans, the U.S.S.R. has been able to borrow technology from abroad on an extraordinary scale."[5] A more extreme version of this viewpoint is expressed by Antony Sutton in his studies of the earlier period of Soviet technology borrowing: "...without assistance from capitalist countries, the Soviet Union would not have had the technical resources to make any economic progress in the 1930s and 1940s."[6] Sutton's thesis is in direct contradiction to the views generally expressed by contemporary Soviet observers. For example, V. I. Kasianenko maintains that "concessions and agreements for technical assistance did not play an important role in Soviet industrial development."[7]

Has the Soviet Union succeeded in absorbing Western technology on a large scale? If so, how was this accomplished in view of the absence of key factors generally believed to facilitate technology transfer? A central purpose of this study is to attempt an answer to this apparent paradox.

4

SCOPE AND LIMITATIONS

The focus of this research is on Soviet foreign economic policy. Consequently, it concentrates on attitudes toward foreign economic relations and methods of borrowing technology, rather than on technological developments in the Soviet automotive industry. The latter is discussed in order to illustrate the extent of Soviet technology borrowing, Soviet ability to absorb Western technology and Soviet ability to generate indigenous technological innovation. However, the emphasis is on the technology transfer process and not on Soviet automotive engineering.

Moreover, the focus on Soviet policy precludes an exhaustive inquiry into the marketing strategies of Western firms vis-a-vis the Soviet market or Western government policy issues surrounding the transfer of technology to the Soviet Union. Although the conclusions clearly have implications for Western corporate and government policy issues, a thorough examination of such issues is outside the realm of the study. Thus, for example, while Western export controls on high technology exports to the Soviet Union are identified as part of the international economic environment in which Soviet decision makers operate, no attempt is made to weigh the costs and benefits of such policies.

The research is also limited chronologically. The periods 1928-1937 and 1966-1975 were selected because they are periods of intensive technology borrowing from the West, uninterrupted by war or revolution. Other technology transfers, such as the occasional passive imports of technology during the interim period, receive only peripheral attention.

METHODOLOGY

A case study of the Soviet automotive industry provides the basis for analyzing Soviet mechanisms for borrowing foreign technology. An attempt is made to identify the kinds of automotive technology imported from the West and to describe the institutions involved in the technology transfer process. The Soviet leadership's rationale for importing technology and the industry's effectiveness in absorbing foreign technology are examined. The case study is used to illustrate overall Soviet policies and techniques related to technology transfer.

The Soviet automotive industry was selected as a

case study because it has been one of the high-priority areas of Soviet technology borrowing and provides examples of technology transfer in the two periods of intensive Soviet interest in Western technology. The case study concentrates on three major projects in the Soviet automotive industry: the Gorkii Automobile Plant (built with the assistance of Ford Motor Company in the late 1920s and early 1930s); the Volga Automobile Plant (built with the primary assistance of the Italian firm FIAT in the late 1960s); and the Kama River Truck Plant (built during the 1970s with assistance from a number of Western firms).

Additional case studies of Western technology transfer to other sectors of the Soviet economy would be a useful means of testing the conclusions of this study. One of the advantages of the case study approach is that it allows a close examination of the specialized, technical literature related to a single branch of industry. In the Soviet Union, technical writers frequently have been more candid and outspoken than social scientists and policy makers about Soviet industrial developments. Much of the Soviet technical and specialized literature has not been adequately explored by Western students of the Soviet system. Thus, case studies in other sectors of the economy may provide additional insights into the Soviet experience as a technology borrower.

An overview of the general literature on technology and technology transfer provides a conceptual framework for analyzing Western technology transfers to the Soviet Union. The extensive literature on this subject has not provided general, widely accepted theoretical models of technology transfer which might assist in analyzing Western technology transfer to the Soviet Union. However, it does provide a clearer understanding of the role of technology in economic growth as well as some insights into international movements of technology. In addition, descriptive studies of technology transfers in various parts of the world have highlighted many of the practical problems involved and the prerequisites for making such transfers effective. This study attempts to put the Soviet experience as a technology borrower into perspective by relating it to our general understanding of technology and the technology transfer process. In other words, Western technology transfer to the Soviet Union is viewed as a part of the general phenomenon of international technology transfer.

ORGANIZATION OF STUDY

The broad parameters of international technology transfer and Western technology transfer to the Soviet Union are discussed in Chapters 2, 3, and 4. Together, these chapters are intended to provide perspective to the central themes of this study. They are followed in Chapters 5 and 6 by a case study, which offers more specific and concrete evidence, against which the general propositions are tested. In Chapter 7, the major conclusions of the case study are summarized and related to the main questions of the study.

The general discussion of technology transfer begins with a definition of terms and a brief survey of the major theoretical contributions on technology and economic growth and technology and trade. This is followed by a description of the mechanisms of technology transfer and an analysis of the empirical or "wisdom literature" on the technology transfer process. The problems and issues involved in technology transfers in various parts of the world are described in order to provide a basis for comparing the Soviet experience.

Chapters 3 and 4 provide general evidence to test the major propositions of the study. First, Chapter 3 provides, where possible, quantitative data to illustrate the trends in Soviet technology borrowing. The quantitative data are followed by a discussion of the Stalinist and post-Stalinist models for economic development, with an emphasis on the role of technology. In Chapter 4, two sections, describing the evolution of elite attitudes and institutional arrangements related to Western technology imports, conclude the general analysis of the Soviet Union's economic and technological ties with the West.

In the case study, comprising Chapters 5 and 6, Western technology transfers to the Soviet automotive industry are examined in detail. Chapter 5 concentrates on the construction of the Gorkii Automobile Plant during the First Five-Year Plan, and Chapter 6, on the major automotive projects of the 1966-1975 period--the Volga Automobile Plant and the Kama River Truck Plant. The case study includes a more detailed discussion of Soviet techniques and motivations for borrowing foreign technology and provides evidence of elements of change and continuity in Soviet foreign economic relations.

In Chapter 7, the conclusions, the results of the case study are summarized, and evidence is

presented with regard to: (1) the basic Soviet
orientation to the international economy; (2) the
contribution of Western technology to Soviet industrial development; and (3) the unique and common
features of Soviet techniques for importing foreign
technology.

NOTES
    1. To some extent, all of the hypotheses are
oversimplified and represent composits of the views
of many different observers. No attempt is made here
to identify any of the hypothesis with a single person. However, several works are cited in which views
are expressed which are related, in part, to the
hypotheses.
    2. Alexander Gerschenkron, Economic Backwardness
in Historical Perspective (New York: Frederick A.
Praeger, 1965), pp. 17-18. See also the discussion
of Communist autarky in Alan A. Brown and Egon
Neuberger, eds., International Trade and Central
Planning: An analysis of Economic Interactions
(Berkeley: University of California Press, 1968),
passim.
    3. Glen Alden Smith, Soviet Foreign Trade:
Organization, Operations and Policy, 1918-1971 (New
York: Praeger Publishers, 1973), pp. 284-286;
J. Wilczynski, The Multinationals and East-West
Relations: Towards Transideological Collaboration
(Boulder, Colorado: Westview Press, 1976), pp. 191-
195; Herbert S. Levine et al., Transfer of U.S.
Technology to the Soviet Union: Impact on U.S.
Commercial Interests (Stanford Research Institute
SRI Project 3543, February 1976), pp. 36-50.
    4. A. Frumkin, "O nekotorykh burzhuaznykh
vzgliadakh na sovetskuiu torgovliu," Vneshniaia
torgovlia, October, 1974, p. 49; Iu. N. Kapelinskii,
Torgovlia SSSR s kapitalisticheskimi stranami posle
vtoroi mirovoi voiny (Moscow: Isdatel'stvo
"mezhdunarodnye otnosheniia," 1970). Michael R.
Dohan places primary emphasis on the economic factors in "The Economic Origins of Soviet Autarky
1927/28-1934," Slavic Review, LXV (December, 1976),
603-635.
    5. Abram Bergson, Economic Trends in the Soviet
Union (Cambridge, Mass.: Harvard University Press,
1963), p. 34.
    6. Antony C. Sutton, Western Technology and
Soviet Economic Development, Vol. II: 1930 to 1945
(Stanford, California: Hoover Institution Press,
1971), p. 286.

7. V. I. Kasianenko, <u>How Soviet Economy Won Technical Independence</u> (Moscow, Progress Publishers, 1966), p. 153.

2. The International Transfer of Technology: A General Discussion

To some extent, special practices and institutions determine the volume of Soviet imports of Western technology and the manner in which foreign technology is assimilated by the Soviet economy. However, Western technology transfer to the Soviet Union is also a part of the overall phenomenon of international technology transfer. Thus, general studies on technology and the experiences of Western countries as recipients of foreign technology should provide insights into the Soviet experience. What is technology and why is it sold across international boundaries? What problems have confronted other countries attempting to borrow foreign technology and how have they attempted to solve them? A short discussion of these questions is intended to provide perspective to the general themes of this study.

DEFINITION OF TERMS

Technology denotes knowledge or information of how to perform tasks, solve problems or produce products or services. The relationship between technology and science is imprecisely understood and difficult to define. Franklin Huddle defines technology as "the development and social use of information," a definition which encompasses basic and applied science.[1] Other observers distinguish between science, which "organizes and explains data and observations by means of theoretical relationships," and technology, which "translates scientific relationships into 'practical' use."[2] Thus, for example, the development of a gasoline engine to power an automobile is the "practical" application of the scientific knowledge comprising the thermodynamic principles of the internal combustion engine. It is sometimes

10

assumed that there is a direct and strong interrelationship between the development of science and
industrial technology. However, recent studies have
suggested that the two kinds of knowledge develop
quite independently.[3] One study, for example, concluded that new scientific knowledge develops from
earlier science, while new technology tends to build
on earlier technology, and that direct ties between
the two are unusual.[4] One implication of this conclusion is that a country may have at the same time
an extensive program for basic science research and
a technologically backward industrial sector.

The term technology is often used to denote
tangible items, such as machines. The definition of
technology as knowledge suggests that machines are
not the totality, but only a physical manifestation
of technology. The design of machines, or any other
products, reflects the human knowledge about physical relationships that we term technology. The product design, however, is only one element of industrial technology. In order to reproduce a product,
two other elements--production techniques and managerial systems to organize and carry out production
plans--are needed.[5] Production techniques, con-
sisting of "a vast array of technical knowledge and
manufacturing knowhow,"[6] are essentially the capability of transforming technical documentation,
labor, machines, and materials into finished products. Managerial systems are the means of planning,
scheduling and controlling the production process.
Studies of the technology gap between U.S. and West
European industries, carried out under the auspices
of the Organisation of Economic Co-operation and
Development, provided evidence of the importance of
the element of managerial systems. A major finding
of the studies was that one of the important causes
of the technology gap was a significant lead by some
U.S. firms in the techniques of management, including the management of research and development (R & D)
and the coupling of R & D with marketing and production.[7]

To some extent, each of the elements of technology is embodied in the finished product. They may
also be described partially in blueprints and technical documentation. However, technology is ultimately derived from the minds of people. Moreover,
much technology is unembodied in machinery and equipment and undescribed by words and diagrams: it
exists only as knowledge or information.

The diverse nature of technology suggests the
difficulty of studying or measuring it very precisely.

11

Much of what we have learned about technology has been observed indirectly. Thus, technology's contribution to economic growth is defined as a residual--what is left over after the contribution of other factor inputs is measured. Differences in the level of technology are described only approximately by differences in factor productivity. International technology transfers can be represented only imprecisely as the value of machinery and equipment shipments or by royalty payments for use of technology.

The focus of this study is the technology that is used by industrial enterprises to organize and rationalize the production of goods and services. G. R. Hall and R. E. Johnson have categorized industrial technologies into three types--general, system-specific, and firm-specific.[8] They defined general technology as knowledge that is common to an industry and is possessed by all firms in that industry. General technology is the basic knowledge and skills needed to begin a certain industrial activity. System-specific technology is the knowledge that is required to manufacture a certain product. It "comprises ingenious procedures connected with a particular system, solutions to unique problems or requirements, and experiences unlike those encountered with other systems."[9] Firm-specific technology is the knowledge and skills that are accumulated as a result of a firm's particular experience and activities, but that are not attributable to any specific item produced by the firm. It differentiates the products and production processes of various firms in an industry. Technology transfer may involve the movement of any of these types of technology.

Technology transfer is "a process by which a given technique (i.e., technology) is substantially moved from one set of users to another."[10] In the context of this study, it is the process by which innovations (new products or processes) made in one country are subsequently brought into use in another country. It is essentially a communication process which involves an active role for both the transferor and the recipient. Technology may be transferred so that it can be applied to the solution of a problem other than the one for which it was developed. An example is the transfer of a product or process developed by the government for defense programs to a private firm producing consumer goods. Technology may also be transferred in order to apply it in the same way in another geographical location--either within a country or across international boundaries.

This study is concerned with the geographical movement of technology from the industrial West

12

(i.e., the advanced industrial countries of Western Europe, North America and Japan) to the Soviet Union. When technology is transferred across international borders, it is usually moved not only from one set of users to another, but from one environment to another. International technology transfer is complicated by the need to adapt new products or processes to the economic factor endowment of the recipient country. Equally important is the adaptation of foreign technology to the economic, political and social systems of the recipient. In the case of Western technology transfer to the Soviet Union, the adaptation of technology to a radically different environment has been a crucial element of the technology transfer process.

TECHNOLOGY TRANSFER AND ECONOMIC THEORY

Why is technology bought and sold in international markets? Since the 1950s, economic theorists have focused increasing attention on the role of technology in the general economy and on its influence in international trade. Their findings, while not providing a full explanation of the technology transfer process, have given some new insights into the motivations for technology transfer and the influence of technology on international trade.

Technology and Economic Growth

Perhaps the major reason for the increased interest in international technology transfer is a clearer understanding among economists and policy makers of the role of technology in economic growth. To say that technology is a major contributing factor to economic growth is almost commonplace today. Its importance has long been understood in a general and nebulous way by both economic policy makers and economists. Yet, it is only recently that economists have paid great attention to the causes and consequences of technological change. The classical economists tended to explain economic growth as primarily the result of increases in labor and capital. To be sure, technology was not toally ignored. John Stuart Mill, for example, suggested that the "productiveness" of labor, capital and materials was related to, among other things, the skills and knowledge of workers and managers.[11] Karl Marx wrote extensively of the effect of technological change on profits, wages, and working conditions under

capitalism.[12] In the early Twentieth Century,
Joseph Schumpeter theorized about the central role
of technological innovation in the development of
capitalism.[13]

Moreover, economists have generally recognized
that economic growth was not merely the product of
increments of capital and labor. Other phenomena,
including technological change, were considered to
play a role, though a decidedly minor one, in economic growth. However, until recently, economists did
not go beyond that vague generalization to explore
the dynamics of the technological variable. Technology was considered to be simply an unexplained
residual of growth, and its contribution tended to
be underestimated.

Systematic research into the relationship
between technology and economic growth did not begin
until the 1950s. Of several important studies in
this period, a 1957 paper by Robert Solow was perhaps the most influential.[14] Based on data on the
non-farm U.S. economy from 1909-1949, Solow found
that increases in per capita output had averaged
1.5 percent per year. His measurements of increases
in capital inputs during the forty-year period
suggested that they could account for only about one-
eighth of the increase in output per capita. Thus,
he concluded, about seven-eighths of the increase in
output per capita was attributable to technical
change.

Solow's findings stimulated much discussion and
helped to direct the attention of economists to technology as a factor of economic growth. His findings
were subsequently challenged and modified by other
economists. In particular, his assumption that all
growth in output not attributed to increases in labor
or capital was due to technological change was reexamined.[15] In 1962, Edward Denison made similar
estimates of the effects of technological change on
U.S. economic growth, but included other variables,
such as the improved quality of labor associated with
education, training and improved health.[16] Still,
he estimated that the effect of technological change
on economic growth was substantial: he concluded
that during 1929-1957, the advance of technological
and managerial knowledge was responsible for 40 percent of the increase of national income per person
employed in the United States. Denison, assisted by
Jean-Pierre Pouillier, also made estimates for a
number of West European countries with similar results.[17] Their estimates of the percentages of
growth of national income per person employed during

1950-1962 that was attributable to advances in knowledge and "changes in the lag in the application of
knowledge" ranged from 20 percent (for Denmark) to
46 percent (for the United Kingdom).

Denison's methodology can be summarized by the
following production function:[18]

$$\Delta Y = \alpha \Delta L + \beta \Delta K + \gamma \Delta A + \Delta R, \text{ assuming } \alpha + \beta + \gamma = 1$$

where:

    Y = Real national income
    L = Labor input, adjusted for quality
    K = Capital input
    A = Land input
    R = Output per unit of input
    Δ = Rate of increase, α, β, γ (= respective
        shares L, K, and A)

Denison's unique contribution is his detailed explanation of how changes in factor inputs and factor
productivity influence changes in national income.
Of particular interest in assessing the role of technology in economic growth is his analysis of output
per unit of input (ΔR). It is this variable which
most directly reflects the impact of technological
progress. For example, Denison found that in the
1948-1969 period, advances in knowledge contributed
67 percent of the growth rate of output per unit of
input in the United States.[19]

Economists who have attempted to measure the
contribution of technology to economic growth generally acknowledge the crudeness of their estimates.
To some extent technological change is an intangible
phenomenon which defies precise measurement. However,
probably most economists would agree with Simon
Kuznets' characterization of the relationship between
technological progress and economic growth:

    The major capital stock of an industrially
    advanced nation is not its physical equipment;
    it is the body of knowledge amassed from tested
    findings of empirical science and the capacity
    and training of its population to use this
    knowledge effectively. One can easily envisage
    a situation in which technological progress
    permits output to increase at a high rate with-
    out any additions to the stock of capital
    goods.[20]

Kuznet's statement suggests the positive impact of
technological change on labor productivity (i.e.,
the ratio of labor inputs to output), which is, in
turn, a major contributing factor to economic growth.
Increases in labor productivity are perhaps the most
important economic consequence of advances in technology. Labor productivity is sometimes used as a
proxy or an indicator of the level of technology.[21]
    Most economists have focused on the contribution
of indigenous technology to the economic growth of a
country. One exception is Stanislaw Gomulka, who
distinguishes between the effects of foreign and
indigenous technology and concludes that the importation of technology is the major determinant of
economic growth in medium-developed countries.[22]
Noting that the medium-developed countries, such as
the Soviet Union, usually have the highest growth
rates, Gomulka concludes that those countries tend
to benefit more from foreign technology than do the
highly developed and less developed countries. Thus,
as a country develops through various stages of economic development, it proceeds from an initial stage
at which it benefits little from foreign technology,
to a middle ground at which it receives maximum
benefits, and finally to a highly developed stage
at which it again receives little benefit.[23]

Technology and International Trade

    Although international movements of technology
may take place through a variety of channels, it has
generally been recognized that it is in the commercial realm that the industrial technologies most
important to economic growth are transferred. This
is true because commercial enterprises, either private or government controlled, are the developers
and proprietors of so many of the important new technological innovations. The managers of these enterprises regard their technology as both a crucial
factor input in their production processes and a
salable commodity.
    There is considerable evidence that commercial
transfers of technology are becoming an increasingly
important element in international trade. For example, technology developed in one country is being
transferred to other countries more rapidly than in
the past. It has been estimated that, since the mid-
1950s, the international transfer of technology has
been increasing at a rate of more than 10 percent
a year.[24] There is a growing technological interdependence, an increasing tendency to rely on the

16

foreign sector as a source of technological progress, among countries. To some extent, the pattern of technological innovation in various countries appears to determine the kinds of goods and services imported and exported.

In recent years, international trade theorists have attempted to refine traditional trade theory to take into account the role of the technology factor. Modern international trade theory is founded on the theory of comparative advantage, initially developed by David Ricardo in the early Nineteenth Century, and subsequently modified and refined most notably by two Swedish economists, Eli Heckscher and Bertil Ohlin.[25] In its modern form, the theory of comparative advantage explains the composition of a country's foreign trade in terms of its relative endowments of labor and capital. According to the Heckscher-Ohlin "factor proportions theory," a country exports goods the production of which uses intensively the factor which is relatively plentiful and consequently inexpensive within its boundaries. Conversely, a country imports those goods the production of which requires relatively more of its scarce, expensive factor. Thus, a country with a relatively high capital/labor ratio, such as the United States, would have a comparative advantage in producing and exporting capital-intensive goods, while a country with a high labor/capital ratio, such as Indonesia, would have a comparative advantage in labor-intensive goods. The theory also provides an explanation of the motive for countries to engage in international trade: by specializing in the lines of production in which it is relatively efficient, each country gains more than it gives up in the international exchange of goods.

In this simple and seemingly commonsensical form, the theory of comparative advantage went largely unchallenged until it was apparently contradicted by the findings of a 1953 study by Wassily Leontief.[26] In studying the factor composition of commodities in U.S. foreign trade, Leontief found that U.S. exports were less capital-intensive than U.S. imports. Since the United States is a capital-rich country, Leontief's findings represented the opposite of what conventional international trade theory predicted. Leontief explained this apparent paradox by pointing out that U.S. labor was more skilled and more productive than foreign labor. Thus, he suggested that his findings might conform to the traditional theory of comparative advantage, when one takes into account that the United States is relatively well-endowed with skilled labor.

A number of subsequent studies supported Leontief's explanation of the paradox by adding a third factor--labor skills or "human capital"--and, in some cases a fourth, natural resources, to the factor proportions theory. In particular, several articles by Donald Keesing refined the concept of labor skills and showed a close correlation between U.S. export performance and the level of skills required to produce various goods and services.[27] Specifically, he found that in 1962, production of U.S. exports required inputs of many more scientists and engineers (the most skill-intensive labor) than did U.S. imports. The empirical work of Keesing and a number of others[28] went far toward explaining the Leontief paradox and, at the same time, helped to refine the Heckscher-Ohlin theory as an explanatory model of international trade patterns.

Others were stimulated by Leontief's paradoxical findings to seek alternative explanations of international trade. The attention of some scholars was focused on the static nature of the Heckscher-Ohlin theory and particularly on the assumption that all countries had similar technologies. Collectively, the approach of these scholars has been referred to as the "neo-technology" critique of traditional trade theory. The best known approach of this school is the product cycle theory, originally proposed by Raymond Vernon[29] and subsequently developed by others. Vernon's theory introduces a dynamic element, allowing explicitly for technological changes, and eliminates the assumption of similar technologies for countries engaged in international trade.

Vernon's explanation of the content of a country's foreign trade concentrates on the characteristics of the domestic market and on the ease of communication between potential consumers and producers of new products. Specifically, he found that because the United States is a high income and high labor cost economy, it tends to produce new products that are either income elastic or labor saving. Production of such new products, he found, formed the basis for U.S. comparative advantage. Because the innovation of these types of goods takes place first in the U.S. economy, U.S. producers initially have monopolistic power in selling them in world markets. Over time, as the new products become more standardized, and the foreign market grows, production begins abroad. Eventually, the country of least cost (particularly labor cost) begins to have a comparative advantage in producing and exporting the new product.

Some observers have stressed the importance of technology gaps among countries as a determinant of trade patterns. Michael Posner, for example, noted that some countries tend to produce new products and export them to foreign markets until foreign producers see the new products as a threat to their market.[30] After a period of time (which he called "imitation lag"), foreign producers react and begin to produce the same product locally. Several studies of specific industries have supported the notion that a country's exports of new products are more a function of technological progress than factor costs.[31]

In summary, since the 1950s, there have been several important developments in economic theory which helped to explain the role of technology in the economy in general and in international trade in particular. These developments largely explain the heightened interest of economists and economic policy makers in the phenomenon of technology transfer. First, new data on the central role of technology in economic growth provide a clear rationale for governments intent on growth to pursue policies designed to facilitate the absorption of the latest foreign technology. The importance of technological progress to factor productivity suggests a particular need for countries which cannot depend on mere increments of capital and labor as a source of economic growth to create optimal conditions for innovating and borrowing foreign technologies.

In addition, refinements in international trade theory have gone far toward highlighting the importance of the technology factor in international trade and explaining the direction of international technology flows. Specifically, trade in technology-intensive goods or in new goods is seen as a function of the relative levels of technological development, as measured, for example, by labor skills or research and development activity. The commodity composition of trade among countries is explained in part by differing capacities to innovate and to market new products.

MECHANISMS OF TECHNOLOGY TRANSFER

Technology is transferred across international boundaries in a wide variety of ways. Transfers of technology may occur as the result of intentional actions by a firm, government or individual, or they may take place unintentionally.[32] Technology transfer is a more commonplace phenomenon than is generally recognized. Most of the technologies used

19

in a given country originated abroad and not as a
result of domestic innovation. They are brought into
a country through both international commercial transactions and non-commercial means. In the transfer of
industrial technologies, the focus of this study,
the commercial mechanisms are the most important.

Among the non-commercial mechanisms, the following are the most common channels for transferring
technology internationally: (1) the flow of books,
journals and other published information; (2) the
movement of persons from country to country (such as
attendance of conferences or emigration); (3) education and training at foreign universities or technical schools; (4) exchange of information and personnel through technical cooperation programs of
international organizations or individual governments.[33] Individually, such non-commercial mechanisms are rarely important or effective means of
transferring technology. However, their cumulative,
long-term effect in raising the general technological
level of a recipient country is undoubtedly quite
significant.

Commercial mechanisms for transferring technology have undergone considerable evolution in the
post-World War II era. In general, there is a growing tendency for the recipient of technology--either
the local enterprise or government--to maintain more
control over or to be more actively involved in the
technology transfer process. Despite this evolution,
the most important commercial mechanisms are forms
of variations of international commercial arrangements
that have been in use for many years. The most frequently used commercial mechanisms are: (1) foreign
direct investment; (2) licensing agreements;
(3) management contracts and technical services
agreements; and (4) exports of products.[34]

Foreign direct investment involves full or
majority ownership of a subsidiary in a foreign country by a transferor firm. The subsidiary is created
and operated under the law of the host country and
owned and managed by the parent company. The foreign
owner typically provides capital and technology
(often under a separate licensing agreement) and
uses domestic material and labor resources. Such
arrangements have been traditionally the primary
commercial mechanism for transferring technology and
probably remain so, although other mechanisms are
becoming increasingly popular.

Foreign investment may be in the form of a joint
venture--an enterprise that is partially owned by
local public or private interests and partially by

20

a foreign investor. Management, control and profits are thus shared in proportion to the number of shares owned by each party. In joint ventures between Western industrial firms and enterprises in developing countries, the Western firm generally provides technology in the form of managerial and technical expertise and licenses. Joint ventures are most often formed in production facilities. However, they may be formed for other purposes, such as joint research and development undertakings or joint marketing companies.

License agreements involve the sale of "naked" or unembodied technology to a foreign firm. The licensee receives certain rights to produce and sell specific products which incorporate inventions and processes developed by the licensor. License agreements may also include the transfer of trademark rights or the sale of knowhow. The licensor usually receives payment for the technology in a lump-sum payment, royalty payments based on a percentage of resultant sales, or both. The license lasts for a definite period of time specified in the contract. It may involve a one-time disclosure of trade secrets or may require a continuing flow of new technical innovations developed during the life of the contract. Generally, the licensor supplies only part of the technology needed to start up production, usually firm-specific or system-specific technology. Sometimes a licensing agreement includes the transfer of general technology, in the form of extensive training programs.

A pure license agreement involves no management by the foreign licensor. There is also no direct foreign control, although restrictions on the use of the resultant output are common. The most common restrictions are limitations on the level of output and on the export of output to foreign markets. The license may also restrict the time period in which the technology may be employed.

Management contracts and technical services agreements are contractual arrangements between a technology transferor (manufacturing firm, consulting firm, or individual) and a recipient firm under which the transferor agrees to perform specified services over a definite period of time. Such contracts involve no foreign ownership and no obligations on either side after the expiration of the contract. They do, however, involve varying degrees of control over the operations of the recipient firm by the foreign transferor. The typical management contract gives operational control and management of

the local enterprise (or part of the enterprise) to
the transferor firm for the life of the contract.
It involves a definite delegation of planning and
decision making authority.[35] Technical services
agreements (or technical assistance contracts) provide for the transfer of a variety of technical skills,
such as feasibility studies, design of plants, machinery and equipment, installation of machinery and
start-up assistance. Thus, while the management contract provides for the performance of major corporate
functions, the technical services agreement provides
for the transfer of engineering skills. The latter
is product- or process-oriented.[36]

     The normal sale of products across international
boundaries frequently involves some transfer of technology. The sale of goods can transfer technology
in two ways: (1) the operation of purchased machinery and equipment which embodies technology; and
(2) imitation and reproduction of the product through
reverse engineering. In addition, the mere attempt
to sell a product through detailed proposals, participation in trade exhibits and commercial visits may
result in the inadvertent transfer of technology.
The sale of sophisticated machinery and equipment
frequently includes the provision of additional
services, such as installation and training in the
operation of the product. However, sales generally
involve no obligations on the part of the seller
beyond normal guarantees on operation and servicing.
They also include no control on the part of the
seller.

     It should be emphasized that these mechanisms
for the transfer of technology exist in a great
variety of contractual forms and frequently are used
in some combination. In East-West economic relations,
for example, new kinds of commercial relations, now
generally referred to as "industrial cooperation,"
have begun to play a central role in the transfer of
technology. A general definition of industrial
cooperation is provided in a 1973 United Nations
study:

     Industrial co-operation in an east-west context
     denotes the economic relationships and activi-
     ties arising from (a) contracts extending over
     a number of years between partners belonging
     to different economic systems which go beyond
     the straightforward sale or purchase of goods
     and services to include a set of complementary
     or reciprocally matching operations (in pro-
     duction, in the development and transfer of

technology, in marketing, etc.); and from (b)
contracts between such partners which have been
identified as industrial co-operation contracts
by Governments in bilateral or multilateral
agreements.[37]

The study also provides descriptions of six major
categories of East-West industrial cooperation:

- Licensing with payment in resultant products;
- Supply of complete plants or production lines
  with payments in resultant products;
- Co-production and specialization;
- Sub-contracting;
- Joint ventures;
- Joint tendering or joint construction of similar
  projects.[38]

When the aspects of these arrangements involving
technology transfers are examined closely, it is
clear that they are essentially variations or com-
binations of the traditional mechanisms described
above.

THE TECHNOLOGY TRANSFER PROCESS

        There is a consensus among international econo-
mic policy makers on the importance of international
technology transfer. It is assigned a crucial role
in the economic development strategies of developing
countries and is considered a necessary ingredient
of the economic policies of advanced industrial
countries which wish to stay abreast of the rapid
pace of technological change, spur domestic economic
growth, and maintain their competitive positions on
international markets. The heightened awareness of
the importance of technology transfer has been accompanied by a growing debate over every aspect of the
technology transfer process.[39] Technology transfer
is a difficult and controversial process which tests
the technical skills of both transferors and recipients. For policy makers in recipient countries,
the importation of technology is often a mixed bless-
ing: it offers clear economic benefits; but may
threaten domestic institutions. Moreover, the
effects of technology transfer frequently transcend
the commercial realm: technology has an impact on
basic economic, political and social institutions.
        There are special problems and issues associated
with each aspect of the technology transfer process.

23

The manner in which these problems and issues have
been confronted has in large part determined the
degree of success which various countries have had
in borrowing foreign technology. While various
approaches have succeeded, certain preconditions
appear to be critical to the ultimate success of an
attempt to transfer technology.

To survey the experiences of Western industrial
and developing countries in importing foreign technology, it may be useful to divide the technology
transfer process into two phases: (1) the initial
planning and purchase of technology, and (2) the
absorption of technology. The first phase relates
primarily to the immediate interface between a recipient firm or country and a foreign transferor of
technology. It includes the selection of technology
and the transfer mechanism, the negotiation of a
contract, and financing. The second phase, including design and adaptation, construction and installation, training, operation of the imported technology
and domestic diffusion, relates primarily to the
interaction of the imported technology with domestic
economic institutions.

TABLE 2.1
The Technology Transfer Process

I.	Initial Planning and Purchase of Technology	choice of technology selection of mechanism negotiation of contract financing
II.	Absorption	design and adaptation construction and installa- tion training operation of plants, machinery domestic diffusion

The two phases are intimately interrelated. The
manner in which problems in the initial phase are
addressed to a large extent predetermines the kinds
of policies and institutions which must be employed
in the second. For example, if a country rejects an
active role for foreign firms, managers, and technicians it is forced to depend on domestic resources in

24

the absorption phase. If, on the other hand, an active role of foreigners is accepted, domestic technical resources are taxed less heavily, though they still play an important role.

Initial Planning and Purchase of Technology

From the recipient's standpoint, the first stage of the technology transfer process is the selection of the kind of technology that is appropriate for the conditions in the domestic economy. Basically, this means choosing a technology which uses intensively the available factors of production--capital, labor (skilled and unskilled), land, and materials--and which accords with the preferences of domestic economic decision makers, whether consumers on the market place or economic planners. While this may appear to be a simple proposition, the problem is sometimes a complex one.[40] It may involve choosing between: a variety of foreign technologies or a domestic technology; the most modern technology available or an "intermediate" or less sophisticated variant (or a combination of modern and intermediate technologies); a large scale or small-scale technology.

The problem is further complicated by certain constraints on the ability or willingness of a recipient to select the imported technology on the basis of rational economic criteria.[41] The constraints derive in part from the fact that the transferor-- frequently a large multinational corporation--has substantial, and sometimes the predominant, decision making power in this matter. The transferor may be ignorant of local factor and market conditions or indifferent to certain externalities that might exist. Furthermore, a transferor might profit by selling capital-intensive technology to a recipient, even if it is located in a labor-abundant country. Other constraints are related to the "technological fixity" of many modern industrial processes. Many of the industrial technologies originating in the advanced industrial countries are developed for the capital-rich, large market conditions that exist in those countries. For some lines of production, a recipient country with different economic conditions, may have no alternative to such inappropriate technologies. Moreover, the adaptation of these technologies may be too costly to be worthwhile. In some cases, non-economic criteria may be predominant in official decision making. For example, modern factories may be imported for prestige or for national defense purposes. Foreign technologies which promise improvements in economic efficiency may also be rejected on the grounds that they threaten domestic cultural and social institutions.

Perhaps the major prerequisite for making rational choices of technology is knowledge--both of the range of technologies available abroad and of domestic technological capabilities and economic conditions and needs. This implies a need for considerable technical expertise among decision makers. Ideally, they should be aware of the frontiers of a given industrial technology and able to determine the feasibility of absorbing it under local conditions.

A second important aspect of the initial planning state is the selection of a mechanism for transferring the technology. This is a crucial decision, not only because of its economic consequences, but because it determines the degree of foreign involvement and control in the domestic economy. In addition the choice of a mechanism frequently has a profound impact on domestic political, social and cultural institutions. Thus, two central issues have dominated decision making on technology transfer mechanisms--the degree to which foreign owners of technology will control key sectors of the domestic economy and the potential impact on the domestic population of an influx of foreign managers, engineers and technicians with new and possibly alien attitudes and ideas.

The possibility that alien ideas might have an adverse impact on the domestic population is seldom debated openly among policy makers in technology recipient countries. There is a reluctance to openly discuss this issue, possibly because such concerns may be construed as a sign of weakness of officially prescribed or accepted ideas. It does, however, appear to be an important underlying issue which influences the structure of contractual arrangements between recipients and transferors of technologies. The influence of this issue is frequently manifested in efforts by the recipient government to limit the exchange of people involved in the technology transfer project. Another manifestation is the isolation of technology transfer projects and foreigners who accompany them from the rest of the economy.

The control issue, on the other hand, has been a hotly debated subject in technology transfers among Western industrial and developing countries. The debate is often couched in economic nationalist terms. Economic decision making is widely perceived as an essential ingredient of national sovereignty.

Thus, foreign control over a country's means of production is naturally perceived as a threat. This is particularly true when foreign control extends over a significant part of the economy. The issue of control is commonly perceived as a special problem of small developing countries which rely on large multinational corporations as sources of technology. In fact, the issue is also important in economic and technological ties among advanced industrial countries. The concerns of West European and Canadian policy makers about the dominant position of U.S.-based companies in sectors of their economies are well documented.[42] The issue has also dominated Japanese policy on technology imports.[43]

A related issue is the question of technological independence. Leaders of developing countries, for example, have an understandable desire to develop their own technological capabilities. They frequently complain that some arrangements for technology transfer tend to perpetuate the role of foreign managers and technicians and provide few opportunities for training domestic personnel.

Of the technology transfer mechanisms,[44] direct foreign investment generally has been singled out for criticism by economic nationalists as the one which reserves the most control for the foreign transferor firm. It combines ownership with indefinite managerial control over the operation of production facilities and disposition of profits. Such control is typically limited only by local laws concerning such matters as working conditions and taxes. One-time sales of plants or equipment, on the other hand, transfer technology without control. Policy makers have become aware, however, of an important tradeoff involved. Direct investment provides the necessary incentives and long-term framework to make technology transfers effective. One-time sales of technology have generally proven to be much less effective transfer mechanisms, particularly for advanced technologies or for relatively unsophisticated recipients.

A Department of Defense task force, studying high-technology transfers to Communist countries concluded that "active" relationships between transferors and recipients of technology are generally required for effective transfers.[45] Such mechanisms, according to the task force, have the following general characteristics:

'Active' relationships involve frequent and specific communications between donor and

27

receiver. These usually transfer proprietary
or restricted information. They are directed
toward a specific goal of improving the technical capability of the receiving nation.
Typically, this is an iterative process: the
receiver requests specific information, applies
it, develops new findings, and then requests
further information. This process is normally
continued for several years, until the receiver
demonstrates the desired capability.[46]

"Passive relationships," involving short-term sales
or transfers of information or products that the
transferor already has disseminated widely, were
found to be ineffective technology transfer mechanisms.

In the Defense Department study, a survey of
four areas of high technology transfers confirmed a
direct relationship between active participation
by the transferor and the effectiveness of technology transplants. Direct investment (joint ventures),
extensive training programs, and other arrangements
involving long-term and continuous contacts were
among the highly effective mechanisms. These are
precisely the types of mechanisms which involve
the greatest control by foreign firms or the greatest exchange of personnel. On the other hand,
passive mechanisms involving little control and
personnel exchange, such as commercial literature,
trade shows and product sales, were found to be
ineffective means of transferring technology. (See
Table 2.2.)

A survey of corporate executives by James R.
Basche, Jr. and Michael G. Duerr suggests that the
effectiveness of direct foreign investment as a
technology transfer mechanism is widely supported by
managers of transferor firms. The surveyed executives also tended to concur on the importance of
other active mechanisms. The authors reported wide
agreement on the proposition that: "technology can
be transferred most effectively when buyer and
seller maintain their relations with each other for
a long period of time."[47]

The need for active mechanisms depends in part
on the type of technology which must be imported from
abroad. Hall and Johnson[48] point out that the transfer of general technology is the most difficult and
requires the most personal contacts because it involves intensive and broad training in the practices
and procedures peculiar to an industry. Frequently
the least developed countries require transplants

28

of general technology; it "blends into the process of general education for development."[49] Firm-specific technology can also be difficult to transfer because it consists in part of the knowhow which results from interpersonal working relationships within a firm and must be communicated directly by those involved in the work. System-specific technology, which is more often embodied in patents, designs or machinery and equipment is more easily transferred and may require little personnel exchange if the recipient is relatively sophisticated. The transfer of system-specific technology involves essentially the communication of how to do something differently that was already done before. In other words, this kind of transfer presupposes the existence of an operating firm in the recipient country. System-specific technology must either be transferred to a country that is realtively advanced industrially or be accompanied by general and firm-specific technology.

The Defense Department and Basche-Duerr surveys include certain types of licensing arrangements--those involving training and transfer of manufacturing knowhow--among the highly effective mechanisms. Licensing has received increasing attention among many recipient countries as the most desirable alternative to direct investment. Licensing agreements provide some of the same advantages as direct investment, often without the degree of control inherent in foreign ownership. By purchasing a license, a firm avoids duplicating expensive research and development work on a new product or process. If successful, a licensing agreement can result in considerable savings of time and money. While effective licensing arrangements must include extensive personal contacts, national policy makers frequently cite the absence of the degree of control that accompanies direct investments. Licenses generally involve little interference in the management of the recipient firm and, aside from royalty obligations, do not involve control over profits. However, as noted above,[50] licensing agreements may include many restrictions. In fact, such restrictions seem to be commonplace and sometimes very comprehensive.[51] Moreover, it has been noted that licensing (vis-a-vis direct investment) may actually increase a country's dependence, from a macroeconomic standpoint on foreign technology because licensed technology tends to displace domestic research and development.[52]

Direct investment has distinct advantages as a technology transfer mechanism. It provides for the transfer of managerial skills and provides an

TABLE 2.2
Effectiveness of Technology Transfer According to Industry and Transfer Mechanism

Active ← Donor Activity

Transfer Effectiveness	Transfer Mechanism	Airframe	Jet Engine	Semiconductor	Instrumentation
Highly Effective (Tight Control)	Turnkey Factories	H	H	H	H
	Licenses with Extensive Teaching Effort	H	H	H	H
	Joint Ventures	H	H	H	H
	Technical Exchange with Ongoing Contact	H	H	H	H
	Training in High-Technology Areas	H	H	H	H
	Processing Equipment (with knowhow)	M	M	H	MH
Effective	Engineering Documents & Technical Data	MH	MH	H	M
	Consulting	MH	MH	H	M
	Licenses (with knowhow)	M	M	MH	M
	Proposals (documented)	M	M	L	L
Moderately Effective	Processing Equipment (w/o knowhow)	L	L	MH	L
	Commercial Visits	L	L	IM	L

30

	Passive
Low Effectiveness (Decontrol)	L L L L
Licenses (w/o knowhow)	L L L L
Sale of Products (w/o Maintenance & Operating Data)	L L L L
Proposals (undocumented)	L L L L
Commercial Literature	L L L L
Trade Exhibits	L L L L

L   =   Low Effectiveness

LM =   Low to Medium Effectiveness

M   =   Medium Effectiveness

MH =   Medium to High Effectiveness

H   =   Highly Effective

Source: U.S. Department of Defense. Office of the Director of Defense Research and Engineering. Defense Science Board Task Force on Export of U.S. Technology. An Analysis of Export Control of U.S. Technology--A DoD Perspective, Washington, D.C., February 4, 1976.

31

incentive for the transferor to operate the technology efficiently. However, by combining licensing
with some other forms of technology transfer, such
as technical and managerial assistance, the same
result can often be received. Incentives for the
transferor firm can often be incorporated by tying
royalty payments to performance, rather than lump
sum payments, and by including provisions for up-
dating technology.

Naturally, the preferences of transferor firms
are frequently a major determinant of the type of
mechanism selected. The transferor's marketing
strategy, profit-maximizing possibilities and willingness to divert managerial and technical personnel
to the technology transfer process may dictate a
preference that is different than the recipient's.
If the interests of transferor and recipient diverge,
the relative bargaining power of the two becomes a
critical factor.[53]

A major issue in foreign purchases of technology
has been the pricing policies of the proprietors of
industrial technologies. A debate has raged over
the question of how to determine a fair price for
technology. Predictably, representatives of those
countries which are heavily dependent on technology
imports, particularly resource-poor developing countries, argue that prices for technology are too high,
while the exporters of technology argue that prices
are fair or too low. The issue is a complex one,
owing primarily to the absence of a free market (in
the classical economic sense) for technology. The
owners of a given technology have monopolistic control over their market. Domestic laws and international conventions protect their exclusive right
to exploit their technology or to sell it on their
own terms. Though they may face some competition
from owners of alternate technologies, the purchaser
frequently either has a narrow range of technologies
from which to choose or is unaware of alternatives.

Owners generally cite the high cost of research
and development for new technologies and the benefits
accruing to the recipient as evidence of the fairness
of prices.[54] Moreover, there is evidence that the
costs of transferring technology are substantial,
particularly when the recipient does not have the
necessary skills to absorb the technology.[55] Technology purchasers maintain that research and development costs are usually recouped in domestic exploitation before the sale of technology. They frequently
maintain that technology is, or should be, a "public
good"; i.e., its utility and availability to a

proprietor is not reduced when it is used by a recipient firm.[56] Thus, the incremental cost of transferring the technology to another firm is said to be near zero.

One of the most frequent complaints about technology pricing concerns the practice of "packaging" technology, or requiring the recipient to purchase capital goods and technical services along with the desired technology. Critics of this practice maintain that it raises the price of technology unnecessarily. The accompanying capital goods and services, they claim, can often be obtained elsewhere at a lower price, or may not be needed at all. Transferor firms generally maintain that the technology "package" is necessary to make the transfer effective.[57]

There is a consensus among sellers and purchasers on one aspect of international technology sales--the critical importance of financing. Large sales of technology and related goods and services are seldom made on a cash basis. Few countries are able or willing to make large outlays before startup of a new plant or machinery. It is more common to pay after the new technology begins to produce. A country's ability to finance technology imports is generally a major determinant of the volume of technology imports. In this regard, the selection of a transfer mechanism is important. For example, a recipient may tie imports of technology to exports of the resultant output. Likewise, domestic expenditures are minimized for direct foreign investment.

In addressing the myriad of problems related to the initial phase of technology transfer, two "models" or approaches to technology transfer have been employed by the more successful technology recipient countries in the West. In the first model, the recipient government creates a propitious environment for foreign direct investment and relies heavily on foreign transferor firms to effect the technology transplant and solve the problems of domestic absorption. In the second model, the recipient government plays an active role in the initial planning and purchase of technology and limits the role of the transferor firm in the domestic absorption process. James Brian Quinn has used the examples of Belgium and Japan, respectively, to illustrate the two models.[58]

Belgium began to promote direct foreign investment by multinational corporations in the early 1960s. Using a variety of tax and other incentives, the Belgian government offered special inducements to modern, high-technology industries. Both the establishment of wholly owned subsidiaries by foreign

firms and mergers between foreign and local firms
were encouraged. Foreign managers and technicians
were allowed in without work permits, and barriers
to the import of capital equipment were removed.
The liberal government attitude toward foreign investment was complemented by efforts to improve the
domestic technological infrastructure. Among the
measures undertaken were expansion of technical training programs, improvement of transport and communications facilities, and encouragement of domestic
industries needed to supply the foreign owned firm.
Belgium's membership in the Common Market, providing
access to a large market, was another important
incentive for foreign firms.
    In the 1950s and 1960s, the Japanese government
developed policies and institutions designed to
encourage the importation of "unpackaged" technology.
Although technical assistance was often included in
Japanese technology purchases, foreign managerial
participation or direct foreign investment was discouraged. Teams of technicians were sent to the
United States and other Western countries (with
combined government and private support) to study
the most advanced technologies in their industries.
Their mission was to look for proprietary and non-
proprietary technologies which could be licensed
or copied. The initial negotiations with potential
licensors of technology were carried out directly by
private Japanese firms. However, the Japanese
Ministry of International Trade and Industry (MITI)
became involved in all negotiations, and its ultimate approval had to be obtained for technology purchases. MITI gained renown as a hard bargainer in
the Japanese company's and the nation's interest.
A particular concern was to remove restrictions on
exporting the products of the licensed technology so
that Japanese firms would be free to aggressively
develop markets. The development of substantial
export capacity has been a key feature of the
Japanese model. The Japanese government followed a
policy of severely restricting foreign ownership
and control over imported technology. At the same
time, the government made a major effort to improve
the absorptive capacity of the domestic economy and
to spur indigenous technological progress.[59]
    Some of the key features of the Japanese model
have eroded in recent years. In reaction to pressures from its major trade partners, Japan has
gradually liberalized its restrictions on foreign
investment since 1967.[60] Still, the original model
has great appeal among policy makers in developing

34

countries, who are moving perceptibly away from the
Belgian direct investment approach and toward the
Japanese model. Japanese success in using foreign
technology to achieve a rapid rate of economic and
technological progress has become the "inspiration"
of many of these policy makers.[61] Argentina, Brazil,
India, Mexico, and others, have introduced some government controls over the selection and purchase of
technology in order to monitor price, quality, and
adaptability to local conditions.[62] While few
governments are attempting to block direct investment completely, many are following Japan's lead in
using government institutions to try to enhance their
bargaining power on prices, control and other matters.

Absorption

In the final analysis, the most appropriate model
for a given country depends on the capacity of its
economy to deal with the difficult problems of absorption. Solution of these problems is left largely
to the transferor firm when the direct investment
mechanism is used, whereas less active mechanisms
require greater efforts by domestic institutions.
Despite the apparent attractiveness of the Japanese
model from a political standpoint, it is not one
that is easily imitated. Japanese success is largely
a result of an extensive technological infrastructure.
This infrastructure, developed over a period of
several decades, includes a highly trained work
force, competent managers and engineers, and sophisticated, capital-rich industries. In addition,
Japanese success has depended on extensive domestic
R & D activity. In particular, Japanese firms have
devoted considerable resources to studying the kinds
of technologies available in foreign countries and
to modifying and adapting imported technologies.[63]
In short, Japan, like a number of other industrially advanced countries, has most of the important
prerequisites for successfully absorbing foreign
technology. It has not needed to rely as heavily
as some countries on foreign assistance during the
absorption process. While the experiences of technology recipient countries are varied, it is possible to make generalizations about the prerequisites
for successful absorption of imported technology.
Listed below are some of the important factors which
have been identified in the Western literature on
this subject:[64]

1. developed infrastructure, such as transportation and communications facilities;
2. trained workers, engineers and managers;
3. domestic research and development capabilities to assist in adaptation and exploitation of new technologies;
4. domestic supplies or convenient foreign sources of vital raw materials;
5. domestic or foreign markets for goods produced with the imported technology;
6. willingness to promote active mechanisms, with extensive contacts between domestic and foreign technical and managerial personnel;
7. flexible domestic industrial organization, including a managerial system which provides incentives to innovate, minimize costs and take risks, and to promote diffusion of imported technologies throughout the economy;
8. information about the technological state of the arts in foreign industries;
9. complementary industries and a reliable supply system to provide necessary inputs for new industries;
10. effective patent services, quality standards and technical documentation centers;
11. financial institutions to assist in establishment of new industries or access to foreign credits.

Most developing countries lack these prerequisites. Indeed, even developed economies, such as Japan and West European countries, can effectively absorb "unpackaged" technology only by diverting substantial technological resources from other parts of the economy. Technology transfers that are unaided by the transferor tend to make greater demands on domestic resources. With active arrangements, on the other hand, the transferor firm may assist in adaptation of products and production techniques, construction and management of factories, training of domestic personnel, domestic diffusion of new technologies, and even marketing of the output on domestic and international markets. Thus, for most recipient countries, the most active mechanisms offer the advantages of economizing on scarce technological resources. The rapidity and breadth of technological change in the world increase the importance of a more active interrelationship with the world economy. Even the most advanced countries may not

have the prerequisites in sufficient quantity and
quality to stay abreast technologically in all areas.
Thus, direct investment and other active mechanisms
can supplement the technological efforts of local
enterprises. The more active arrangements, although
they may be costly in both economic and political
terms, can make a greater technological contribution
to the recipient.

The imposing list of prerequisites for successful technological absorption suggests why the
"advantages of being backward" are often elusive
for less developed countries. It is true that late-
comers in the economic development process have
access to a vast array of industrial technologies
that have been developed at a great cost and over a
long period of time in the industrially advanced
countries.[65] However, they frequently do not have
the means to assimilate such technologies. The
experiences of many developing countries suggest that
those countries which are technologically backward
are least able to absorb foreign technology effectively. Gomulka's finding that less-developed
countries tend to benefit less than medium-developed
countries from foreign technology[66] is probably best
explained by the absence of these important prerequisites.

NOTES

1. U.S. Congress, House, Committee on Science
and Technology, Science Policy, A Working Glossary,
by Franklin P. Huddle. Committee Print (Washington,
D.C.: Government Printing Office, March 1976), p. 82.
2. G. R. Hall and R. E. Johnson, "Transfer of
United States Aerospace Technology to Japan," in The
Technology Factor in International Trade, ed. by
Raymond Vernon (New York: National Bureau of Economic Research, 1970), p. 306. Cf., Edward P. Hawthorne,
The Transfer of Technology (Paris: Organisation for
Economic Co-operations and Development, 1971), p. 19.
3. Derek J. de S. Price, "The Structures of Pub-
lication in Science and Technology," in Factors in
the Transfer of Technology, ed. by W. H. Gruber and
D. G. Marquis (Cambridge: The M.I.T. Press, 1969),
pp. 91-104; J. Langrish et al., Wealth from Knowledge:
A Study of Innovation in Industry (London: MacMillan,
1972); C. C. Gallagher, "Manufacturing Technology in
Planned and Market Economies," (paper presented at the
Conference on Technology and Communist Culture,
Bellagio, Italy, August 22-28, 1975).

4. Price, p. 97.

5. Jack Baranson, Industrial Technologies for Developing Economies (New York: Frederick A. Praeger, 1969), pp. 28-31.

6. Ibid., p. 29.

7. Organisation for Economic Co-operation and Development. Gaps in Technology: Analytical Report (Paris, 1970).

8. Hall and Johnson, p. 308.

9. Ibid.

10. U.S. Congress, House, Committee on International Relations, Subcommittee on International Security and Scientific Affairs, Science and Technology in the Department of State: Bringing Technical Content Into Diplomatic Policy and Operations, by Franklin P. Huddle. Committee Print (Washington, D.C.: Government Printing Office, June 1975), p. 6.

11. John Stuart Mill, Collected Works. Vol. II-III: Principles of Political Economy (Toronto: University of Toronto Press, 1963). Book 4, Chap. 1, Section 2.

12. Karl Marx, Capital, Vol. I, Chap. 13, passim. (New York: E. P. Dutton & Co., Inc., 1957).

13. Joseph Schumpeter, "The Instability of Capitalism," Economic Journal, XXVIII, (September, 1928), 361-86.

14. Robert Solow, "Technical Change and the Aggregate Production Function," Review of Economics and Statistics, XXXIX (August, 1957), 312-20.

15. Edwin Mansfield, "Economic Impact of International Technology Transfer," Research Management, XVII (January, 1974), 8.

16. Edward Denison, The Sources of Economic Growth in the United States and the Alternatives Before Us (New York: Committee for Economic Development, 1962).

17. Edward Denison, assisted by Jean-Pierre Pouillier, Why Growth Rates Differ: Postwar Experience in Nine Western Countries (Washington, D.C.: The Brookings Institution, 1967), pp. 296-319.

18. Denison, The Sources of Economic Growth; Stanley H. Cohn, "The Soviet Path to Economic Growth: A Comparative Analysis, Review of Income and Wealth, March 1976, p. 49.

19. Edward F. Denison, Accounting for United States Economic Growth, 1929-1969 (Washington, D.C.: The Brookings Institution, 1974), p. 80.

20. Simon Kuznets, Toward A Theory of Economic Growth (New York: W. W. Norton and Co., Inc., 1968), pp. 34-35.

21. Some economists prefer to use factor productivity--the ratio of combined inputs of capital, labor and land to output--as an indicator.

22. Stanislaw Gomulka, *Inventive Activity, Diffusion and the Stages of Economic Growth* (Aarhus, 1976).

23. *Ibid.*, pp. 50-59.

24. Organisation for Economic Co-operation and Development, *Gaps in Technology*, Book IV.

25. David Ricardo, *Principles of Political Economy and Taxation* (New York, E. P. Dutton & Co., 1948); Eli Heckscher, "The Effect of Foreign Trade on the Distribution of Income," *Ekonomisk Tidskrift*, XXI, 1919; Bertil Ohlin, *Interregional and International Trade* (Cambridge, Mass.: Harvard University Press, 1933).

26. Wassily Leontief, "Domestic Production and Foreign Trade: The American Position Reexamined," *Economia Internazionale*, VII (February, 1945), 9-45.

27. Donald Keesing, "Labor Skills and International Trade: Evaluating Many Trade Flows with a Single Measuring Device," *Review of Economics and Statistics*, XLVII (August, 1965), 287-94; "Labor Skills and Comparative Advantage," *American Economic Review*, LVI (May, 1966), 249-254; and "Labor Skills and the Structure of Trade in Manufactures," in *The Open Economy: Essays on International Trade and Finance*, ed. by Peter B. Kenen and Roger Lawrence (New York: Columbia University Press, 1968), 3-18.

28. For a survey of this literature, see John F. Morrall, III, *Human Capital, Technology and the Role of the United States in International Trade* (Gainesville, Fla.: The University of Florida Press, 1972).

29. Raymond Vernon, "International Investment and International Trade in the Product Cycle," *Quarterly Journal of Economics*, LXXX (May 1966), 190-207.

30. Michael Posner, "International Trade and Technical Change," *Oxford Economic Papers*, XIII (October, 1961), 323-41.

31. G. C. Hufbauer, *Synthetic Materials and the Theory of International Trade* (Cambridge, Mass.: Harvard University Press, 1966).

32. The unintentional flow of technology across international boundaries is frequently referred to as international diffusion of technology.

33. United Nations, Conference on Trade and Development, Secretariat, *Guidelines for the Study of the Transfer of Technology to Development Countries* (New York, 1972), p. 8.

34. For a general discussion of these mechanisms, see United Nations, Department of Economic and Social

Affairs, The Acquisition of Technology from Multi-national Corporations by Developing Countries (ST/ESA/12), New York, 1974, pp. 28-37; and United Nations, Institute for Training and Research, The International Transfer of Technology in the Establishment of the Petrochemical Industry in Developing Countries, by Robert B. Stobaugh, (UNITAR Research Report No. 12), New York, 1971, pp. 16-19.

35. Peter P. Gabriel, The International Transfer of Corporate Skills: Management Contracts in Less Developed Countries (Boston: Harvard Business School, 1967), pp. 22-37.

36. Ibid., p. 29.

37. United Nations, Economic Commission for Europe, Analytical Report on Industrial Co-operation among ECE Countries (Prepared by the Executive Secretary pursuant to Commission resolution 4 (XXVII) for submission to the Twenty-Eighth Session of the Economic Commission for Europe, Geneva, 1973), p. 2.

38. Ibid., pp. 7-14.

39. For a summary of the official Soviet position on various technology transfer issues, see E. Obminskii, "Rynok tekhnologii i razvivaiushchiecia strany," Mirovaia ekonomika i mezhdunarodnye otnosheniia, September, 1975, pp. 40-50.

40. For a useful survey of this problem, see Sara Jackson, Economically Appropriate Technologies for Developing Countries (Washington, D.C.: Overseas Development Council, 1972).

41. R. Hal Mason, "The Selection of Technology: A Continuing Dilemma," Columbia Journal of World Business, IX (Summer, 1974), 29-34.

42. See, for example, J. J. Servan-Schreiber, The American Challenge (New York: Atheneum, 1968).

43. Terutomo Ozawa, Japan's Technological Challenge to the West, 1950-1974: Motivation and Accomplishment (Cambridge: The M.I.T. Press, 1974), pp. 16-20.

44. Supra, pp. 19-23.

45. U.S. Department of Defense, Office of the Director of Defense Research and Engineering, An Analysis of Export Control of U.S. Technology--A DoD Perspective, a Report of the Defense Science Board Task Force on Export of U.S. Technology (Washington, D.C., February 4, 1976, pp. 4-8.

46. Ibid., p. 4.

47. James R. Basche, Jr. and Michael G. Duerr, International Transfer of Technology: A Worldwide Survey of Chief Executives (New York: The Conference Board, 1975), pp. 13-14.

48. Hall and Johnson, p. 312.

49. Ibid.

50. Supra, p. 21.

51. Constantine V. Vaitsos, "Strategic Choices in the Commercialization of Technology: The Point of View of Developing Countries," Social Science Journal, XXV, No. 3 (1973), 370-386.

52. John H. Dunning, "Technology, United States Investment, and European Economic Growth," in The International Corporation: A Symposium, ed. by Charles P. Kindleberger (Cambridge: The M.I.T. Press, 1970), p. 169.

53. Jack Baranson, "Technology Transfer Through the International Firm," American Economic Review, LX (May, 1970).

54. Basche and Duerr, pp. 3-5.

55. David J. Teece, The Multinational Corporation and the Resource Cost of International Technology Transfer (Cambridge, Mass.: Ballinger Publishing Company, 1976), p. 4.

56. Vaitsos, p. 371.

57. Basche and Duerr, pp. 3-7; Vaitsos, p. 375; and United Nations Conference on Trade and Development, Guidelines, pp. 20-27.

58. James Brian Quinn, "Technology Transfer by Multinational Companies," Harvard Business Review, XLVII (November-December, 1969), 160-161.

59. For a detailed description of the Japanese government's role in the technology transfer process, see Terutomo Ozawa, "Imitation, Innovation and Trade: A Study of Foreign Licensing Operations in Japan," (unpublished Ph.D. dissertation, Columbia University, 1966).

60. Ben Crain, "The Regulation of Direct Foreign Investment in Australia, Canada, France, Japan and Mexico," unpublished report, Library of Congress, Congressional Research Service (74-52E), February 28, 1974, pp. 30-53.

61. Miguel S. Wionczek, "Changing Attitudes in the Developing World," Intereconomics, No. 1, 1973, pp. 7-8.

62. Ibid., pp. 7-8; and United Nations, Department of Economic and Social Affairs, The Acquisition of Technology.

63. Richard E. Caves and Masu Uekusa, Industrial Organization in Japan (Washington, D.C.: The Brookings Institution, 1976), p. 126.

64. See especially, Hawthrone, and Daniel L. Spencer and Alexander Woroniak, "The Feasibility of Developing Transfer of Technology Functions," Kyklos, XX, No. 2 (1967).

65. Alexander Gerschenkron, Economic Backwardness in Historical Perspective, (New York: Frederick A. Praeger, 1965).

66. Supra, p. 20.

3. The Role of Western Technology in the Stalinist and Post–Stalinist Economic Systems

The importance of Western technology in Soviet economic development has varied over the years of Soviet rule. While one cannot quantify precisely the varying volumes of Western technology transfers to the Soviet Union, it is useful to define the historical record as much as possible in quantitative terms. The first section provides some quantitative data, albeit incomplete and imprecise, as proxies or indicators of the level of Soviet technology imports during the two periods which are the focus of this study. The subsequent sections explore the rationales for Soviet technology borrowing during the Stalinist and post-Stalinist eras. It is suggested that the two periods of Soviet economic development are characterized by fundamentally different growth strategies, which include different roles for foreign technology.

QUANTITATIVE DATA

The discussion in Chapter 2 highlights some of the difficulties in quantifying technology transfer. In general, technology is not easily defined, and economists have quantified its role in economic growth with only the crudest approximations. It is transferred from country to country through a variety of mechanisms, many of which are informal and unmeasured by official statistics. In the case of Soviet technology imports, the difficulties are compounded by the scarcity of data which are routinely collected in other countries.

Nevertheless, there are some quantitative data which provide useful indicators of the trends in Western technology transfer to the Soviet Union. Three kinds of data are presented. First, Soviet imports of machinery and equipment (which are the most technology-intensive goods) from the West provide one readily available indicator. Secondly, the discussion in Chapter 2 suggests that active technology transfer mechanisms are the most effective means of transferring commercial technologies. Data are presented for several kinds of active mechanisms--concessions and technical assistance contracts in the earlier period, and various forms of industrial cooperation agreements in the later period.[1] The critical role of people exchanges in the technology transfer process suggests the importance of measuring the movement of people, especially businessmen and other technical personnel, between the Soviet Union and the West. Such data are presented, although, unfortunately, only the sketchiest statistical data are available.

The machinery and equipment import statistics for the earlier period show a gradual increase of imports until the First Five-Year Plan (1928-1932), when there was an extraordinary upsurge. (See Table 3.1.) Imports peaked in 1931, and there was a sharp cutback, beginning in 1932 and accelerating in 1933. In the five years preceding the First Five-Year Plan, annual imports of machinery and equipment averaged approximately .3 billion rubles. During the First Five-Year Plan, they averaged 1.4 billion rubles, and during the Second Five-Year Plan, they fell back to the previous level of .3 billion rubles.

There has been a steady increase in Soviet machinery and equipment imports in the post-War period. Since 1955, annual imports have increased from a little over $100 in 1955 to approximately $4 billion in 1975. (See Table 3.2.) There has been an acceleration of the increase in machinery and equipment imports in the 1960s and 1970s and a quantitative jump during the Ninth Five-Year Plan (1970-1975). Overall, Soviet foreign trade, although a relatively small share of total economic activity, has been growing more rapidly than the economy as a whole. The industrial countries of the West have been increasing gradually their share of Soviet imports since the 1950s.

Published Soviet statistics on the numbers of concessions and technical assistance agreements in effect during the 1920s and 1930s are incomplete. Moreover, various Soviet sources cite different numbers. However, the statistics in Table 3.3 suggest the general trends. Concessions began in the early 1920s and peaked just before the First Five-Year Plan began. The number of technical assistance agreements

44

Table 3.1
Soviet Imports of Machinery and Equipment
(Value in 1000 Constant 1950 Rubles)

Year	Value
1921/22*	203,402
1922/23	110,887
1923/24	108,059
1924/25	344,256
1925/26	542,145
1926/27	547,176
1927/28	787,975
1928 (Oct-Dec)	172,114
1929	923,225
1930	1,726,561
1931	2,076,197
1932	1,366,946
1933	521,891
1934	202,900
1935	198,052
1936	419,459
1937	278,464

*From 1921-1938, official Soviet statistics were compiled by fiscal year, beginning in October of each year

Source: U.S.S.R. Ministerstvo vneshnei torgovli. Glavnoe tamozhennoe upravlenie. Vneshniaia torgovlia SSSR za 1918-1940 gg. Statisticheskii obzor. Moscow: Vneshtorgizdat, 1960.

TABLE 3.2
Soviet Imports of Western Machinery and Transport
Equipment, 1955-1975 (Millions of U.S. Dollars,
Current Prices)

1955	104
1956	139
1957	128
1958	123
1959	717
1960	310
1961	390
1962	436
1963	402
1964	489
1965	366
1966	395
1967	457
1968	639
1969	889
1970	905
1971	840
1972	1,113
1973	1,566
1974	2,100
1975	4,000*

*Estimate.

Source: Philip Hanson, "International Technology
Transfer from the West to the U.S.S.R.," in U.S.
Congress, Joint Economic Committee, Soviet Economy
in a New Perspective, Joint Committee Print (Washington, D.C.: Government Printing Office) October 14,
1976, p. 795.

in effect grew gradually during the 1920s and then
rapidly in the first years of the First Five-Year
Plan. They then began to decline sharply after peak-
ing in 1931. By the end of the 1930s, there were few
of either kind of agreement in effect.

The Soviet Government maintains secrecy about
the number of license agreements signed in recent
years, but some information has been published. One
Western estimate is that 250 licenses had been purchased from the West by 1973.[2] A Soviet source in
early 1974 stated that 120 new products and processes
had been introduced into production by that date

TABLE 3.3
Concessions and Technical Assistance Agreements in
Effect, 1925-1937

	Concessions	Technical Assistance
1925/26	NA	6
1926/27	NA	14
1927/28	73	17
1928	68	22
1929	59	70
1930	39	104
1931	30	124
1932	23	74
1933	21	46
1934	19	NA
1935	17	NA
1936	11	NA
1937	11	NA

NA--not available.

Sources: Vasilii Ignat'evich Kas'ianenko, Zavoevanie
ekonomicheskoi nezavisimosti SSSR (1917-1940 gg.)
(Moscow: Politicheskaia literatura, 1972), pp. 143-
191; Antony C. Sutton, Western Technology and Soviet
Economic Development, Volume I, 1917 to 1930, p. 9,
and Volume II, 1930 to 1945, p. 10 (Stanford:
Hoover Institution on War, Revolution and Peace,
1968 and 1971).

under license.[3] Soviet sources also suggest that
purchases of foreign licenses are expanding at a
rapid rate. The Soviet Union bought five times as
many licenses during the Eighth Five-Year Plan
(1966-1970) as it had in the preceding post-war
years.[4] During the Ninth Five-Year Plan, the value
of Soviet purchases of foreign licenses again increased rapidly, by 4.5 times.[5]
     Two other statistics indicate the rapid expan-
sion of Soviet technological ties to the West in
the 1960s and 1970s. In the mid-1960s, the Soviet
Government began to conclude various kinds of industrial cooperation agreements with Western firms. In
less than a decade, they are estimated to have concluded about 160 contracts with Western firms.[6] In

the same period, the Soviet Government signed approximately 105 scientific and technological cooperation
agreements with major Western firms.[7]
   There is little reliable data on travel between
the Soviet Union and the West by businessmen, engineers, technicians and workers. The available information suggests that, for the earlier period, such
travel peaked during the First Five-Year Plan and
declined rapidly thereafter. An official count of
foreigners working in the Soviet Union in November
1928 revealed that there were 379 specialists
(engineers and technicians) and 505 workers.[8]
Another count in September 1932 found that there were
1910 specialist and 10,655 workers.[9] The 1932 total
was clearly an extraordinarily large number by Soviet
standards, reflecting Soviet reliance on relatively
active technology transfer mechanisms during the
First Five-Year Plan. Soviet industrial specialists
also traveled abroad, though in smaller numbers.
Nine hundred Soviet specialists reportedly traveled
abroad in 1928-29, and 485, in 1931.[10] While
personal contacts with the West were numerous, they
were short-lived. Travel between the West and the
Soviet Union declined rapidly after 1932, as concessions and technical assistance agreements were
liquidated and other technical ties were broken.
   The data on travel by businessmen, engineers
and other technology transfer agents are also sketchy
for the current period. Various Soviet sources pub-
lish statistics on foreigners visiting the U.S.S.R.
and Soviet citizens traveling abroad. However, the
figures lump together tourists, diplomats, businessmen and all other categories of travelers. The
travel statistics for the Ninth Five-Year Plan, broken down by travel between the Soviet Union and
socialist countries and between the Soviet Union and
non-socialist countries, are provided in Table 3.4
During the five-year period, a total of 14.4 million
foreigners traveled to the Soviet Union, and 10.6
million Soviet citizens traveled abroad. By comparison, approximately the same number of Soviet and
foreign citizens crossed the Soviet border in the
previous 15 years.[11] Although, one cannot determine
exactly what share of the rapid increase is related
to economic and technological exchanges, Soviet press
accounts of the latter suggest that it is quite
substantial.

TABLE 3.4
Numbers of Foreigners Visiting the USSR and of Soviet Citizens Traveling Abroad 1971-1975 (Figures in Thousands)

Year	Foreigners Entering the USSR ——— Origin ———			Soviet Citizens Going Abroad ——— Destination ———		
	Total	Socialist Countries	Other Countries	Total	Socialist Countries	Other Countries
1971	2,000	1,300	700	1,817	1,000	817a
1972	2,317	1,442	875	1,972	1,118	854
1973	2,909	1,599	1,310	2,083	1,214	869
1974	3,446	1,888	1,558	2,225	1,332	893
1975	3,700	2,108	1,592	2,500	1,517	983
TOTAL	14,372	8,337	6,035	10,597	6,181	4,416

a - Figure for 1970

Source: Radio Liberty Research, "The USSR's Plans for Tourism in 1976-80," RL 34/77, February 3, 1977, p. 2.

THE STALINIST MODEL OF ECONOMIC DEVELOPMENT

What has come to be known as the Stalinist
model for economic development was initiated during
the First Five-Year Plan and lasted until well after
Stalin's death. The model was quintessentially a
strategy for rapid industrialization. Stalinist
economic planners began with an economy which had
a large capacity for producing agricultural products
and a relatively small capacity for producing machinery, equipment and the other industrial goods which
provide the means for industrialization. Their task
during the First Five-Year Plan was to restructure
the economy in order to provide an industrial base
for future growth. This required both a major
reallocation of resources and a fundamental change
in Soviet industrial technology. These structural
changes were to be largely accomplished by 1932. A
corollary prerequisite was to create a new economic
administrative apparatus which could exert the necessary controls over economic resources.

The reallocation of resources was accomplished
largely by channeling labor, capital and materials
into the "leading sectors" of the economy (primarily
heavy industry), while minimizing outlays on non-
growth promoting and non-defense sectors. Soviet
planners operated with what has been described as a
simple set of imperatives:

1. allocate to the military the resources
   needed to fulfill strategic goals, and lay
   aside the minimum requirements for consumption and the development of the economic
   infrastructure;
2. maximize the flow of resources into heavy
   industry and specify how the resources are
   to be combined to maximize output; and
3. distribute the residuals to non-priority
   sectors, such as agriculture and light
   industry.[12]

Implicit in these imperatives was an unbalanced
growth pattern, with some parts of the economy growing at the expense of others. Another essential element was a very high investment (and savings) rate,
with the consequent deprivation of the consumer.

In changing Soviet industrial technology, Soviet
planners relied heavily on foreign trade during the
First Five-Year Plan and made little use of it thereafter. Large amounts of raw materials--particularly
timber, petroleum products and grain--were exported

to pay for a massive influx of new machinery, equipment and industrial materials from the industrial West. Western technology transfers, which had already begun to play a significant role in the Soviet economy, increased dramatically. Like domestic resources, imports of capital and technology were concentrated in a small segment of the economy. As described by Soviet economists and policy makers, there were two major aspects of Soviet foreign trade policy. First, Soviet foreign trade was import oriented: it was valued primarily for the contribution imports could make to the industrialization process. Goods were exported only to pay for imports. In the words of a Stalinist foreign trade official, "...the main task of Soviet exports is to accumulate foreign exchange resources through the sale of Soviet goods abroad to pay for Soviet imports."[13] Secondly, the goal of foreign trade was import substitution-- to rid the Soviet Union of the need for further imports:

> ...The necessity of faster tempos of industrial-
> ization, of a creation of high-powered metal-
> lurgical and machinebuilding industries in the
> shortest possible time demanded an expansion of
> our trade relations with capitalist countries in
> order to utilize their advanced technology for
> the quickest realization of our goals. This
> posed the problem of not wasting foreign ex-
> change on items of secondary importance, but
> importing as much as possible as quickly as
> possible the machinery and metals needed to
> create heavy industry and to free the country
> from the need to import machinery and equip-
> ment...[14]

Given such an import substitution strategy, a cutback of imports at some time in the future was predictable. In fact, the curtailment of imports was more abrupt than planned. Eugene Zaleski's calculations of foreign trade plan fulfillment show that Soviet import plans were substantially over-fulfilled until 1931 and seriously underfulfilled in the later years of the First Five-Year Plan.[15] Several constraints confronted by Soviet planners help to explain this development. The accelerated growth rate of the economy created new demands for machinery, equipment and industrial supplies which could only be met by imports. Moreover, major industrial projects, the output of which had been planned to sub-stitute for imports, were not finished on time. The

problems of absorbing Western technology were greater
than anticipated. Imported machinery and equipment
lay idle during construction delays, domestic supply
plans were not met, and there were frequent break-
downs after startup of new enterprises.[16]

On the export side, production goals for exportable goods, particularly agricultural products were
seriously underfulfilled. The situation was exacerbated by a sharp reduction in world market prices
for Soviet raw material exports and an adverse shift
in Soviet terms of trade.

Instead of a five-year surplus of 791.9 million
rubles anticipated in the five-year plan, a deficit
of 389 million rubles accumulated from October 1928
through December 1932.[17] The desire of Soviet
planners to reduce the trade deficit contributed to
the decision to restrict imports in the last years
of the First Five-Year Plan. The deficit might have
been financed by taking greater advantage of credits
from supplier countries. However, this option had
been rejected by Soviet planners:

> The problems of the first two years [of the
> five-year plan] are a result of the fact that,
> during the drafting of the five-year plan,
> attention was not paid to the possibility of
> increasing long-term foreign trade credits; it
> would have been improper to include in the draft
> of the five-year plan an increase in foreign
> trade credits, for this would have signified
> the dependence on foreign credits for achieving
> the intended tempo of development of the econo-
> my; it was more proper and correct to calculate
> only on domestic resources.[18]

Thus, the balance of payments constraint was exacerbated because planners had feared becoming dependent
on capitalist lenders.

In choosing the kinds of industrial technologies
upon which Soviet industrialization would be based,
Soviet planners were confronted with a fundamental
dilemma. Their perceived need to import the most
advanced Western technology came into conflict with
their factor endowment (i.e., a severe capital shortage coupled with a relatively unlimited supply of
unskilled labor). Since new technologies tend to be
capital-intensive and labor-saving, reliance on them,
at least in the short run, would appear to be an
inefficient use of available resources. This problem
received considerable attention from Soviet economists
in the 1920s and early 1930s. It was an element of

the important economic debates of the 1920s on basic
economic growth strategy and of a subsequent debate
on the "effectiveness of capital investment."[19]

Still, Soviet technology imports revealed a
clear preference for the most advanced technologies
in the West. In the conditions of the late 1920s,
this meant a preference for capital-intensive, American mass-production techniques over the relatively
labor-intensive, European model of small-batch production. Reliance on the European approach, while
probably more appropriate for Soviet factor proportions, was rejected on the grounds that it would
condemn the Soviet Union to an inferior technological
status for years to come. Soviet planners stressed
the longer term advantages of adopting the most
modern technologies. They believed that only by
transplanting these new technologies to the Soviet
Union could they ever catch up and overtake the
capitalist industrial powers. David Granick points
out that because of the rapid tempo of industrialization, it was especially important for the latest
technologies to be chosen. Investment in the high-
priority sectors would be necessarily lumpy: those
sectors would be the beneficiaries of major capital
investments for a period of only a few years and
could thereafter expect relatively little attention.
Thus, Soviet industry had to make a quantum jump
technologically "if only to compensate for the almost
inevitable falling-behind in the following decade
or decades."[20]

In selecting foreign technologies, Soviet officials frequently had quite limited choices. To a
large extent, Soviet planners were confronted by the
same kind of technological fixity of production processes which policy makers in developing countries
face today. Charles Wilber argues persuasively that
the choice of Soviet planners was frequently not
between labor-intensive and capital-intensive techniques, but between labor-intensive and more productive techniques.[21] Thus, in many cases, Soviet
importers had a limited choice of technologies; their
task was simply to choose between the most modern,
efficient technology and an obsolete, inefficient
one. Norton Dodge's study of the tractor industry
supports this notion. He found that the Soviet
decision to model the Stalingrad tractor plant after
modern, mass-production American plants resulted not
only in substantial savings in labor but also savings
in capital (compared to old, small-scale Soviet
tractor plants).[22] Thus, Wilber and Dodge suggest
that Soviet planners maximized output and economized

on capital by adapting the most advanced techniques to their own factor proportions.

A major element in Soviet adaptation of advanced Western technologies during the First Five-Year Plan was the employment of a dual technology strategy in industry. The most advanced Western techniques were chosen for basic production processes, such as furnaces, foundries, forges and assembly lines, while older, labor-intensive techniques were used for auxiliary processes, such as materials handling, repairs, and clerical work. By using new technologies in the most capital-intensive operations, Soviet industry succeeded in lowering the capital-output ratio of many kinds of production. At the same time, abundant labor could be employed in industrial operations where capital-saving potential was relatively limited. This approach allowed Soviet industrial managers to take advantage of their plentiful labor supplies, while attempting to maximize capital productivity.[23]

The dual technology strategy was not followed consistently by Soviet planners, particularly in the mid- to late 1930s. There were numerous cases of huge, mass-production plants, modeled after U.S. facilities, which resulted in highly inefficient uses of capital because of inadequate labor and management skills, small size of local markets, or inadequate supplies of material inputs.[24] A narrow, engineering approach to production frequently resulted in the irrational construction of large-scale, vertically integrated facilities which could not be managed efficiently. The inefficiencies of mindless devotion to such large, capital-intensive projects became apparent to Soviet planners and leaders in the 1930s. A campaign against "gigantomania" ensued, which led to some moderation in the immediate prewar period.

Another aspect of Soviet absorption policy which helped to economize on scarce capital was the high utilization rate for new machinery and equipment.[25] In part, this was accomplished through the use of multiple shifts in the operation of plants and equipment. The use of two shifts was a common feature in Soviet factories in both the pre-war and post-war periods. In addition, the Soviets kept plants and equipment in operation for longer periods than elsewhere. Thus, they avoided investments for new capital at the expense of keeping obsolete and inefficient machinery and equipment in operation.

When machinery and equipment were replaced, little attention was given to technological improvement of the production process. Soviet planners minimized capital investments for research and development and tooling up for new kinds of machinery and equipment and new production processes. They also minimized hard currency expenditures by not importing new generations of machinery. Likewise, products tended to be standardized, with relatively little variety and little improvement over time. These were elements of what Soviet economists now refer to as an extensive economic growth strategy (i.e., reliance on increases of capital and labor inputs for economic growth, with relatively little attention to improving the productivity of those inputs through technological progress).

One significant departure from the extensive growth strategy was heavy Soviet emphasis on vocational and technical training. While they were temporarily dependent on "bourgeois specialists"-- engineers and managers of prerevolutionary days who were kept on the job--the Soviets made a great effort to replace them as soon as possible with "Red experts." Formal education, from the early grades through universities and vocational schools was emphasized, particularly during the First Five-Year Plan. A somewhat unusual aspect of Soviet training policy was heavy emphasis on on-the-job training in factories, including modern facilities imported from the West. The employment of unskilled workers as operators of advanced machinery and equipment, which they could not operate properly, frequently resulted in production delays and damage to machines. In part, this situation appears to have resulted from a lack of appreciation of the difficulties of absorbing new technology. However, there may have been an element of deliberate design. For example, Stalin claimed that this approach hastened the process of developing technical skills in the work force.

> We proceeded openly and consciously to the inevitable outlays and over-expenditures associated with the shortage of sufficiently trained people who knew how to handle machines. True, we destroyed many machines at the same time, but at the same time we won the most important thing--time--and we created the most precious thing in the economy--Cadres.[26]

The Stalinist growth strategy in the First Five-Year Plan must be judged a success in one important respect: it changed radically the structure of the Soviet economy. From a basically agricultural economy, the Soviet Union emerged as a major industrial power. The overall economic growth rate was modest in the First Five-Year Plan, but quite rapid during the Second. Richard Moorsteen and Raymond Powell estimate that Soviet gross national product grew at a rate of 6.2 percent per year (in 1937 prices) for the entire period 1928-1937.[27] Most of the increased output came in the industrial sector. Moreover, by the mid-1930s, high priority industries had achieved a relatively high degree of technological sophistication. Partially on the basis of acquired Western technology, the Soviets had built the necessary base to increase industrial output at a rapid rate. Thus, their primary goal--rapid industrialization--was largely achieved.

However, there were distinctive shortcomings in Soviet economic performance. First, performance in the Soviet economy was uneven. The concentration of resources in heavy industry predictably resulted in the neglect and consequently poor performance in agriculture, light industry, and infrastructural activities. More importantly for long-run Soviet needs, performance with respect to technological progress was poor. This is evidenced by Soviet productivity performance. Soviet industry seriously underfulfilled the First Five-Year Plan goals for increases in labor productivity. While Soviet planners had anticipated a doubling of productivity, the actual increase by the end of 1932 was only 41 percent (according to Soviet estimates).[28] In his history of the period, Maurice Dobb notes that the planned productivity improvement was expected to come from new plant and equipment and more rationalized industrial organization, but that "there had evidently been excessive optimism as to the speed with which many of the new plants could be brought into full and successful operation...".[29] Estimates by Moorsteen and Powell confirm that Soviet factor productivity performance during this period was disappointing. After rising by 6 percent from 1928 to 1930, productivity fell by 10 percent from 1930 to 1932, then rose by 24 percent from 1932 to 1937. (It fell again in the late 1930s and during the War, and began to increase after the War.) While acknowledging that their productivity estimates are crude, they found that the growth rate of Soviet productivity "does not appear unambiguously high" for the period they studied (1928-1961).[30] Their estimates for the entire period range from 0.1 percent to 3.2 percent. This represents the same order of productivity growth rates as the advanced industrial countries. (By comparison, the U.S. productivity advances during the same period averaged 1.5 to 2 percent.) They conclude that Soviet productivity performance was surprisingly poor, when the potential productivity gains which might have been derived from technology imports from the West are considered. Only a part of this poor performance can be accounted for by the setbacks during World War II. Their estimates show no large increases in the prewar period when technology imports were heavy. Moorsteen and Powell attribute the relatively poor performance to managerial inefficiency, to the concentration of technology imports and other resources in a relatively small part of the economy, and to the limited capacity of the Soviet economy "to obtain and make use of new techniques."[31]

In an extensive study of the contribution of Western technology to Soviet economic development, Antony Sutton concludes that "Western technical assistance was the major causal factor in Soviet economic growth for the period 1928-1945."[32] This view, generally expressed in less extreme terms, has gained considerable currency among many observers in the West. However, Sutton's finding is contradicted by Moorsteen's and Powell's estimates of Soviet productivity performance. An important conclusion of their study is that Soviet economic growth during the 1928-1961 period was extensive; i.e., that growth can be attributed primarily to increments of capital and labor, rather than increases in factor productivity. They thus suggest that technology, including technology imports from the West, accounted for a relatively small part of Soviet growth. While Western technology is assigned an important role by Moorsteen and Powell and most other Western students of Soviet economic growth, its contribution was undoubtedly limited by Soviet absorption problems and by Soviet measures to restrict economic and technological ties to the West. Naturally the Moorsteen-Powell estimates pertain to the economy as a whole. If one looks at individual Western-assisted projects, one may find huge gains from Western assistance. It is important to keep in mind, however, that the benefits of Western technology were concentrated in certain sectors and limited primarily to particular periods of time. Western technology contributed relatively little to some Soviet economic activities, and the cutback of technological ties to the West in the 1930s reduced the potential gains from technology imports.

THE POST-STALINIST MODEL

The extensive pattern of economic development which characterizes the Stalinist model far outlived its chief architect. Indeed, Stalin's legacy in economic planning is felt acutely by Soviet economists today. For a number of years, a major theme in Soviet economic literature has been the need to shift from an extensive to an intensive growth strategy. The continuation of an extensive growth pattern in the post-World War II Soviet economy has been clearly demonstrated by Stanley Cohn, who applies Denison's methodology to explain Soviet economic growth and compare it with economic growth with economic growth in Western industrial countries.[33] Cohn finds that the Soviet growth rate has not been unusually high: it is only slightly higher than Denison's estimates for Northwest European countries and barely half that of Japan. The most distinctive feature of Soviet growth performance, he finds, is the comparatively low rate of growth of output per unit of input, i.e., joint factor productivity. Japan, France, Germany and Italy had substantially higher rates of increase, while the United States and the United Kingdom had somewhat lower rates. At the same time, the Soviet Union had rapid rates of increase for all three factor inputs--land, labor, and capital--rates which were exceeded only by Japan. Cohn further shows that in terms of proportionate contribution to economic growth, factor productivity accounted for a smaller percentage in the Soviet Union than in any other country compared.

Not only is the growth rate of Soviet productivity comparatively low, it is also declining. According to estimates by Rush V. Greenslade, Soviet labor productivity, after growing rapidly in the 1950s, slowed to a still respectable 3.4 percent average annual growth rate in the 1960s and then to a disappointing 1.8 percent during 1971-1975.[34] Productivity growth rates for the other factors of production have also slowed noticeably. The reasons for declining factor productivity growth in the Soviet economy are numerous. Poor agricultural performance, inefficient planning and management, the end of the rapid productivity increases associated with recovery from World War II, and declining marginal returns to large infusions of capital are among the major contributiong factors.[35]

From the standpoint of increasing economic growth, the Soviet predicament is exacerbated by less favorable trends in resource availabilities. Shorter work hours and a slowdown in the growth of the work force are expected to create a substantial labor shortage in the Soviet Union in the late 1980s and 1990s. According to Western estimates, increments in the able-bodied ages in the Soviet Union during the 1980s will be only about one-fifth of the numbers of the period 1971-1975. Increments in the 1990s will also be lower than the current period.[36] Since the traditional sources of new labor supplies--migration of labor from the agricultural section and increased participation of women in the labor force--are almost exhausted, this trend will be a serious constraint on future growth.

At the same time, Soviet planners are finding it difficult to maintain the high rates of capital investment which characterized the Stalinist model.[37] Moreover, the number of claimants on Soviet capital investments has grown. The needs of agriculture, defense, and the infrastructure are diverting resources away from the growth-promoting heavy industrial sector. In addition, the needs of Soviet consumers can no longer be overlooked; quality consumer goods must be made available to meet rising expectations and to provide incentives to increase labor productivity.

The net effect of factor input and productivity trends has been to create a declining Soviet growth rate. After averaging between 5 and 6 percent increases in GNP in the 1950s and 1960s, the average growth rate in 1971-1975 slipped to 3.8 percent. (See Table 3.5.) This trend is particularly disturbing to Soviet leaders, who have long emphasized high growth rates as the key success indicator of the Soviet economy and who stress the need to surpass the capitalist economies.

These adverse economic trends have created the rationale for adoption of an intensive growth strategy. Abram Bergson maintains that the Stalinist model's influence on Soviet planning, which has been waning since Khrushchev's reign, has finally given way to a "new growth model."[38] The major elements of the new model are a more balanced growth pattern, with more resources being allocated to formerly low-priority sectors of the economy, and reliance on increasing productivity to bring about economic growth. Central to the intensive growth strategy is an increasing emphasis on technological progress in the economy. The attention to technological progress has become increasingly prominent in Soviet economic plans. Thus, the Ninth Five-Year Plan projected ambitious growth rates for industry and

TABLE 3.5
U.S.S.R.: Average Annual Rates of Growth of Total GNP Production, Factor Inputs, and Factor Productivity, 1951-75 (Percent)

	1951-55	1955-60	1961-65	1966-70	1971-75
Total GNP	6.0	5.8	5.0	5.5	3.8
Inputs:					
Labor (man-hours), capital, and land[a]	4.5	3.9	4.1	3.9	4.1
Man-hours	1.9	.6	1.6	2.0	1.9
Capital	9.0	9.8	8.7	7.5	7.9
Land	4.0	1.3	.6	-.3	.9
Factor productivity:					
Labor (man-hours), capital, and land	1.4	1.8	.9	1.5	-.2
Man-hours	4.6	5.1	3.4	3.4	1.8
Capital	-2.7	-3.6	-3.3	-1.9	-3.8
Land	1.9	4.4	4.4	5.8	2.9

[a]Inputs have been combined using a Cobb-Douglas (linearly homogeneous) production function with weights of 60.2, 36.7, and 3.1 percent for labor, capital, and land, respectively.

Source: Rush V. Greenslade, "The Real Gross National Product of the U.S.S.R., 1950-1975," in JEC, p. 279.

60

agriculture which were to be accomplished largely by
productivity gains and introduction of new technology. In his foreword to the published version of
the Ninth Five-Year Plan, Nikolai K. Baibakov, Chairman of the State Planning Committee, reaffirmed the
24th Party Congress's directive that the "main task"
of the plan was:

> ...to ensure a substantial rise in the material
> and cultural standard of living on the basis
> of high rates of development of socialist pro-
> duction, a rise in production efficiency,
> scientific and technical progress, and a
> faster growth of labor productivity.[39]

Some of the specific goals of the plan, such as
planned labor productivity growth, proved to be
overly optimistic and were not met.

The Tenth Five-Year Plan again placed major
emphasis on technological progress. The "Basic
Guidelines of Development of the USSR National
Economy in 1976-1980," issued at the Twenty-Fifth
Party Congress, make it clear that most of the
anticipated growth is expected to come from increases in productivity. Brezhnev, in his report to
the Congress, said, "The first order task remains
the speeding up of scientific and technical progress."
He called the new Five-Year Plan "the Five-Year Plan
of effectiveness and quality."[40] According to a
Soviet planning official, increases in labor productivity are expected to account for 90 percent of
the increase in industrial output and practically
the entire increase in agricultural production and
construction and assembly operations.[41] The Plan
directives indicate that most of the productivity
increase is to be achieved through technological
progress--both by increasing the tempo of domestic
innovation and by importing foreign technology.

Productivity increases have also been linked
by Soviet economists to economic reform. Since
Stalin's death, Soviet leaders have experimented
with a variety of reforms designed to improve national economic planning through improved collection of
statistical data and application of mathematical
techniques. At the microeconomic level, they prom-
ised more efficient enterprise management through
various decentralization schemes and more effective
incentive structures. Judging from both Soviet
press commentary and Soviet economic performance,
the results of the reforms have been disappointing.
Since 1973, emphasis has been placed on creation of

large industrial associations--conglomerates of
enterprises with similar or complementary output.
Associations are designed primarily to give managers
some degree of independence in decision making and
to improve coordination of inputs and outputs of
related enterprises. In addition, Soviet leaders
hope that this reform will improve technological
performance in Soviet industry.
Foreign trade has clearly been assigned a central role in the new growth strategy. According to
the Soviet economist I. Ivanov, the following goals
in foreign trade have been discussed in relation to
Soviet long-term planning (i.e., for the period
1975-1990):

- Ensuring a growth of foreign trade surpassing
  that of national income;
- expanding export specialization in the most
  advanced industries and industrial capacities
  oriented to exports;
- evaluating new products and technology for the
  reduction in practice exclusively on the basis
  of conforming to the world technological level
  and world market requirements;
- the USSR taking a major place as an exporter
  not only of raw materials but also of machinery
  and technology, including "research-intensive"
  ones and ones destined for Western markets;
- setting up a well-established foreign trade
  infrastructure abroad (transport, service,
  financing, insurance facilities, commercial
  representation network, etc.);
- expanding the geography of foreign trade relations;
- evaluating imports as an alternative source
  while making decisions on domestic investments;
- allocating to imports a larger share in improving the technological level of Soviet agriculture, the service sector, and the economy as
  a whole;
- incorporating international technological
  exchange in R & D plans and programmes.[42] [sic]

Efforts to implement many of the goals identified by Ivanov are evident. During the Eighth and
Ninth Five-Year Plans, foreign trade was one of
the most dynamic sectors of the Soviet economy.
For example, from 1971-1975, it grew about two and
one-half times faster than Soviet GNP. While the
planned growth rate of foreign trade during that
period was 35 percent, the actual growth rate was

186 percent. The Tenth Five-Year Plan goal of a
further 30-35 percent increase in foreign trade also
seems likely to be exceeded.[43] Trade with Western
industrial countries is accounting for an increasingly large share of total Soviet trade. From an
average of less than 20 percent in the 1960s, trade
with the West rose to 31 percent of total trade
turnover in 1974-1975.[44] While some of the increased
trade with the West can be accounted for by larger
grain imports, high-technology imports have also
increased rapidly and are playing an increasingly
important role in Soviet investment plans. Imports
have accounted for 10-12 percent of total Soviet
investment in machinery and equipment in the 1970s.[45]

Donald Green and Herbert Levine have attempted
to quantify the contribution of Western technology
to Soviet economic growth during the 1958-1973 period.
Their analysis, based on the Soviet Econometric Model
constructed by the Stanford Research Institute and
Wharton Econometric Forecasting Associates, suggested that increases in Western technology transfers to the Soviet Union during this period had
made a major contribution to Soviet economic growth.
Specifically, they concluded that without the new
Soviet emphasis on importing Western machinery, 15
percent of the Soviet industrial growth rate during
1968-1973 would have been foregone.[46]

Soviet imports of Western technology tend to be
much broader based than in the past. A wide spectrum
of Soviet industries have benefitted from Western
technology transfers. For the first time, these
include consumer industries, such as passenger cars,
food-processing, tableware, and tourist facilities,
as well as producer goods industries. In addition,
Soviet agriculture has been the recipient of Western technology in the chemical fertilizers, farm
machinery and animal husbandry sectors.[47]

The changing role of foreign trade in the new
growth model goes beyond a mere increase in volume
and diversification of imports. Soviet economists
are paying increasing attention to the advantages
of progressive integration of the Soviet economy
into the world economy. There has been particular
interest in international specialization or international division of labor in industrial production.
One of the clearest expositions of what Soviet
economists mean by these terms is provided by the
Soviet economist N. P. Shmelev.[48] He bemoans the
predominance of "national industrial complexes" in
the industrialized world, which include "if not all,
at least a significant part of all the branches of

modern industry." In obvious reference to the development strategies of the Soviet Union and other socialist countries, Shmelev notes the negative consequences of building parallel, duplicative and relatively small-scale industries in separate countries. While maintaining that this pattern of development was the logical result of political tensions between socialist and capitalist countries, he claims that the new international environment dictates a new strategy of international specialization to include industrial enterprises in both economic systems. This, he explains, means specializing investments in such a way as to allow long production runs and economies of scale. It entails cooperative industrial relations between all advanced industrial countries, taking advantage of a common market for supplies of raw materials, manufactured goods and the results of research and development.

To put Soviet discussions of international specialization into perspective, it should be noted that this process of international specialization has not proceeded very far in Soviet economic policy. Even within the confines of the Council of Mutual Economic Assistance (CEMA), where policy makers have long talked of coordinating their annual and long-term plans, there has been relatively little specialization. However, traces of such a process are already evident. Several kinds of industrial cooperation agreements, such as those involving long-term Soviet commitments to deliver raw materials in exchange for Western technology, fit into this framework. Another important manifestation of a new approach to international specialization is the development of special export capacity in some Soviet manufacturing industries.

Soviet foreign trade planners no longer rely on commodities that happen to be in surplus to meet their export needs. There has been a concerted drive to produce high-quality manufactured goods which can compete successfully on international markets.[49] This new approach has led to assignment of a high priority for exportable products, which sometimes results in higher quality for exports than for domestic goods.[50] Large projects assisted by imports of Western technology often earmark a part of their output for foreign markets in order to repay hard currency credits. Exports of manufactured goods are seen as a means of promoting Soviet economic growth by allowing Soviet industry to reap the benefits of comparative advantage and

international specialization. The emphasis on exports of manufactured goods is largely a result of
the increasingly high cost of exploiting domestic
natural resources. This rationale is particularly
compelling because major new sources of traditional
Soviet raw material exports--wood products, oil and
other minerals--are located in remote areas of
Siberia.
    The Soviet drive to expand exports of manu-
factured goods to the West is necessitated in part
by continual Soviet hard currency balance of trade
deficits. In the ten-year period 1966-1975, the
Soviet Union had only one surplus in its hard currency trade. (See Table 3.6.) At the end of 1976,
the Soviet Union had accumulated an estimated hard-
currency debt of $14 billion, and the debt is ex-
pected to continue growing in the immediate future.
This aspect of Soviet trade with the West bears
strong resemblance to Soviet foreign trade problems
of the early 1930s. However, the current response--
allowing indebtedness to grow while developing export industries--is in sharp contrast to Soviet
policy in the earlier period.

TABLE 3.6
U.S.S.R.: Hard Currency Trade Deficit (In millions
of U.S. dollars)

	Exports	Imports	Balance
1966	1,517	1,755	-238
1967	1,711	1,616	+95
1968	1,909	2,018	-109
1969	2,125	2,436	-311
1970	2,197	2,711	-514
1971	2,652	2,955	-303
1972	2,815	4,171	-1,356
1973	4,818	6,566	-1,748
1974	7,630	8,541	-912
1975	7,800	14,081	-6,281

Source: John Farrell and Paul Ericson, "Soviet
Trade and Payments with the West," in JEC, p. 728

The export of manufactured goods is also seen as a means of promoting domestic technological progress. On the one hand, increased foreign exchange earnings allow greater imports of Western technology. One of the means developed in recent years to provide incentives for Soviet enterprises to export is to return a part of the hard currency earnings to the enterprise. These earnings are allotted to the acquisition of new foreign licenses, technical specifications and machinery. The primary purpose of the acquired technology is the production of additional exports and improving their quality.[51] The Soviets are also becoming aware of the importance of competition on international markets as an incentive to produce higher quality, more sophisticated goods. One Soviet economist has described the international market place as a "filter" which allows only high-quality goods to pass. This filtration process, he says, has a beneficial influence on the structure and quality of domestic production. It encourages the production of goods which meets the highest world standards.[52] The development of Soviet export industries is in its formative stages. There are still formidable problems in industrial organization, quality control, marketing skills, servicing and other matters that must be solved in order to succeed in this endeavor.[53]

The new export orientation of Soviet foreign trade suggests an effort to imitate the Japanese example of using foreign technology to create export industries. Indeed, the Soviet press reflects a keen Soviet interest in this aspect of Japanese economic development.[54] There is a particular Soviet interest in the contribution of foreign technology to Japan's high growth rate and Japan's success in capturing export markets in both high technology and mature manufacturing industries. Some Soviet observers betray a scarcely hidden admiration of the Japanese government's role in screening technology imports, Japanese industry's ability to put new ideas rapidly into the production process and the quality control and marketing techniques of Japanese managers.[55] Perhaps underlying Soviet interest in the Japanese model is the recognition that Japan has borrowed technology without allowing substantial control by foreign firms in the domestic economy.

In the current period, Soviet planners face different problems than their Stalinist counterparts in choosing among foreign technologies to import. Since Soviet factor proportions are similar to those in Western industrial countries, the choice between

66

labor-intensive and capital-intensive technologies is no longer a serious problem. The current Soviet emphasis on labor-saving technologies for both basic and auxiliary production processes makes the Stalinist dual technology strategy irrelevant to the new model. Current Soviet planners show an absolute predilection to import the most modern, largest scale technologies from the West.

A new option for Soviet planners is the choice between foreign and domestic technologies. Heavy Soviet research and development in some high-priority sectors of the economy have resulted in the development of sophisticated technologies which can compete with those developed in the West. For example, in selected industries, the transfer of technology from the military sector may be a realistic alternative to importing.[56]

Even when Soviet technology is inferior, it may be chosen to economize on hard currency expenditures. In addition, unlike the situation which pertained at the beginning of the First Five-Year Plan, there is a broad-based industrial structure in the Soviet Union. Consequently, the choice of technology may hinge on a decision of whether to build an entirely new plant or to modernize existing facilities.

A common feature of the Stalinist and post-Stalinist development models is the heavy emphasis on technical training to raise the technical level of domestic workers, engineers and managers. However, unlike the earlier period, investment in manpower training is now coupled with a major investment in domestic research and development. While Soviet planners have been disappointed in the returns to investments in domestic R & D, continued large expenditures in this area are central to the new development strategy. In contrast to the Stalinist approach, Soviet managers are now encouraged to replace obsolete and unproductive machinery with new models embodying the latest technological advances.[57] (Although the incentive structure for enterprise managers sometimes works at cross-purposes.) The pressure to introduce more productive and efficient machinery and equipment leads inevitably to simultaneous efforts to increase domestic production of new machinery and equipment and increasing the importation of new generations of machinery and equipment.

The major departure in Soviet economic growth strategy portends a continued expansion of Western technology transfers to the Soviet Union. The underlying economic conditions which inspired the new

67

strategy will not change in the foreseeable future.
Because of its inability to generate major increases
in factor inputs, the Soviet economy will have to
rely on technological change as a source of continued
growth. Indeed, the logic of the new growth model
will become more compelling in the 1980s. The need
for technological progress, in turn, provides an
incentive for continued technological interchange
with the West. Thus, Soviet leaders will be unable
to change courses, as they did in the 1930s, without considerable economic costs.

NOTES

    1. See Chapter 4 for definitions and further
discussions of these mechanisms.
    2. J. Wilczynski, Technology in Comecon:
Acceleration of Technological Progress through
Economic Planning and the Market (New York: Praeger
Publishers, 1974), p. 301.
    3. Pravda, March 12, 1974, p. 1.
    4. M. L. Gorodisskiy, Licenses in U.S.S.R.
Foreign Trade, trans. by the National Technical
Information Service (Moscow: Mezhdunarodnyye
otnosheniia, 1972), p. 18.
    5. M. M. Maksimova, SSSR i mezhdunarodnoe
ekonomicheskoe sotrudnichestvo (Moscow: Izdatel'stvo
"Mysl'," 1977), p. 59.
    6. Maureen R. Smith, "Industrial Cooperation
Agreements: Soviet Experience and Practice," in
U.S. Congress, Joint Economic Committee, Soviet
Economy in a New Perspective, Joint Committee Print
(Washington, D.C.: Government Printing Office,
October 14, 1976), p. 768. (Hereinafter referred
to as JEC.)
    7. Lawrence H. Theriot, "Governmental and
Private Industry Cooperation with the Soviet Union
in the Fields of Science and Technology," in JEC
pp. 739-766. (See Appendix A.)
    8. A. Kolomenskii, Kak my ispol'zuem zagranichnuiu
tekhniku (Moscow: Gosudarstvennoe izdatel'stvo, 1930),
p. 17.
    9. V. I. Kas'ianenko, Zavoevanie ekonomicheskoi
nezavisimosti SSSR, 1917-1940 gg. (Moscow:
Politicheskaia literatura, 1972), p. 186.
    10. Ibid., p. 190.
    11. Pravda, August 10, 1977, p. 3.
    12. John P. Hardt and Carl Modig, "Stalinist
Industrial Development in Soviet Russia," in Kurt
London, ed., The Soviet Union: a Half Century of

Communism (Baltimore: The Johns Hopkins Press, 1968),
p. 310.

13. Dmitrii Dmitrievich Mishustin, Vneshniaia
torgovlia i industrializatsiia SSSR (Moscow:
Izdatel'stvo Mezhdunarodnaia kniga, 1938), p. 88.

14. Dmitrii Dmitrievich Mishustin, Sotsialisticheskaia monopoliia vneshnei torgovli SSSR (Moscow:
Izdatel'stvo Mezhdunarodnaia kniga, 1938), pp. 4-5.

15. Eugene Zaleski, Planning for Economic Growth
in the Soviet Union 1918-1932, trans. from the French
by Marie-Christine MacAndrew and G. Warren Nutter,
Chapel Hill: The University of North Carolona Press,
1971), p. 253.

16. Kas'ianenko, Zavoevanie, Chapters 3 and 4,
passim.

17. Zaleski, pp. 254.255.

18. M. Kaufman, "Itogi i perspektivy vneshnei
torgovli," Planovoe khoziaistvo, April, 1929, p. 94.

19. See Alexander Erlich, The Soviet Industriali-
zation Debate, 1924-1928 (Cambridge, Mass.: Harvard
University Press, 1960), pp. 151-153; and Gregory
Grossman, "Scarce Capital and Soviet Doctrine,"
Quarterly Journal of Economics, LXVII (August, 1953),
315-316.

20. David Granick, Soviet Metal-Fabricating and
Economic Development: Practice versus Policy
(Madison: The University of Wisconsin Press, 1967),
p. 24.

21. Charles K. Wilber, The Soviet Model and
Underdeveloped Countries (Chapel Hill: The University
of North Carolina Press, 1969), p. 93.

22. Norton T. Dodge, "Trends in Labor Productivity in the Soviet Tractor Industry: A Case Study
in Industrial Development" (unpublished Ph.D.
dissertation, Harvard University, 1960), Chapter
VIII.

23. Granick, p. 111, and Wilber, p. 94.

24. Granick, p. 111.

25. Wilber, pp. 95-97.

26. Pravda, December 29, 1934, cited in Joseph
Berliner, "The Economics of Overtaking and Surpassing," in Industrialization of Two Systems: Essays
in Honor of Alexander Gerschenkron, ed. by Henry
Rosovsky (New York: John Wiley & Sons, Inc., 1966),
p. 173.

27. Richard Moorsteen and Raymond P. Powell,
The Soviet Capital Stock, 1928-1962 (Homewood, Ill.,
Richard D. Irwin, Inc., 1966), p. 286.

28. Maurice Dobb, Soviet Economic Development
Since 1971 (London: Routledge and Kegan Paul Ltd.,
1948), p. 239.

29. _Ibid_.
30. Moorsteen and Powell, p. 283.
31. _Ibid_., p. 294.
32. Antony Sutton, _Western Technology and Soviet Economic Development_ Vol. II: 1930-1945 (Stanford: Hoover Institution Press, 1971), p. 339.
33. Stanley H. Cohn, "The Soviet Path to Economic Growth: A Comparative Analysis," _Review of Income and Wealth_, March, 1976, pp. 49-59.
34. Rush V. Greenslade, "The Real Gross National Product of the U.S.S.R., 1950-1975," in _JEC_, p. 279.
35. Cohn, pp. 56-57, and Abram Bergson, "Soviet Economic Perspectives: Toward a New Growth Model," _Problems of Communism_, March-April, 1973, pp. 2-4.
36. Murray Feshbach and Stephen Rapawy, "Soviet Population and Manpower Trends and Policies," in _JEC_, pp. 113-154.
37. Bergson, _passim_.
38. _Ibid_.
39. N. K. Baibakov, ed. _Gosudarstvennyi piatletnii plan razvitiia narodnogo khoziaistva SSSR na 1971-1975 godu_ (Moscow: Izdatel'stvo politicheskoi literatury, 1972), p. 9.
40. _Pravda_, February 25, 1976.
41. N. I. Rogovskiy, "Proizvoditel'nots' nashego truda," _Pravda_, June 9, 1976, p. 2.
42. I. Ivanov, "Foreign Trade Factors in the USSR's Economic Growth and Some Perspectives for the U.S.-Soviet Economic Cooperation," paper presented at the Conference on U.S.-U.S.S.R.; Problems and Opportunities, sponsored by Stanford Research Institute and the Institute of World Economy and International Relations, Arlington, Virginia, April 17-19, 1973).
43. U.S. Central Intelligence Agency, _Soviet Economic Plans for 1976-80: A First Look_ (ER 76-10471), August 1976, p. 29.
44. U.S. Central Intelligence Agency, _The Soviet Economy: Performance in 1975 and Prospects for 1976_ (ER 76-10296), May 1976, p. 17.
45. CIA, _Soviet Economic Plans_, p. 26. Similar figures are cited by Soviet economists. See, for example, O. Bogomolov, _Izvestiia_, February 26, 1976.
46. Donald W. Green and Herbert S. Levine, "Implications of Technology Transfers for the USSR," in _East-West Technological Co-operation_. (Main Findings of Colloquium held 17th-19th March, 1976 in Brussels NATO, Directorate of Economic Affairs, 1976, p. 56.
47. U.S. Congress, House, Committee on Foreign Affairs, Subcommittee on National Security Policy

and Scientific Developments, U.S.-Soviet Commercial Relations: The Interplay of Economics, Technology Transfer, and Diplomacy, by John P. Hardt and George D. Holliday (Washington, D.C.; Government Printing Office, June 10, 1973), pp. 15-22 and 45-47.

48. N. P. Shmelev, ed., Ekonomicheskie sviazi Vostok-Zapad: problemy i vozmozhnosti (Moscow: Izdatel'stvo "Mysl'," 1976), pp. 16-18.

49. Paul Ericson, "Soviet Efforts to Increase Exports of Manufactured Products to the West," in JEC, pp. 709-726.

50. "Planirovanie i upravlenie nauchno-tekhnicheskim progressom v X piatiletke," Voprosy ekonomiki, No. 8. 1975, p. 118.

51. Iu. Samokhin, "Stimulirovanie eksportnogo proizvodstva," Ekonomicheskaia gazeta, No. 12, March 1975, p. 20.

52. P. S. Zavialov, Nauchno-tekhnicheskaia revoliutsiia i mezhdunarodnaia spetsializatsiia proizvodstva pri kapitalizme (Moscow: Izdatel'stvo "Mysl'," 1974), pp. 13-14.

53. Ericson, pp. 724-726.

54. See, for example, B. Komzin, "Iaponskii put' nauchno-tekhnicheskogo razvitiia," Mirovaia ekonomika i mezhdunarodnye otnosheniia, June, 1973, pp. 51-62; and N. N. Smeliakov, S chego nachinaetsia rodina (Moscow: Izdatel'stvo politicheskoi literatury, 1975), pp. 472-505.

55. Smeliakov, passim.

56. Karl F. Spielmann, "Defense Industrialists in the USSR," Problems of Communism," XXV (September-October, 1976), 67.

57. S. A. Kheinman, "Mashinostroenie: perspektivy i reservy," Ekonomika i organizatsiia promyshlennogo proizvodstva, No. 6, 1974, pp. 37-62.

4. Evolution of Soviet Attitudes and Institutions

The development of a new Soviet model of economic growth has been accompanied by an evolution of Soviet attitudes and institutions related to the absorption of foreign technology. In reviewing the changes in this realm, it is important to keep in mind that, in the Soviet Union as elsewhere, such evolution seldom moves forward in an uninterrupted straight line. For example, one finds in Soviet policy elements of economic isolationism and elements of internationalism coexisting at any given time. There is no unanimity among Soviet policy makers on questions involving Soviet foreign economic relations and institutional reform. Nevertheless, a review of the Soviet literature on foreign economic and technological relations reveals important changes in emphasis in both official pronouncements and statements by Soviet economists. Moreover, there have been substantial changes in Soviet institutions involved in various aspects of technology transfer.

ATTITUDES OF SOVIET POLICY MAKERS

The early Bolsheviks were influenced by Marx's assessment of the technological prowess of capitalism. Marx wrote extensively and positively of the technological achievements of capitalist society. However, he believed that a capitalist economy could continue to progress only up to a point, at which certain institutional barriers inherent in private ownership of the means of production would impede further technological development. In Marx's terminology, the modern productive forces created by capitalism would come into conflict with capitalist conditions of production.

72

>...The productive forces at the disposal of
> society no longer tend to further the develop-
> ment of the conditions of bourgeois property;
> on the contrary, they have become too powerful
> for these conditions, by which they are fettered,
> and so soon as they overcome these fetters,
> they bring disorder into the whole of bourgeois
> society, endanger the existence of bourgeois
> property. The conditions of bourgeois society
> are too narrow to comprise the wealth created
> by them.[1]

At this point, further progress would depend on
changes in the social order, specifically the advent
of the socialist economic order. The superior form
of economic organization would enable a socialist
country to surpass the technological level achieved
by capitalism.

These ideas were reflected in the writings of
V. I. Lenin. Soon after the Bolsheviks came to
power, Lenin was forced to think seriously about
building a technological base for the Soviet economy.
His first major initiative in this area was the policy of granting concessions to capitalist firms in
Soviet Russia. The concessions policy, announced
on November 23, 1920, was one of the most controversial aspects of Lenin's New Economic Policy proposals. Many Bolsheviks opposed the concessions on
the grounds that they would provide a foothold for
the revival of capitalism. Lenin's defense of the
concessions policy reveal three major elements of
his thinking about borrowing Western technology.
First, he believed that a period of borrowing the
latest capitalist technology was inevitable and
necessary. However, this need would presumably dis-
appear at some point because of technological stagnation in capitalist countries:

>...capitalist monopoly inevitably give rise to
> a tendency to stagnation and decay. As monopoly
> prices become fixed, even temporarily, so the
> stimulus to technical .and, consequently to all
> progress, disappears to a certain extent, and
> to that extent, also the economic possibility
> arises of deliberately retarding technical
> progress.[2]

Secondly, Lenin acknowledged the dangers of allowing
capitalists to operate in Russia, but believed that
their influence could be contained:

> Economically, we have a vast deal to gain
> from concessions. Of course, when settlements
> are created, they will bring capitalist customs
> with them, they will demoralize the peasantry.
> But watch must be kept, we must put up our
> communist influence in opposition at every step.
> This also is a kind of war, the military rival-
> ry of two methods, two formations, two kinds of
> economy--communist and capitalist. We shall
> prove that we are the stronger.[3]

Finally, Lenin showed a great awareness of the difficulties of assimilating advanced technology in a
backward economy. His concessions policy was
designed to provide an extensive opportunity for
Soviet industrial managers and technicians to learn
from the capitalists.

> ...side by side with the concession land, the
> concession square of territory, there will be
> our square, and then again their square; we
> shall learn from them how to organize model
> enterprises by placing our own side by side with
> theirs. If we are incapable of doing that, it
> is not worth talking about anything. To procure
> the last word in technology in the matter
> of equipment at the present time is not an easy
> task, and we have to learn, learn it in prac-
> tice; for this is not a thing to be got from
> schools, universities or courses. And that is
> why we are granting concessions on the checker-
> board system: Come and learn on the spot.[4]

On one occasion, Lenin intimated that this learning
process, while temporary, would last for an extended
period. He claimed that, if successful, the concessions policy would result in the construction of
a small number of the most advanced, large-scale
enterprises, and added that "in a few decades these
enterprises will be transferred entirely to us."[5]
Stalin obviously shared the view that the Soviet
Union had much to learn technologically from the
capitalists. He made frequent references to his
speeches to "American efficiency," which was held up
as a model for Soviet industry.[6] A central element
of his First Five-Year Plan was to import massive
amounts of Western technology. Like Lenin's,
Stalin's perception of the need for Western technology was strongly influenced by the Marxist notion
of technological stagnation as an inevitable consequence of advanced capitalism. Thus, he once

contrasted the "periodic breaks in technical development, accompanied by destruction of the productive
forces of society," under capitalism, with the "un-
broken process of perfecting production on the basis
of higher techniques" under socialism.[7]
Statements by Stalin and his subordinates made
it clear that they considered the heavy reliance on
technology imports from the West to be a temporary
measure. For example, one element in the debate
over "socialism in one country" that dominated the
Fourteenth Party Congress in 1925 was the fear of
becoming an "appendage" to the capitalist world
economic system. The Congress passed a resolution
pointing out that the expansion of imports had
temporarily aggravated the Soviet Union's dependence
on capitalist countries and instructed the Central
Committee to take steps to secure the Soviet Union's
future economic independence.[8]
The drastic reduction in commercial relations
with the West after the First Five-Year Plan is an
important indicator of official attitudes of the
time. To be sure, the causes were complex. In the
first place, there was an element of deliberate
planning; as the resolution at the Fourteenth Party
Congress and many other official pronouncements of
the time suggest, the large-scale import of Western
technology was intended to be a temporary phenomenon.
Economic factors--the completion of the First Five-
Year Plan and the beginning of the extensive
Stalinist growth models; the change in Soviet terms
of trade and the inability to earn sufficient foreign exchange--were important, particularly in deter-
mining the timing of the curtailment.[9] Current
Soviet commentators frequently stress the existence
of a "capitalist encirclement"--a hostile capitalist
world--as a primary reason for the cutback.[10] However, the timing of the rapid curtailment, beginning
in 1931-1932 suggests that this is more a post-hoc
rationalization than a primary motivating factor.
While Soviet leaders were undoubtedly suspicious of
capitalist governments, there was no reason to per-
ceive an immediate threat from the West. Relations
were, in fact, improving with some Western governments, including the United States. Relations with
Germany, while uneasy, were good enough to permit
extensive military and commercial ties even after
the cutback.[11]
Another factor emphasized the Soviet observers--
the perception that the Soviet Union had attained the
means to insure continued economic and technological
progress without substantial ties to the West--

probably reflects more accurately Soviet attitudes
and motivations in the 1930s. Indeed, some Soviet
writers assert that this was the most important
factor:

> The reduction in scale of foreign technical
> assistance at the end of the Five-Year Plan
> was not a manifestation of an attempt by the
> Soviet Government to fence itself off from the
> capitalist countries. This step was necessi-
> tated by objective reasons. In the capitalist
> countries, anti-Soviet campaigns continued.
> In the Soviet Union, the hard currency problem
> worsened. In 1931-1932 the Soviet Government's
> debt to foreign firms and banks became exacer-
> bated. In order to reduce the consequences
> of the economic crisis and strengthen the
> position of the monopolies, foreign firms
> broke agreements on technical assistance in
> some instances. And finally, most importantly--
> in the years of the First Five-Year Plan, the
> U.S.S.R. achieved outstanding successes in pre-
> paring engineering-technical cadres. The
> government also succeeded in redirecting the
> activities of the scientific-research institutes
> and organizations to the needs of socialist
> production.[12]

The perception that the Soviet Union could
develop independently enabled Soviet planners to
undertake the Stalinist economic development model
with a great degree of confidence. The Stalinist
political elite in particular was infused with a
kind of technological naiveté--a lack of understanding of the prerequisites for technological change--
which shaped their attitudes toward economic and
technological relations with the West. There were
three central elements of this technological naiveté:
(1) an underestimation of the speed of technological
change and the future technological prospects of the
Western economies; (2) an underestimation of the
difficulties of absorbing foreign technology; and
(3) a lack of understanding of the prerequisites
for domestic technological progress.
The onset of the Depression in the West strengthened the conviction among the Stalinist political
elite that capitalism had little or nothing more to
offer a socialist economy. Furthermore, there was a
belief that technological progress would be more or
less automatic under socialism. For example, the
editors of Planovoe khoziaistvo wrote in 1932:

> ...the "latest word" in capitalist technology
> is only a point of departure for socialist
> technology; socialism makes possible a com-
> pletely different, incomparably more rapid and
> comprehensive development of technology than
> that which takes place in even the most pro-
> gressive capitalist countries.[13]

The conviction that socialism had superior technological capabilities frequently resulted in what
appear in retrospect to be unreasonable boasts. For
example, in 1929 a Soviet economist expressed the
belief that within ten years, the level of Soviet
technology could reach and possibly surpass that of
the most advanced capitalist countries.[14] Similarly,
Sergei Orjonikidze claimed in 1932 that "The times
when we had to go to Europe or America to have our
tractor and motor factories designed have gone
forever."[15]

The conclusion that technological progress
would be more rapid under socialism than under
capitalism removed the rationale for maintaining
long-term, large-scale economic and technological
ties to the West. In particular, it obviated the
continuation of the relatively active mechanisms--
technical assistance contracts and concessions--
which had been used to absorb Western technology in
the 1920s and early 1930s. The occasional technological advance in the West could be borrowed by more
casual methods. The use of active technology transfer mechanisms was also undermined by the notion
that borrowing foreign technology was not a difficult undertaking. In Stalin's words:

> They say that it is difficult to master tech-
> nology; that is incorrect. There are no
> obstacles which the Bolsheviks cannot over-
> come...
>
> The most important things with respect to con-
> struction we have already done. There remains
> little for us to do: learn techniques, master
> science. And when we do this, we will attain
> tempos which we cannot dream about now. And
> we will do this if we really want to.[16]

The technological naiveté of the Stalinist
political elite had been manifest in other policies.
For example, the purges of Soviet engineers, because
of their alleged bourgeois or technocratic leanings,
were carried out on the assumption that "red experts"--

Communist Party members who had received technical training (frequently hurried and incomplete)--could immediately take their place.[17] These purges began with the Shakhty trial of 1928 and reached their peak with the Industrial Party trial of 1930, when perhaps several thousand engineers were arrested. The arrests came at the height of the First Five-Year Plan, when their technical expertise was desperately needed by Soviet industry. Similarly, the naiveté of Soviet policy makers undoubtedly contributed to the lack of attention given to research and development activities in Soviet industrial enterprises. The importance of allocating substantial resources to research and development was not fully appreciated by the political elite.

This technological naiveté was not the only reason for the Soviet decision to cut back economic and technological relations with the West. However, in the face of other political and economic problems, it appears to have predisposed the political leadership toward an isolationist policy. The attitudes of the political elite were not shared by many managers and engineers in Soviet enterprises. There is considerable evidence that many of the latter did not agree with the cutoff of active technological ties with the West. Their recalcitrance led to a country-wide campaign beginning in 1930 against "bureaucratism and opportunist lack of faith in socialist industry"--the Party leadership's characterization of the allegedly unnecessary import of machinery and equipment when domestically produced alternatives were available. A number of people at some factories were dismissed for "serious blunders in planning machine imports."[18]

The attitudes of the pre-War period persisted in the early post-war years and through much of the 1950s. The leadership found it necessary to import technology in certain previously neglected sectors, such as the chemical industry, but by and large their attitudes seemed typified by Premier Nikita Khrushchev's boasts about the achievements of Soviet science and technology and about the prospects of overtaking and surpassing the capitalist countries. However, gradually the boasts began to be mixed with a growing awareness of achievements abroad. This development coincided with a slowdown in the Soviet economic growth rate. Khrushchev began to speak of the need for a more active technology import policy:

It is essential that we make use of everything that science and technology give us in our country more rapidly and exhaustively and take more boldly all the best that foreign experience can give.[19]

These themes were developed further and given much more emphasis by Khrushchev's successors, Premier Alexei Kosygin and Communist Party Secretary Leonid Brezhnev. In 1965, Kosygin candidly admitted that "The pattern of production of machinery and equipment being turned out by many branches of Soviet industry does not conform to modern standards."[20] In 1966, at the Twenty-Third Party Congress, he asserted:

> Heretofore, we have underestimated the importance of trade in patents and licenses. At the same time, throughout the world such trade is playing an increasingly noticeable role and is developing more rapidly than the trade in manufactured goods. Our scientific and technical personnel are capable of creating-- and this has been proven in practice--advanced machinery and equipment. Therefore, we can and should hold a worthy place on the world license market. In turn, in a number of cases it is more profitable for us to purchase a license than to work on the resolution of a given problem. During the new five-year plan, the purchase of patent rights abroad will make it possible to save hundreds of millions of rubles on scientific research.[21]

Brezhnev has also been outspoken about the relationship between foreign trade and technological progress. For example, in his report to the Twenty-Fifth Party Congress, Brezhnev stated:

> Like other states, we strive to use the advantages provided by foreign economic ties to mobilize extra possibilities for the successful solution of economic tasks and to gain time to increase the efficiency of production and speed up the progress of science and technology.[22]

Another theme of both Brezhnev and Kosygin in recent years is the need for new forms of commercial relations, going beyond ordinary trade. They place emphasis on large-scale and long-term projects. In Brezhnev's words:

...today it is simply not advantageous and
unreasonable to limit economic cooperation to
trade. Staying abreast of the times and meeting
the needs and possibilities of the scientific-
technical revolution can be accomplished only
on the basis of a wide international division
of labor. Today this is perhaps axiomatic.
Thus, the need for mutually beneficial, long-
term, large-scale economic cooperation--both
bilateral and multilateral.[23]

In summary, the new attitude, as reflected in
the speeches of Brezhnev, Kosygin and others contains
several key elements which distinguish the new
approach from the old policy. There is increasing
awareness and concern about the slowness of technological progress in the domestic economy and a willingness to become more actively involved in the
international division of labor as a means of spur-
ring technological progress. There is also an
emphasis on the rapidity and broadness of what is
called the scientific-technical revolution, which
makes it impossible for any one country to lead on
all technological fronts. In particular, there is
an acknowledgement of the existence of rapid technological progress in Western capitalist countries
and of the need to import technology in areas in
which the Soviet Union is behind. Finally, there is
an emphasis on the need to find new ways to improve
the technology transfer process.

EVOLUTION OF SOVIET INSTUTIONAL ARRANGEMENTS

Generally speaking, changes in Soviet institutional arrangements for borrowing technology have
reflected a central dilemma for Soviet policy
makers. On the one hand, there has been a perceived
need to protect Soviet citizens from alien ideas and
to maintain the economic and technological independence of the Soviet economy. On the other hand, they
have valued the potential economic benefits of
absorbing Western technology. Thus, Soviet technology import policy has largely reflected a balancing
of political costs and economic benefits. Many
organizational features which tend to isolate the
Soviet economy have persisted throughout Soviet rule.
However, during periods of great interest in borrowing foreign technology, there has been considerable
flexibility in adapting institutions to the needs of
the technology transfer process.

In recent years, there has been evidence of three kinds of institutional changes aimed at improving the interface between foreign technology and the Soviet domestic economic environment: development of new technology transfer mechanisms; modifications in the Ministry of Foreign Trade's monopoly; and subtle, foreign-trade oriented changes in domestic industrial organization. These changes have been evolutionary, developing primarily in the 1960s and 1970s. They do not represent a drastic departure from the traditional organizational forms and techniques for borrowing foreign technology; many of the latter continue to be used. However, changes have been made, and they illustrate a willingness by Soviet officials to experiment with new institutional arrangements. In some cases, further changes have been actively discussed, but not yet implemented.

Traditional Technology Transfer Arrangements

The central institution in the Soviet Union's efforts to borrow foreign technology has been the foreign trade monopoly administered by the Ministry of Foreign Trade (MFT). The monopoly of foreign trade has traditionally meant that all Soviet foreign trade transactions are executed by agencies of the MFT--currently more than fifty specialized foreign trade organizations (FTO's). In the past, Soviet officials have emphasized that the foreign trade monopoly entailed a concentration of foreign trade powers not only in the hands of the government, but in the hands of a single government agency:

> Thus, the definition of foreign trade monopoly as the concentration of foreign trade in the hands of the government does not capture the full meaning of foreign trade monopoly. The foreign trade monopoly, in excluding capitalist elements from foreign trade, at the same time creates a situation in which even government organizations and enterprises cannot have direct and independent foreign trade relations. The monopoly of foreign trade concentrates the administration of foreign trade affairs in one government organ that is all-powerful in that field. That organ is the Ministry of Foreign Trade. No Soviet enterprise can conduct trade operations...[24]

Established in 1918, the foreign trade monopoly
initially was opposed by some Soviet policy makers,
but is now considered "the keystone of the foreign
trade system in the U.S.S.R."[25] All official Soviet
pronouncements on the subject lavish praise on its
accomplishments and steadfastly maintain that it
will remain the basis for Soviet foreign trade.
Despite its preeminence, the MFT's monopoly has been
successfully challenged at times. In periods when
Soviet policy makers have attached great importance
to technology imports, the power of the foreign
trade monopoly has tended to wane. Although the
foreign trade monopoly has been successful in insu-
lating the Soviet economy from the vicissitudes of
the Western economy, carefully controlling the influx
of people (and ideas), and allocating scarce foreign
exchange to meet the leadership's highest priorities,
it has not proved to be the most effective means of
absorbing foreign technology. The MFT's concentration on simple import and export operations has made
it ill-suited to administer the diversity of technology transfer mechanisms. Consequently, the responsibility for conducting Soviet foreign economic
relations at times has been decentralized.
       John Quigley has chronicled the early debate
over the concept of a foreign trade monopoly and has
shown how the monopoly was circumvented, particularly
in the 1920s.[26] While Lenin's strong advocacy
apparently saved the monopoly, the opposition of
many Party leaders and government officials resulted
in the adoption of a decree by the All-Russian Central Executive Committee on March 13, 1922, which:
(1)   provided direct exporting and importing by
state enterprises, provincial executive committees
and all-Russian cooperatives with the permission of
the People's Commissariat of Foreign Trade (the
predecessor of the MFT); and (2)   provided for the
formation of "mixed" joint stock companies, part of
whose capital would be contributed by the Foreign
Trade Commissariat and part by private source,
including foreign.[27]
       While the Foreign Trade Commissariat conducted
the greatest volume of trade, a number of government
agencies, cooperatives, private citizens, mixed and
state-owned companies continued to maintain direct
trade ties with Western companies. Within the Soviet
Government, officials at the Supreme Economic Council (VSNKh) were the most activist opponents to the
Foreign Trade Commissariat. VSNKh, the highest
authority in the industrial bureaucracy and legally
superior to the Commissariat, constantly tried to

expand its control over foreign trade relations. In 1922, VSNKh created a special Foreign Trade Section to supervise the Commissariat. Moreover, it often conducted negotiations with foreign firms without going through the Commissariat.[28]

In addition, during the 1920s and since, Soviet policy makers have resorted to a wide variety of technology transfer mechanisms which have tranceded and sometimes breached the foreign trade monopoly. For example, they have made extraordinary efforts to absorb technology by canvassing Western technical literature.[29] They have permitted travel to and from the Soviet Union by scientists, managers and engineers, though on a smaller scale than most governments. There have also been numerous charges of Soviet industrial espionage in the West. In short, they have resorted to the full range of non-commercial technology transfer mechanisms in borrowing technology from the West.

More importantly, the most active Soviet technology transfer mechanisms have operated with varying degrees of independence from the foreign trade monopoly. The most active mechanisms employed by the Soviet Union in the 1920s and 1930s were concessions and technical assistance agreements. Concessions were first authorized in Soviet Russia in 1920 and were the dominant active mechanism during the early and mid-1920s.[30] Technical assistance agreements began in the early 1920s, but were not widely employed until the First Five-Year Plan, when they rapidly replaced concessions as the favored technology transfer mechanism. Soviet observers and Western students agree that these mechanisms accounted for only a small portion of total Soviet economic activity during this period.[31] However, their important technological contribution to a number of Soviet industries has been extensively documented.[32]

The pure concession was an agreement between the Soviet state and a foreign company, which allowed the foreign firm to invest capital (both money and equipment) in the Soviet Union and to repatriate a part of the profits from its investment. Typically, the contract stipulated what kinds of machinery and equipment would be imported and the schedule for start-up of the concession. The concessionaire was obligated to pay a share of its profits to the Soviet Government, usually stipulated as a percentage of sales. It also paid taxes on a progressive scale, increasing with the rate of profits. At the end of the concession, all equipment, buildings, and inventory were transferred to the Soviet Government.

The unique (in Soviet experience) aspect of concessions was the Soviet Government's relinquishing of operational control and management rights to foreigners. Once the concession was granted, the Soviet Government had little control, except that the foreign concessionaire was subject to Soviet law. Moreover, the Government did not go to great efforts to establish priorities for technology imports. Concessions were dispersed throughout the economy, their distribution reflecting primarily the attractiveness of various opportunities to foreign firms. A variant was the mixed concession, in which the initial investment was made jointly by a Soviet agency and a foreign firm. In such cases, control and management was shared in accordance with the number of shares controlled by each.[33]

Responsibility for signing concessions agreements and overseeing their operation was vested in the Chief Concessions Committee (Glavnyy Kontsessionnyi Komitet). The Committee was attached directly to the Council of People's Commissariats and was thus independent of the foreign trade monopoly. However, in December 1937, the Chief Concessions Committee was eliminated because of the reduced number of concessions. The remaining concessions were transferred to the Foreign Trade Commissariat where a Concessions Department was created.

Like concessions, technical assistance contracts were signed and executed outside the framework of the foreign trade monopoly. Responsibility for bringing technical specialists into the Soviet Union and overseeing their work was vested in the Central Bureau of Foreign Consultation, established in May 1929 under the Construction Department of VSHKh.[34] VSNKh officials set rigid priorities for technical assistance contracts, concentrating them in projects considered crucial for industrialization. Central planners also played a strong role in directing and overseeing implementation of the contracts.

Separation of technical assistance agreements from the foreign trade monopoly was necessitated by the complexity of some of the arrangements. Many technical assistance agreements involved packaged technology transfers, in which foreign firms were employed to provide a variety of services: preparation of designs for projects or consultation on designs prepared by Soviet engineers; preparation of blueprints for buildings and production lines; cost calculations; patent rights; supervision of construction and training of workers and technicians; and assumption of responsibility for successful startup.[35] Purchases of machinery and equipment and licenses were also included in many contracts.

Technical assistance agreements, unlike concessions, did not provide for repatriated profits or royalty payments to the Soviet Government. Instead, the Government paid a set fee for services provided by the Western partner. The fee was usually either a percentage of the cost of the project or a percentage of the economies achieved as a result of the technical assistance.[36]

While technical assistance agreements provided extensive personal contacts among foreign and domestic workers and technicans, they had some limitations as technology transfer mechanisms. They provided no management role for the Western firm. Although technical assistance inevitably involved some Western advice on managerial matters, the contracts were essentially vehicles for transferring engineering skills. Moreover, technical assistance agreements generally covered shorter periods than concessions, most often three to five years. A key feature of these agreements was the provision of a schedule for the Soviet factory to achieve progressive independence from the Western partner. The ultimate success for the Soviet enterprise or industry involved was to rid itself of the need to import from the West or to rely on Western technology.[37] The relatively short duration of the contracts removed the possibility of paying for technology imports by exporting part of the output of the project. Although the Soviet Government sometimes reserved the right to sell output to third parties, especially to Soviet trade partners in Asia,[38] exports from Western-assisted projects were never an important factor in Soviet foreign trade. In these important respects—the absence of a foreign managerial role and shorter duration of contracts—the use of technical assistance agreements represented a step back from the concessions policy of limited interdependence with the West.

Between 1930 and 1935, the Foreign Trade Commissariat gradually established more completely its monopoly of foreign trade. A number of reforms in those years reshaped Soviet foreign trade institutions into a form which remained essentially unchanged until the 1960s. Private individuals and companies were excluded from foreign trade, and other government agencies began to play a smaller role. A sharp separation between domestic and foreign trade was effected. (For a short period before 1930, the Commissariat had authority for both foreign and domestic trade.) FTO's were given some operational authority, while the central staff of the Commissariat became more concerned with policy matters. Operations were transferred to Moscow whenever possible. The government encouraged the FTO's to negotiate sales, inspect imports and exports, make payments and arbitrate disputes in Moscow. This meant that fewer Soviet trade representatives were sent abroad.[39] Moreover, the phasing out of concessions and the reduction in the number of technical assistance agreements strengthened the Foreign Trade Commissariat's monopoly.

One practical effect of the strengthening of the foreign trade monopoly was a greater reliance on more passive technology transfer mechanisms. The passive mechanisms which predominated in Soviet efforts to import technology after the mid-1930s, consisted of transactions in which the Ministry of Foreign Trade's FTO's specialized--simple imports of unpackaged machinery and equipment and other goods. Purchases of accompanying technical services and knowhow were deemphasized. There was little training involved, either in the Soviet Union or abroad. Contacts between Soviet and Western firms were almost always short-term and generally were carried out through intermediaries in the foreign trade bureaucracy. Such passive mechanisms served the Soviet Union's primary foreign trade needs, as perceived by the Stalinist bureaucracy. They reduced the foreign exchange expenditures on foreign technology, minimized contacts between foreign and domestic specialists and provided selected goods which could not be produced domestically.

The Western literature on Soviet foreign trade and technology absorption has given great emphasis to Soviet copying of Western technology via passive mechanisms, such as buying machinery and "reverse engineering" (i.e., dismantling in order to determine how it is produced), industrial espionage, and careful screening of Western technical literature. Many cases of such passive borrowing have been documented by a number of Western observers. Thus, Antony Sutton describes a common Soviet pattern in acquiring advanced Western technology: (1) acquisition of prototypes; (2) duplication and standardization; and (3) dependence on domestic production.[40] Such techniques are frequently cited as evidence of Soviet technological backwardness and total dependence on the West for technological progress. However, in view of the experiences of

86

other countries in borrowing technology, it is evident that borrowing technology through such passive mechanisms is a very difficult process. Successful absorption of foreign technology requires many of the same prerequisites as domestic innovation.[41] It is a costly, resource-consuming process, requiring a major expenditure of domestic technological resources. Because passive mechanisms do not include transfers of engineering and managerial knowhow, they require greater domestic efforts. They do not help to solve the central problems of technology absorption, which concern not how to put something together, but how to mass produce it efficiently. Nor do they help to solve traditional Soviet problems in the innovation process, such as moving from the prototype stage to mass production, maintaining quality control, and keeping apace with technological change. Moreover, borrowing technology through passive mechanisms is a slow, time-consuming process. It is likely to be more successful in technologically advanced rather than backward countries. For the latter, it virtually assures a considerable technological lag behind the innovating countries.

Soviet Problems in Borrowing Technology

Since the 1960s, Soviet observers have begun to acknowledge serious shortcomings in the efforts of Soviet enterprises to borrow foreign technology. While the Soviet economy has had notable successes, the technology transfer process had tended to be slow, inefficient, and costly, and has contributed to the persistent technology gap with the West. To a large extent, current complaints of inadequacies in the technology transfer process are reminiscent of similar complaints in the 1920s and early 1930s. While the Soviet Union had overcome some of the problems of technological backwardness and economic underdevelopment of the earlier period, many of the institutional problems persisted, and in some respects worsened in the interim period. Thus, on the one hand, the economic and technological infrastructure had made great progress. In particular, the Soviet Government had been successful in educating and training workers, engineers and scientists. Transportation, communications, and other infrastructure, while not up to the standards of the Western industrial countries, no longer resembled their relatively underdeveloped, post-Revolution states. Exploitation of the Soviet Union's massive

raw material riches was well underway, and a huge
capital stock had accumulated.

On the other hand, some of the problems of the
earlier period, particularly those associated with
domestic economic institutions and policies, have
persisted. Despite the increase in technical manpower, research and development facilities for
civilian industries are ill-equipped and ineffi-
ciently managed. Technology transfer projects are
serviced by an undependable supply system. Soviet
enterprises lack adequate incentives to take risks
or to introduce innovations, whether of domestic or
foreign origin. Moreover, reliance on passive technology transfer mechanisms have created special
problems--inadequate provision for long-term, extensive exchange of personnel; lack of knowledge about
technological developments in the West; necessity
of dealing through intermediaries in the foreign
trade bureaucracy; and lack of ties to the Western
financial community. Ironically, when improvements
in the Soviet economic and technological infrastructure should have facilitated the acquisition of
Western technology, the Soviet Government began to
eliminate another essential ingredient to successful technology transfers--active ties between Soviet
enterprises and Western industry.

It is instructive, in this context, to examine
specific complaints in the Soviet literature about
the methods and results of acquiring Western technology. The problems encountered by Soviet institutions have received attention at the highest
policy making level. In his keynote address to the
Twenty-Fifth Party Congress in February 1977,
Brezhnev criticized the performance of Soviet industry in this regard and said that a greater "sense of
responsibility" was needed by FTO's, industrial
ministries, enterprises and construction firms. He
added that, unless Soviet workers could be relied
upon to complete buildings on time and deliver
products which met quality standards, the Soviet
Union could not "speak of any advantages gained by
cooperating with the West."[42]

Brezhnev's statement highlights one of the most
frequently cited problems in the technology absorption process--delays in introducing foreign technology after it has been purchased. There are numerous
examples. The Soviet press reported that a foreign
license had been purchased for the automobile industry for production of disk brakes and brake equipment. However, the Ministry of Automotive Industry
did not carry out the necessary organizational and

technical preparation, and the license expired before
the industry could start up production.[43] In another
case, in 1967, the Soviet Union brought the license
for the technologically superior glass-making Pilk-
ington float-glass process. (It acquired the license
later than most Western countries.) It took forty-
one months from purchase of the license to start
up of production. The average of sixteen other purchasers of the license was twenty-seven months.[44]

Similarly, foreign machinery and equipment often
sits idle because of delays in Soviet technology
transfer projects. The Soviet press reported that
on January 1, 1973, there was 1.4 billion rubles
worth of uninstalled imported machinery on hand in
Soviet industry.[45] Such problems are frequently
related to construction delays, which are commonplace in Soviet technology transfers projects, as
they are in strictly domestic projects. Soviet
complaints about slow introduction of foreign technology are strikingly reminiscent of similar problems encountered by Soviet industry during the First
Five-Year Plan.[46]

Another set of problems relates to the inefficient operation and poor management of projects
after they start up. In 1969, a Soviet economist
gave an example of the failure of a technology transfer project to accomplish one of its main goals--
economizing on labor. Six chemical projects were
designed for the Soviet Union by a Western firm.
The Western firm recommended on the basis of experience in the West, that each project employ ninety-
one auxiliary workers. The Soviet projects operated
with 723, eight times more than the Western design
called for. The Soviet projects also employed three
and one-half times more engineering and technical
workers and fifty-five percent more chief technicians
than stipulated in the design.[47]

There are also frequent complaints of the failure
of suppliers to provide high-quality inputs, of the
inability of new projects to maintain the rate of
technological progress in the West and of slow diffusion of newly imported technologies to other parts
of the economy.[48] The increasing emphasis of new
technology transfer projects on exports, has brought
complaints about new management problems--insufficient
quality control and lack of foreign marketing knowhow.

Another problem lies in the inability or unwillingness of Soviet enterprises to take full advantage
of available foreign technology. Soviet industry
sometimes spends large sums on development of technologies that could be purchased less expensively in

the West. In part, this problem results from igno-
rance of developments in Western industry. However,
sometimes purchases of foreign technology are re-
sisted by Soviet research and development because
of professional pride:

> There are many shortcomings in the work con-
> nected with the purchase of licenses. Con-
> siderations of prestige often take precedence
> over economics. The directors of a number of
> enterprises and organizations frequently re-
> gard the decision to buy a foreign license as
> a mark of their own scientific and technical
> incompetence and as a slur on the honor of
> their department. That is why a certain per-
> centage of them strive to solve every new
> scientific and technical problem with their
> own resources, which leads to an unjustified
> proliferation of research topics, the scatter-
> ing of funds and a considerable delay in the
> creation of new manufactured articles.[49]

Similarly, Soviet industrial officials sometimes in-
sist on buying unpackaged technology from the West,
and supplying part of the technology from their own
resources in order to economize on hard currency
expenditures. This can create special problems of
coordinating unlike technological inputs and lead
to further delays.

A Soviet study of foreign license acquisition
attributes delays in the process to inadequate
planning and organization in the preliminary stages.

> The practice of buying and using foreign
> licenses indicates that the delay in putting
> licenses to use results mainly from the late
> placement of orders for equipment, assembly
> components, and materials and from insuffi-
> ciently thorough drafting of proposals for
> cooperation with other ministries and depart-
> ments and for determining the extent of license
> agreements...
>
> In some cases putting licenses to use is held
> up because of inadequate analysis of the capa-
> bilities of domestic industry. One cause of
> the slow incorporation of licenses lies in
> the fact that production preparations are not
> started immediately after the conclusion of
> the license agreement, but only after the
> entire volume of technical and technological

documents has been received. This inevitably
leads to a delay of 1.5-2 years in putting
the license to use.[50]

The lack of preparation and prior planning can
be attributed partially to reliance on inactive
technology transfer mechanisms. Without extensive
collaboration with the Western firm in the preliminary stages of technology transfer, Soviet
industrial officials cannot plan adequately complementary inputs. At the same time, Western suppliers have great difficulty in designing machinery,
equipment or whole plants without extensive knowledge of the capabilities, needs and constraints of
the recipients.
    The absence of active arrangements also contri-
buted to the poor management of technology transfer
projects. The Western partner generally has little
incentive to insure the successful operation of a
technology. It typically is required only to
guarantee the startup of the production line or
factory which it supplies. Soviet passive mechanisms also do not provide a means of transferring
management skills, a vital part of the technology
transfer process.

New Technology Transfer Mechanisms

    The first departures from the interim model of
technology transfer were purchases of "turnkey"
plants and a new interest in foreign license trade.
These kinds of transactions were in some ways a
continuation of past practices, in that they were
characterized by simple, one-time purchases of foreign technology. However, there were important differences. Turnkey purchases--purchases of complete
plants, with technical assistance in putting the
plant into operation--are necessarily longer term
arrangements. They require foreign participation
in installing equipment, providing technical designs
for work to be carried out by the buyer, training
domestic personnel, and starting up operations. The
increasing Soviet interest in licensing operations
represented a change in emphasis from hardware
purchases, reverse engineering and copying. It also
represented a new respect for industrial property
rights, a change which culminated in Soviet ratifi-
cation of the Paris Convention for the Protection of
Industrial Property in 1965.
    Since the late 1960s, the Soviet Union has
begun to employ more active arrangements for

91

purchasing complete plants and licenses. Licenses
are frequently bought on credits which are repaid
with products that are related to or emanating from
the license. Such repayments may cover the total
value of the license or only a part of it. The
heightened Soviet interest in Western licenses has
also induced the Government to adopt new practices
in license purchases, which have long been standard
in Western license trade. For example, Soviet
organizations have begun to pay royalties, rather
than lump sum payments for foreign licenses. Indeed,
since 1970, royalties have been the main form of
payment.[51]

Increasingly, complete plants or production
lines are also being paid for wholly or in part with
the output or the recipient project. These product
payback arrangements, called compensation agreements
by Soviet specialists, are generally long term,
averaging ten to fifteen years and frequently cover-
ing longer periods. Compensation agreements provide
that all plants, machinery and equipment installed
in the Soviet Union become the property of the Soviet
Government. The agreements frequently include provisions for foreign assistance in planning and construction of new enterprises, development of raw
materials and assistance in start up of production
facilities. For both license and complete plant
purchases, there is a tendency toward longer term
arrangements, with greater exchange of personnel.

The Soviet Union has concluded over fifty
compensation agreements with Western firms, many of
them very large. (See Appendix B.) They have
generally been used for Soviet enterprises producing
raw materials and semi-manufactured goods, especially
natural gas, chemicals, fertilizers and wood products.
Most compensation projects export twenty to thirty
percent of their output for repayment. It has been
estimated that nearly ten percent of Soviet hard
currency exports in the 1975-1980 period will be
under compensation agreements.[52]

Perhaps the most sophisticated forms of industrial cooperation between the Soviet Union and Western firms are coproduction and specialization
arrangements.[53] They involve relationships between
Soviet and Western partners that are more complex
than compensation agreements. Two major variants
have been employed: (1) each partner specializes
in the production of certain parts of a final product, which is then assembled by one of the partners
or by both, each for its own market; (2) each
partner produces a limited number of items in a

manufacturing program which are then exchanged to complete each partner's range of products. Typically, the Western firm provides the technology, though sometimes Soviet technology or technology produced through joint research and development is used. These agreements are generally long-term. They often include joint marketing arrangements, and sometimes involve the transfer of the Western firms trademark rights. Although coproduction and specialization agreements have been employed less widely in the Soviet Union than in the East European countries, the Soviets have had limited experience in cooperation in the machine-building sector with France and Sweden, shipbuilding with Finland, and manufacturing coal mining equipment with Japan.[54]

Soviet officials have signed coproduction and specialization agreements involving only joint research and development more often. Research and development cooperation generally results from a cooperation agreement between a Western firm and the Soviet State Committee for Science and Technology. Most of these agreements are concluded within the framework of inter-governmental agreements on science and technology such as those concluded with the United States and most major Western industrial countries. For example, between the 1972 signing of the U.S.-Soviet Agreement for Cooperation in the Fields of Science and Technology and 1976, fifty-three agreements were signed with U.S. firms.[55] (Well over 100 were signed with all Western firms.)[56] Cooperation agreements have covered a wide variety of industrial activities. Typically they involve exchange of information on research and development and applications to industrial processes. The agreement may go no further than an exchange of information. However, they sometimes lead to other forms of industrial cooperation and to substantial sales of technology and capital equipment. Soviet officials appear to be displeased with the results of many of the agreements and have announced their intention to limit them to agreements that are likely to lead to concrete commercial transactions.[57]

Soviet industrial cooperation agreements with Western firms exist in a variety of configurations. In addition to those described above, leasing of modern machinery and equipment, subcontracting for Western firms and participation in joint ventures located in the West have assumed important roles in the transfer of Western technology to the Soviet Union. Of the common technology transfer mechanisms employed in Western countries, only direct foreign

investment in the domestic economy has been prohibited in the Soviet Union. Private ownership of
the means of production is prohibited by Soviet law,
and consequently the establishment of foreign-owned
enterprises or joint ventures on Soviet soil is precluded. Of the socialist countries, only Yugoslavia,
Romania and Hungary have permitted the establishment
of joint ventures.

Soviet foreign trade officials frequently
emphasize that the absence of opportunities for
direct foreign investment should pose no serious
barrier to Soviet-Western industrial cooperation.
They maintain that Western firms are concerned not
so much with ownership as with a share of the profits and participation in management.[58] Soviet
spokesmen emphasize that these roles for Western
firms are not prohibited. Thus, the Soviet economist N. D. Shmelev remarked:

> ...I think that in the future practice will
> suggest forms of cooperation providing a
> mutually acceptable basis for settling matters
> like guaranteed share of the profits...the
> Western partner's say in the technical and
> commercial policy of the enterprise, repre-
> sentation of his interests in management, and
> so on.[59]

Despite the absence of direct investment
opportunities, some Soviet industrial cooperation
agreements with Western firms have been quite
active. They are frequently long-term and involve
extensive personal contacts between Soviet and
Western specialists during all stages of the technology transfer process. They often involve packaged technology transfers, combining purchases of
machinery and equipment, licenses, knowhow and
training. They are also frequently export-oriented,
sometimes allocating a major portion of their output for exports. Many of the joint ventures
(located in the West) in which the Soviet Union
participates are marketing enterprises which specialize in selling and servicing exports from such
technology transfer projects.[60]

The development of new, more active technology
transfer mechanisms completes a cycle in the history
of Soviet economic and technological relations with
the West. After their initial experience with
relatively active mechanisms--concessions and technical assistance agreements--Soviet leaders chose to
rely on passive mechanisms for a long interim period

(roughly the mid-1930s to the mid-1960s), and then
began to experiment with active mechanisms again.
The new industrial cooperation agreements are
different from the early active mechanisms, but have
common elements. The following schematic outline
shows the essential features of concessions and
technical assistance agreements:

CONCESSION

1. No foreign ownership, but provision for
    repatriation of profits.
2. Payment of royalties and taxes to the
    Soviet Government.
3. Requirement to invest stipulated amount
    of capital and stipulated technology.
4. Long-term contract, sometimes twenty to
    thirty years.
5. Managerial control for Western firm,
    limited only by requirement to obey Soviet
    laws.
6. Extensive training of Soviet engineers and
    workers, both in the Soviet Union and
    abroad.
7. Few priorities for technology imports set
    by the central government; concentrated in
    raw materials development and production
    of consumer goods.

TECHNICAL ASSISTANCE AGREEMENT

1. No foreign ownership; no profits.
2. Soviet Government pays set fee for techni-
    cal assistance.
3. Technology transfers usually packaged,
    including patents, knowhow, machinery and
    equipment.
4. Short- and medium-term contracts with
    definite cut-off date.
5. No managerial authority for Western firm
    and no effort to borrow Western management
    techniques.
6. Extensive training of Soviet engineers and
    workers, both in the Soviet Union and abroad.
7. Concentrated in high-priority heavy industry
    sectors.

In sharp contrast are the major elements of the
passive mechanisms employed during the interim period
(the "interim isolationist model"):

95

INTERIM ISOLATIONIST MODEL

1. No foreign ownership; no profits.
2. Emphasis on importing machinery and equipment without accompanying technical services.
3. Predominance of one-time sales; few medium- or long-term contracts.
4. Extensive efforts to reverse engineer or copy critical Western technologies.
5. Minimum involvement of foreign technicians and managers.
6. Relatively little training, either in the U.S.S.R. or abroad.
7. Preeminence of intermediaries in the foreign trade bureaucracy in negotiations with Western firms.
8. Concentrated in high-priority heavy industry sectors.

The "alternative industrial cooperation model" suggests changes that have been implemented or that are being actively discussed in the Soviet Union:

ALTERNATIVE INDUSTRIAL COOPERATION MODEL

1. Foreign ownership unlikely, but provisions for sharing output and profits.
2. Emphasis on purchase of packaged technology, including machinery, patents, knowhow, trademarks and training.
3. Foreign assistance in various stages of technology transfer, from planning to operation of enterprise.
4. Long-term contractual ties.
5. Application of Western management techniques; allowance for Western managerial participation.
6. In many cases, production for export; frequent repayment on compensation basis.
7. Strict observance of industrial property rights; emphasis on purchase and sale of licenses.
8. Direct contacts between Soviet enterprises and foreign firms during negotiations and subsequent stages of technology transfer process.
9. Some technology imports for formerly low priority sectors of the Soviet economy.

It should be emphasized that the alternative industrial cooperation model is still the exception in

Soviet economic and technological relations with
the West. Much of Soviet technology borrowing is
continuing along the lines of the interim isolationist model. However, the trend appears to be
clearly toward greater reliance on industrial cooperation with the West.

Changes in the Foreign Trade Monopoly

Soviet officials have also responded to the
increase in technology imports and to the problems
of absorbing technology by modifying the traditional
foreign trade bureaucracy. Two parallel efforts,
each reflecting separate bureaucratic interest, have
been underway in the post-Stalinist period. On the
one hand, the organization of the Foreign Trade
Ministry has evolved in an effort to accommodate
the Soviet Union's foreign technology trade needs
and thus to maintain the monopoly it has had in
Soviet foreign trade matters. At the same time,
alternative sources of power and decision making
have been developed and have effectively eroded the
authority of the MFT.

The most apparent change in the organization
of the MFT is the proliferation and increasing
specialization of foreign trade organizations. From
eighteen at the end of World War II, the number has
grown to over fifty. The progressive specialization
of FTO's has been accompanied by an increase in the
number of technical specialists employed by the MFT.
The rapid growth reflects the expanded overall
volume of Soviet trade, the increasing range of
goods imported, and the increasing number of countries with which the Soviet Union trades. In particular, the formation of new FTO's has reflected
increases in Soviet trade in high-technology products and technical data. Thus, for example, in the
immediate post-War period all Soviet imports of
machinery, equipment and complete plants were han-
dled by two FTO's--Mashinoimport (The Machine Importing Company) and Tekhnoimport (Technical Importing
Company). By 1971, six important FTO's had been
added to assist in the import of machinery and equipment and whose plants:[61]

- Sudoimport (Ship Importing Company) was established in 1954 to import ships and shipbuilding technology;
- Tekhmashinimport (Technical Machine Importing
  Company) was established in 1959 to import whole
  plants for the chemical pharmaceutical, sugar
  and soap industries;

97

- Prommashimport (Industrial Machine Importing Company) was established in 1965 for importing technology for the pulp-paper and forest products industries;
- Avtopromimport (Auto Industry Import Corporation) was established in 1966 to import auto manufacturing technology;
- Metallurgimport (Metallurgy Import Company) was established in 1970 to import metallurgical machinery and equipment; and
- Electronorgtekhnika was set up in 1971 to import computers and other electronic equipment.

In addition, Litzensintorg (License Trading Company) was established in 1962 to specialize in the purchase and sale of licenses, especially with Western countries.

Similarly, the efforts of the Soviet Government to expand exports of high-technology goods led to the establishment of exporting FTO's such as Avtoexport (Auto Exporting Corporation) in 1956; Medexport (Medical Exporting Corporation) in 1961; Tekhsnabexport (Technical Supply Export Corporation in 1963; Mashpriborintorg (Machinery Instrument Trading Company) in 1959; Traktoroexport (Tractor Export Corporation) in 1961; and Aviaexport (Aviation Export Company) in 1961. The drive to expand exports has been aided by participation of these FTO's in joint marketing ventures with foreign firms.

The creation of a Main Administration for Import of Machines and Equipment from Capitalist Countries within the MFT in the 1960s (one of seven main administrations to regulate and control the FTO's operating in defined spheres) also reflected the increased interest in high-technology trade with the West. At the same time, it reflected the MFT's emphasis on traditional, passive export and import operations. The increasing emphasis of the Soviet leadership on more active mechanisms led to the creation in 1976 of a Main Administration for Compensation Projects with Capitalist Countries.[62] The purpose of the new Administration is apparently to give the MFT new flexibility to control such projects. It was created in reaction to problems in coordinating the activities of the various Ministries and departments that might be involved in a single compensation project. Specifically, its purpose is to insure that imports and exports from such projects are on schedule and to maintain the necessary long-term supervision for the projects. The creation of a new Main Administration represents an effort by the MFT to establish control over the new forms of foreign commercial relations with the West.

Despite the organizational changes in the MFT, its domination of Soviet foreign economic activities, particularly in the technology import realm, has clearly eroded. The erosion has come about primarily as a result of the increasing role of specialized state committees and other organs, responsible directly to the Council of Ministries, in foreign economic activities. The Council of Ministers began to involve itself more directly in foreign trade in 1957, when it created a subordinate State Committee for Foreign Economic Relations. Its involvement has increased as newly created state committees and other subordinate organs have gained control over foreign trade organizations which were formerly under the jurisdiction of the MFT. According to one Western scholar, eight Soviet FTO's are no longer under the MFT: Intourist (responsible for foreign tourism) is subordinate to the Administration for Foreign Tourism; Skotoimport (cattle and meat), to the Ministry of Meat and Dairy Industries; Sovexportfilm (movie films), to the Committee for Cinematography; Sovfrakht (ocean freight), and Sovinflot (servicing of ships), to the Ministry of Merchant Marine; Soyuzkoopvneshtorg (consumer goods barter), to the Central Union of Consumers; Vneshtorgizdat (publications) to the Committee on the Press; and Vneshtekhnika (technical collaboration), to the Committee on Science and Technology.[63]

In the realm of technology transfer, the erosion of the MFT's monopoly has been especially pronounced. Originally created in 1961 as the State Committee for Coordination of Scientific Research Work, the State Committee for Science and Technology (SCST) has emerged as the dominant force in scientific and technological matters for both the domestic economy and foreign economic, scientific and technological relations. Creation of the State Committee centralized functions that had previously been performed by the Committee on Inventions and Discoveries, various organs of the union republics, and the Ministry of Foreign Trade.[64] In addition to its domestic activities, the State Committee was required "to direct the study, compilation and dissemination of the achievements of domestic and foreign science and technology for the purpose of using their achievements in the national economy of the U.S.S.R." to coordinate "the international relations of ministries, departments, and scientific-research organizations on questions of science and technology," and "in

99

accordance with the policy of the Soviet government, to expand and strengthen collaboration in scientific research with foreign countries."[65] In 1963, the State Committee for Coordination of Scientific Research Work was placed under the newly formed Supreme Council of the National Economy of the Council of Ministers. It was reorganized in 1965 as the State Committee on Science and Technology, directly subordinate to the Council of Ministers, thus regaining its ministerial rank.

As it presently operates, SCST represents the institutionalization of efforts to solve choice-of-technology and technology absorption problems. It is SCST which ultimately decides on which foreign technology is to be imported. In this realm, the MFT has increasingly operated as a technical agency which negotiates and signs contracts after decisions have been made by SCST. For example, no license can be purchased without a decision by SCST. (For licenses of particularly great importance, the decision must be made by the Council of Ministers.)[66] Litsenzintorg's role is confined to negotiating and signing contracts. SCST's involvement in the technology transfer process is not limited to approving or disapproving license purchases. It also reviews proposals for exploiting licensed technology in the domestic economy, and, after a license is purchased, oversees the implementation of the contract.[67]

Moreover, SCST has also assumed some of the MFT's technical functions. At the prompting of SCST, Vneshtekhnika was founded in 1967 "to assist Soviet and foreign scientific organizations, industrial enterprises and firms in purchasing documentation, samples of equipment, instructions and materials."[68] It thus performs the function of other FTO's while remaining subordinate to SCST. SCST also plays an active role in initiating contacts with foreign firms which are potential suppliers of technology to the Soviet Union. It is responsible for concluding the scientific and technical cooperation agreements which precede most major technology transfer agreements. SCST's preeminence in the realm of technology transfer is illustrated by the fact that it may issue obligatory orders within its sphere of operation to all ministries, including the MFT.[69]

Other central economic agencies, particularly the State Planning Committee (GOSPLAN) and the Ministry of Finance, are also playing more active roles in Soviet foreign commercial relations. In recent years, these agencies have engaged in more detailed and comprehensive planning of Soviet foreign trade and financial operations and have developed more sophisticated planning techniques.[70] For example, since 1970, the acquisition and use of foreign licenses have been carried out in accordance with special annual and five-year plans that are integral parts of the State Plan.[71] The Ministry of Finance, through its subordinate Foreign Trade Bank (Vneshtorgbank), appears to be playing an increasingly prominent role in planning and executing compensation agreements.[72]

There is also evidence that Soviet industrial managers, in the ministries, departments and enterprises, are able to exert more influence on Soviet foreign trade operations. Traditionally, the end-user of imports--the domestic enterprise--has had relatively little direct contact with the FTO which actually signed contracts for purchasing foreign goods and services. The enterprise imports by requesting that its needs be included in the annual plan. Once the need to import is confirmed, the Council of Ministers issues a permit, usually to supply-and-sales agencies of the State Committee of Material and Technical Supply. It is the supply-and-sales agencies which actually contract with the FTO for imports. The formal mechanisms for coordinating questions of exports and imports between domestic enterprises and foreign trade organizations are special export-import associations in the industrial ministries. Through these associations, industrial specialists are able to advise foreign trade bureaucrats on their detailed requirements and specifications.

Some exceptions to this cumbersome process have been allowed for imports of technology. Industrial ministries, rather than supply agencies, act as ordering agencies for imports of machinery and equipment which are to be used entirely within the Ministry.[73] Likewise, foreign licenses are ordered directly by the industrial ministries and departments, with the approval of SCST.[74] There has also been a growing tendency to involve industry representatives in negotiations with foreign firms. According to one Soviet specialist, the recipient firm or representatives of the industrial ministry routinely take part in negotiations on purchases of foreign licenses, from the beginning of the search for a foreign supplier until the contract is signed. Together with representatives of Litsenzintorg, and sometimes independently, the recipient frequently travels abroad to exercise supervision over fulfillment by the licenser of provisions of the contract.[75]. Likewise, the various ministries involved in compensation projects are represented in the MFT's new Main Administration for Compensation Projects with Capitalist countries.

The degree to which other institutions have intruded into what was formerly a near exclusive domain of the Ministry of Foreign Trade clearly troubles some Soviet officials. V. S. Posdniakov, a prominent Soviet specialist on Soviet foreign trade law, has called for tighter control by the MFT over all trade and trade-related activities. He complains that "as a result of the recent increase in our country's foreign economic relations, an increased number of ministries, state committees and departments, as well as economic organizations have become involved with state foreign trade agencies, including Soviet trade missions abroad." He proposes that a new foreign trade statute should be enacted which would enable Soviet foreign trade mission, "as agents of the Soviet foreign trade monopoly abroad," to exercise a centralized administration of Soviet foreign trade. "The new statute," he proposed, "should grant the trade missions jurisdiction over all foreign trade operations, including technical assistance, scientific and technical export and import, transport services, rental operations, etc."[76]

One also finds in the Soviet literature, spirited defenses of the traditional foreign trade monopoly:

> Imperialist circles...spare no effort to circumvent the foreign trade monopoly and to establish trade contacts between capitalist firms and individual Soviet enterprises. But it is of course absolutely unrealistic to make the development of economic cooperation between the U.S.S.R. and the capitalist world dependent on change in the economic and foreign trade mechanism of our country. The planned development of the economy of the U.S.S.R. and the state monopoly of foreign trade, far from being an obstacle to extensive and diversified economic, scientific and technical ties between East and West, give them stability.[77]

The reference to "imperialist circles" probably masks a debate within the Soviet economic bureaucracy over the wisdom and efficiency of maintaining the foreign trade monopoly in its traditional form. There have been numerous challenges to the traditional system in the form of proposals to improve the organization of Soviet foreign trade management. Thus, the

Soviet economist and foreign trade specialist
O. Bogomolov, cited with approval the Central
Committee accountability report to the 24th Party
Congress, which called for "specific measures to
improve the management of the entire foreign economic activity, and the elimination of a narrowly
departmental approach in this important matter."
The Central Committee report maintained that foreign
economic activities "must be based, to an ever
greater extent, on the combination of production
with trade functions, so that the needs and possibilities of the world market will be operatively
considered and comprehensively used for the sake
of the development of our economy."[78] Similarly,
in a conversation with U.S. newsmen, Nikolai N.
Inozemtsev, an official of the State Planning
Committee, proposed three areas in Soviet foreign
trade management which needed improvement: a reorganization of foreign trade agencies; closer relations between Soviet industry and the trade agencies,
and greater direct contact between American concerns
and Soviet industrial establishments.[79]
     Another Soviet observer notes that the growing
complexity of Soviet foreign economic relations
necessitates the involvement of many domestic
organizations:

     In former years, when foreign economic relations
     were mostly limited to foreign trade, and for-
     eign trade transactions were essentially of a
     single type, the process of carrying out such
     operations was relatively uncomplicated, and
     was carried out primarily by the Ministry of
     Foreign Trade and its subordinate agencies.

     Now imagine just one of the modern, large-scale,
     long-term projects carried in cooperation with
     foreign countries. In preparing, organizing
     and carrying out such projects in their various
     stages, tens of government organs participate--
     from the Council of Ministers and Gosplan, to
     the Ministry of Foreign Trade, the State Com-
     mittee on Science and Technology, the Ministry
     of Finance, Gosbank, Foreign Trade Bank,
     various industrial, construction, transporta-
     tion and other ministries, departments, asso-
     ciations and enterprises...[80]

Such observations clearly suggest the erosion of the
traditional foreign trade monopoly, in which decision
making authority was centralized in the MFT.

Changes in Domestic Institutions

The problems experienced by the Soviet Union in absorbing foreign technology can be solved only partially by improving technology transfer mechanisms and reorganizing foreign economic institutions. The experiences of other countries suggest that the domestic environment must be appropriate, that certain preconditions must be in place, for the effective absorption and utilization of Western technology. Many Soviet officials and economists do not acknowledge the need to reform domestic economic institutions in order to improve the absorptive capacity of the economy. Indeed, some probably see the importation of technology as a substitute for reform. In the words of Joseph Berliner:

> There is some disposition among the governors of the Soviet economy to regard borrowed technology as the deus ex machina. It offers a way of attaining the high rate of technical advance greatly sought, without having to tamper once again with the fundamental economic structure.[81] *Berliner pS18*

Berliner argues that Soviet planners will be unable to achieve the desired results through technology borrowing alone, and that there is no substitute for domestic economic reform. There are at least some Soviet officials who appear to agree with this assessment. For example, N. N. Smeliakov, Deputy Minister of Foreign Trade, has observed that the success of Japanese technology borrowing is heavily dependent on their domestic technological efforts:

> ...when one states that they [the Japanese] merely copy foreign inventions, machinery and technology, meaning to say that private companies do not spend money on research and development, I cannot agree. When the Japanese buy a license or "know-how", they intelligently improve upon the purchased invention, frequently surpassing the original. They also conduct their own research and development effort. Foreign inventions and licenses are frequently used as a springboard to move forward technologically...[82]

The main features of traditional Soviet domestic economic institutions responsible for absorbing foreign technology have already been noted. Projects utilizing foreign technology tend to be isolated from the rest of the economy. Soviet industrial managers compensate for the shortcomings of the domestic supply system by developing large, vertically integrated plants which produce as many of their needed inputs as possible. Managers act essentially as engineers, maximizing output with given constraints. The incentive structure of the enterprise reflects the priority assigned to increasing output and meeting delivery schedules, rather than improving quality. Industrial research and development is separated from production and largely centralized at the ministerial level.

The isolation of technology transfer projects in the Soviet economy is largely an extension of normal Soviet enterprise management practices. In the absence of a smoothly functioning supply system, the enterprise manager tends to avoid dependence on outside sources of supply. He also eschews innovation, since new input requirements resulting from changes in the production process are unlikely to be fulfilled properly. For the new project utilizing foreign technology, the unreliability of the supply system is exacerbated. Domestic suppliers are likely to be less able to meet the fundamentally new quality standards and specifications for imported technologies. Generally speaking, the interface between the imported technology and the domestic economy does not provide adequate incentives and in some respects creates considerable barriers to effective absorption. The natural response of the industrial managers who import technology is to isolate the recipient enterprises. In addition, they may attempt to overcome systematic problems in high priority technology projects by diverting the best materials, manpower and other inputs from other parts of the economy. Such diversion, however, is a costly, resource-consuming undertaking.[83]

The traditional Soviet approach to industrial management has by no means been eliminated in reaction to the problems of absorbing foreign technology. However, the increasing interest in technological ties to the West and the problems associated with absorbing Western technology has induced Soviet economic managers to make some changes in domestic institutions. For example, in 1973, the Soviet Government amended its industrial property laws to bring them in line with the Paris Convention. Basically, the changes gave foreign patent holders equal treatment with Soviet nationals. In case of conflict with the Paris Convention, the clauses of

the Convention now prevail. There had been considerable debate before the law was passed between
advocates of a patent system appropriate to a socialist economy and those who wanted to conform to international norms. A Western study of the reform concludes that "the statute of 1973 is a victory of
the champions of international cooperation."[84]

Some Soviet economists and managers have proposed more fundamental changes in the approach to the
organization and management of Soviet enterprises.
Their proposals reflect a keen awareness of the
shortcomings of the present system, as well as an
awareness of industrial management practices in the
West. Two particularly noteworthy developments,
which will be discussed further in the case study,
are the efforts to reduce the isolation and degree
of vertical integration of Soviet enterprises and
attempts to develop a new management style in Soviet
enterprises, a style which is likely to be influenced by observation of Western management techniques.

The discussion of whether Western-assisted
plants in the Soviet Union should continue to be
highly concentrated and vertically integrated or
more specialized and decentralized is part of a
general debate about the organization and structure
of the Soviet enterprise. Enterprises in the automotive (see case study) and the general machine-
building industries have been a focal point of the
debate. The question, as posed by the Soviet economist S. A. Kheinman, is whether the Soviet Union
should build "complex plants with a universal collection of large capacity preparatory and auxiliary
shops, or...move toward creation of plants with
technological and component specialization, cooperating with assembly plants producing finished machines."[85]
Kheinman rejects the first variant, which he says
characterizes industry in the Soviet Union and
smaller Western countries such as West Germany, in
favor of the latter, which he associates with U.S.
practice.

Soviet policy has been somewhat ambivalent on
this matter. There is still a tendency toward the
large, vertically integrated plant. However, the
creation of production associations may spur evolution in the opposite direction. If the associations
succeed in making inter-plant deliveries more reliable,
there will presumably be less need for the Stalinist
pattern of enterprise management. However, there
has not been sufficient experience with associations
to know if this will be the case.[86]

The Soviet attempt to develop a new style of
industrial management was an important element of
both the reform measures initiated in 1965 and the
creation of production associations. Soviet economic reforms have aimed at revising success indicators
to induce managers to economize on material, capital
and labor inputs and to improve the quality of output.
They have also emphasized the development of long-
term contractual ties between enterprises in order
to make the supply system more reliable. Most
importantly, they are intended to provide a greater
degree of independence for enterprise managers to
determine their production goals and manufacturing
methods and to enter into contracts with other enterprises. Soviet discussions of these reforms suggest
that they have not proceeded far: the Soviet manager
is frequently thwarted in trying to exercise his
independence because of a plethora of plan targets
set by central planners and by the continued cen-
tralization of the supply system, research and development activities, and other functions.

Despite the slow progress of the domestic reforms, the emphasis on new management techniques has
sparked a heightened Soviet interest in Western
management science. This new development parallels
the attraction of Lenin and the early Bolshevik
leaders to Western management practices in the immediate post-Revolutionary period, which subsequently
waned and gave way to the engineering approach to
business management characteristic of the Stalin
period. It has been suggested that the engineering
approach itself was heavily influenced by Taylorist
and other schools of management science current in
the West in the years preceding and during the first
Soviet Five-Year Plan.[87] Soviet commentators are
quite candid in describing this evolution of Soviet
studies of management science. Speaking of difficulties experienced by Soviet economic managers,
Dzherman Gvishiani, Deputy Chairman of SCST, has
noted:

> ...The Communist Party is steadily overcoming
> these difficulties and resolutely getting rid
> of the defects in production management which
> resulted from a subjective, voluntaristic
> approach to the solution of a number of organi-
> sational problems.
>
> It is a well-known fact that in the USSR scien-
> tific research on the problems of management
> was considerably curtailed at the end of the

thirties, and that little was done in this field until recent times. This inevitably affected the scientific validity of certain organisational decisions and led in practice to an approach to problems of management that was often purely empirical.[88]

Thus far, Soviet attempts to absorb Western management techniques have relied on indirect, passive channels. Courses in management science have been established at a number of Soviet institutions. A new kind of high-level business school has been established to train Soviet managers in management science. The first school at the national level was created in Moscow in 1971, and another was established in Kiev in 1975. The curricula at these schools include studies of the best management techniques developed in the Soviet Union and abroad. A number of Soviet institutes concerned with foreign affairs, such as the Institute of International Economics and International Relations and the Institute for the Study of the U.S.A. and Canada, also devote considerable efforts to studying Western management practices.

There is also increasing interest in direct importation of Western management technology through more active technology transfer mechanisms. Soviet officials are looking more favorably at mechanisms that provide transfers of managerial knowhow. Specifically, they are interested in Western techniques such as computer applications and systems analysis to assist in solving the chronic problems of Soviet management--managing the innovation cycle; quality control; better organization of labor and improvement of the incentive structure of the enterprise; marketing; and coordination of very large industrial projects.

NOTES

1. Karl Marx, "Manifesto of the Communist Party," in Karl Marx and Frederick Engels: Selected Works, Vol. 1 (Moscow: Foreign Languages Publishing House, 1950), p. 38.
2. V. I. Lenin, Selected Works (Moscow, Foreign Languages Publishing House, 1943), Vol. V, pp. 91f., cited by Stefan T. Possony, ed., Lenin Reader (Chicago: Henry Regnery Company, 1966), p. 298.
3. Ibid., pp. 294-295.
4. Ibid., pp. 98-99.

5. V. I. Lenin, "O prodovol'stvennom naloge." Izbrannye proizvedeniia, Vol. 3 (Moscow: Izdatel'stvo politicheskoi literatury, 1972), pp. 547-548. (Emphasis added.)

6. Joseph Stalin, The Foundations of Leninism (Moscow: Foreign Languages Publishing House, 1950), p. 160.

7. Joseph Stalin, Economic Problems of Socialism in the USSR. (New York: International Publishers, 1952), p. 33.

8. V. Kasyanenko, How Soviet Economy Won Technical Independence (Moscow: Progress Publishers, 1966), p. 37.

9. Michael R. Dohan stresses the importance of the economic factors in "The Economic Origins of Soviet Autarky, 1927/28-1934," Slavic Review. XXXV (December, 1976), 604-635.

10. Pravda, December 18, 1975, p. 2.

11. Harvey L. Dyck, Weimar Germany and Soviet Russia, 1926-1933: A Study in Diplomatic Instability (New York: Columbia University Press, 1966).

12. V. I. Kas'ianenko, Zavoevanie ekonomicheskoi nezavisimosti SSSR (1917-1940) (Moscow: Izdatel'stvo politicheskoi literatury, 1927), p. 191. (Emphasis added.) A similar explanation is given in N. P. Shmelev, ed., Ekonomicheskie sviazi Vostok-Zapad: problemy i vozmozhnosti (Moscow: Izdatel'stvo "Mysl'," 1976), pp. 24-25.

13. L. Mertts et al, "GAZ i Ford," Planovoe khoziaistvo, No. 6-7, 1932, p. 237.

14. L. Sabsovich, Ekonomicheskoe obozrenie, May 1929, p. 24, cited by David Granick, Soviet Metal-Fabricating and Economic Development: Practice versus Policy (Madison: The University of Wisconsin Press, 1967), p. 21.

15. Kasyanenko, Soviet Economy, p. 145.

16. Joseph Stalin, cited by B. V. Lavrovskii, Tsifry i fakty za 15 let po avtostroeniiu v SSSR (Moscow: Gosudarstvennoe aviatsionnoe i avtotraktornoe izdatel'stvo, 1932), p. 27.

17. Kendall E. Bailes, "The Politics of Technology: Stalin and Technocratic Thinking among Soviet Engineers," American Historical Review, LXXIX (April, 1974), 445-69.

18. Kasyanenko, Soviet Economy, pp. 131-39.

19. XXII S"ezd KPSS, stenograficheskii otchet, (Moscow, 1961) Vol. 1, p. 63.

20. Alexei Kosygin "On Improving Management of Industry, Perfecting, Planning and Enhancing Economic Incentives in Industrial Production," in New Methods of Economic Management in the USSR (Moscow: Novosti Press Agency Publishing House, 1965), p. 19.

21. Materialy XXIII S"ezda KPSS, (Moscow, 1966), p. 171.

22. Pravda, February 25, 1976.

23. Pravda, October 27, 1973.

24. D. D. Mishustin, Sotsialisticheskaia monopoliia vneshnei torgovli SSSR (Moscow: Izdatel' stvo Mezhdunarodnaia kniga, 1938), p. 13.

25. Alexander Baykov, Soviet Foreign Trade (Princeton: Princeton University Press, 1946), p. 11.

26. John Quigley, The Soviet Foreign Trade Monopoly: Institutions and Laws (n.p.: The Ohio State University Press, 1974).

27. Quigley, p. 27.

28. Ibid., p. 55.

29. Antony C. Sutton, Western Technology and Soviet Economic Development, Vol. I; 1917-1930 (Stanford: Hoover Institution on War, Revolution and Peace, 1968), p. 6; and U.S. National Science Foundation, Office of Science Information, The U.S.S.R. Scientific and Technical Information System: A U.S. View, (report of the U.S. participants in the U.S./ U.S.S.R. Symposium on Scientific and Technical Information, Moscow, June 18-30, 1973, and Washington, D.C., October, 1973), passim.

30 The concession decree, dated November 23, 1920, is reprinted in Ivan Ivanovich Skvortsov-Stepanov, Ob inostrannykh kontessiakh (Moscow; Gosudarstvennoe izdatel'stvo, 1920), pp. 41-43.

31. Alex Nove, An Economic History of the U.S.S.R. (Baltimore; Penguin Books, 1972), p. 89.

32. See especially Sutton, Vol. I, passim.

33. For a detailed description of the contractual obligations and rights of concessions, see G. A. Kuzbasov, Rabota profsoiuzov na kontsessionnykh predpriiatiiakh (Moscow: Gosudarstvennoe izdatel'stvo, 1920), pp. 113-123; and Joseph Watstein, "Soviet Economic Concessions: The Agony and the Promise," ACES Bulletin, XVI (Spring, 1974).

34. Kas'ianenko, Zavoevanie, p. 185.

35. A. Kolomenskii, Kak my ispolzuem zagranichnuiu tekhniku (Moscow: Gosudarstvennoe izdatel'stvo, 1930).

36. Ibid., p. 53.

37. Kas'ianenko, Zavoevanie, passim.

38. Kasyanenko, Soviet Economy, p. 140.

39. Quigley, pp. 60-68.

40. Sutton, Vol. 1-3, passim.

41. Supra, pp. 35-37.

42. Eastern Europe Report, V (March 5, 1976), 65-66.

43. Pravda, March 12, 1974, p. 1.

44. Philip Hanson, "The Diffusion of Imported Technology in the USSR," in NATO, Directorate of Economic Affairs, East West Technological Co-operation, Main findings of Colloquium held 17-19th March, 1976 in Brussels, p. 149.

45. L. Pekarsky, Sotsialisticheskaia industriia, December 19, 1973.

46. Kas'ianenko, Zavoevanie, pp. 130-32.

47. E. Manevich, "Problemy vosproizvodstva rabochei sily i puti uluchsheniia ispol'zovaniia trudovykh resursov v SSSR," Voprosy ekonomiki, 10, 1969.

48. See case study in Chapters 5 and 6.

49. E. Artemiev, "Patenty i litsenzii: vazhnoe uslovie tekhnicheskogo progressa," Pravda, July 30, 1975, p. 2. The same point is made in "Sovershenstvovat' planirovanie vnedrenie nauchno-tekhnicheskikh dostizheniy v proizvodstve," Planovoe khoziaistvo, November, 1975, p. 8.

50. M. L. Gorodisskiy, Litsenzii vo vneshnei torgovli SSSR (Moscow: Izdatel'stvo Mezhdunarodnyye otnosheniia, 1972). Translated by National Technical Information Services, COM-73-10738, May 2, 1972, p. 136.

51. M. Papichev, "Regulirovanie pokupok litsenziy i 'nou-khau'," Vneshniaia torgovlia, No. 10, 1975, p. 49.

52. U.S. Department of Commerce, Bureau of East-West Trade, "Impact of Compensation Agreements on Soviet Exports Through 1930," (unpublished paper, January 18, 1977).

53. Details of the new forms of East-West industrial cooperation are provided in: United Nations, Economic Commission for Europe, Analytical Report on Industrial Co-Operation among ECE Countries, Geneva, 1973, E/ECE/844/Rev. 1, pp. 7-14; and N. P. Shmelev, "Scope for Industrial, Scientific and Technical Cooperation between East and West," (paper presented at the International Economic Association meeting in Dresden, German Democratic Republic, July 1976).

54. Shmelev, "Cooperation Between East and West."

55. Lawrence H. Theriot, "U.S. Governmental and Private Industry Cooperation with the Soviet Union in the Fields of Science and Technology," in JEC, pp. 739-66.

56. See Appendix I.

57. Eastwest Markets, May 3, 1976, p. 2.

58. Some Western businessmen agree with this assessment. See, for example, Interview with David Rockefeller, "How to Trade with the Communists," U.S. News and World Report, August 13, 1973, p. 37.

59. Shmelev, "Cooperation Between East and West."
See also, V. Sushkov, "Dolgosrochnoe torgovo-
promyshlennoe sotrudnichestvo SSSR s razvitymi
kapitalisticheskimi stranami na kompensatsionnoi
osnove," Vneshniaia torgovlia, No. 5, 1977, pp. 17-22.
    60. Jozef Wilczynski, Joint East-West Ventures
and Rights of Ownership, Carleton University, Institute of Soviet and East European Studies. (East-
West Commercial Relations Series, Working Paper
No. 6, October 1975).
    61. Glen Alden Smith, Soviet Foreign Trade:
Organization Operations and Policy, 1918-1971
(New York: Praeger Publishers, 1973), pp. 95-98.
    62. Business Eastern Europe, V (October 15,
1976), 321-22.
    63. Smith, pp. 102-5.
    64. Quigley, p. 78.
    65. Ibid.
    66. Gorodisskiy, p. 131.
    67. E. Ia. Volynets-Russet, Planirovanie i
raschet effektivnosti priobreteniia litsenzii
(Moscow: "Ekonomika," 1973), pp. 128-42.
    68. Soviet Business and Trade, IV, (August 4,
1975), p. 6.
    69. Quigley, p. 78.
    70. Lawrence J. Brainard, "Soviet Foreign Trade
Planning," in JEC, pp. 695-708.
    71. Gorodisskiy, p. 129.
    72. Business Eastern Europe, V (October 15, 1976),
321-22 and (August 5, 1977), 244-45.
    73. Quigley, p. 164.
    74. Gorodisskiy, p. 131.
    75. Ibid., p. 133.
    76. V. S. Posdniakov, "The Legal Status of U.S.S.R.
Trade Missions Abroad," Sovetskoe gosudarstvo i pravo,
March, 1975, pp. 87-94, trans. in Current Digest of
the Soviet Press, XXVII, (November 5, 1975). See
also Quigley, pp. 79-80.
    77. I. Kovan, "Leninskii printsip vneshneekonomi-
cheskikh otnoshenii sovetskogo gosudarstva,"
Vneshniaia torgovlia, No. 4, 1973, p. 8.
    78. O. Bogomolov, "O vneshneekonomicheskikh
sviaziakh SSSR," Kommunist, March, 1974, p. 98.
    79. New York Times, July 10, 1973.
    80. Margarita Matveevna Maksimova, SSSR i
mezhdunarodnoe ekonomicheskoe sotrudnichestvo
(Moscow: Izdatel-stvo "Mysl'," 1977), pp. 192-93.
    81. Joseph S. Berliner, The Innovation Decision
in Soviet Industry (Cambridge: The M.I.T. Press,
1976), p. 518.

82. N. N. Smeliakov, S chego nachinaetsia rodina (Moscow: Izdatel'stvo politicheskoi literatury, 1975), p. 488.

83. See John P. Hardt and George D. Holliday, "Implications of Commercial Technology Transfer between the Soviet Union and the United States," in U.S. Congress, House, Committee on International Relations, Subcommittee on International Security and Scientific Affairs, Technology Transfer and Scientific Cooperation between the United States and the Soviet Union: A Review, Committee Print (Washington, D.C.: Government Printing Office, May 26, 1977), pp. 81-82.

84. M. W. Balz, Invention and Innovation under Soviet Law: A Comparative Analysis. (Toronto and London: Lexington Books, D. C. Heath, 1975).

85. S. A. Kheinman, "Mashinostroenie: perspektivy i reservy," Ekonomika i organizatsiia promyshlennogo proizvodstva, November-December, 1974, p. 61.

86. Alice C. Gorlin, "Industrial Reorganization: The Associations," in JEC, pp. 162-88.

87. John A. Armstrong, The European Administrative Elite (Princeton: Princeton University Press, 1973), pp. 188-90.

88. Dzherman Gvishiani, Organization and Management: A Sociological Analysis of Western Theories (Moscow: Progress Publishers, 1972), pp. 7-8.

5. Western Technology Transfer to the Soviet Automotive Industry: The Gorkii Automobile Plant

   In chapters 5 and 6, a case study--the transfer
of technology to the Soivet automotive industry--
is used to examine the Soviet Union's experience as
a technology borrower. The automotive industry has
been one of the high-priority areas of Soviet technology borrowing in the two periods of intensive
Soviet interest in Western technology--the First
Five-Year Plan (1928-1932) and the current period
(the mid-1960's to the mid-1970's). The case study
is intended to provide a basis for evaluating the
hypothesis that the Soviet orientation to the
international economy has undergone a fundamental
change since the 1930's. Specifically, Western technology transfers to major Soviet automotive projects
in the two periods are analyzed in order to determine
if there is movement toward more active technology
transfer mechanisms, characterized by more permanent
technological ties and more active involvement of
Western firms in the Soviet economy. In addition,
the degrees and kinds of Soviet technological dependence on the West are examined. The case study concentrates on three major projects in the Soviet automotive industry: the Gorkii Automobile Plant (built
in the late 1920s and early 1930s with the assistance
of the Ford Motor Company and other Western firms);
the Volga Automobile Plant (built during the Eighth
Five-Year Plan with the primary assistance of the
Italian firm FIAT); and the Kama River Truck Plant
(begun, but not completed, during the Ninth Five-Year
Plan with assistance from a number of Western firms).[1]
In each case, the study will examine the forms of
cooperation, with Western firms, the criteria for
selection of foreign technology and foreign firms,
the role of foreign companies in the management of
the projects, and the degree of permanency of Soviet
economic ties with the West. The impact of foreign

technology on the industry as a whole will also be
examined.

The use of foreign technology by the Soviet
automotive industry has been in some ways typical
of Soviet industry as a whole. The contractual
arrangements in both periods--technical assistance
contracts in the earlier period and various industrial cooperation arrangements in the 1960s and 1970s--
were similar to those used in many branches of Soviet
industry. Moreover, the rationale for borrowing
foreign technology and the domestic environment into
which the technology was transplanted were similar
for the automotive and other Soviet industries. In
the 1920s and 1930s, Soviet economic planners sought
foreign assistance to transform a backward domestic
industry, with insignificant production, into a
modern mass-production industry capable of meeting
the needs of a rapidly industrializing economy. In
the 1960s and 1970s, purchases of foreign technology
have been viewed by the Soviet leadership as a means
of modernizing a large but in some ways inadequate
industry, improving the productivity of capital and
labor inputs, and overcoming the increasingly evident technology gap between the Soviet Union and the
industrial West. In both periods, efforts in the
Soviet automotive industry paralleled developments in
other sectors of the economy.

In one respect--the scale of Western technology
transfers to the Soviet Union--the automotive industry may be regarded as somewhat atypical. The
Soviet automotive industry has been the recipient of
as much or more Western technology than any other
Soviet industry during the two periods studied.
According to one Soviet source, the Soviets spent
311.4 million rubles of scarce foreign exchange for
machinery and equipment for the Gorkii and Moscow
automobile factories during the First Five-Year Plan
(189.2 million rubles for GAZ and 122.2 million
rubles for Moscow).[2] These two factories alone
accounted for over four percent of all Soviet imports during the First Five-Year Plan and exceeded
the hard currency expenditures for such huge Western-
assisted projects as the Magnitogorsk Metallurgical
Works and the Dnepr Hydroelectric Station. Additional funds were spent for expansion of the Yaroslavl
Automobile Plant and for various suppliers to the
automobile industry (such as producers of glass,
metal, electrical equipment). These expenditures
continued, though at a reduced rate, during the
Second Five-Year Plan.

Similarly large expenditures have been and are

being made for purchasing Western technology for the Soviet automotive industry during the 1960s and 1970s. The construction of the Volga Automobile Plant (VAZ), for example, was assisted by purchases of about $550 million of Western machinery and equipment.[3] The Kama River Truck Plant (KamAZ) is expected to cost over $1 billion in purchases from the West.[4] VAZ and KamAZ represent the major industrial undertakings of the Eighth and Ninth Five-Year Plans respectively. In addition, large purchases of Western technology have been made during the current period to modernize other parts of the Soviet automotive industry. Thus, it appears that the Soviet automotive industry has been the beneficiary of a disproportionate share of Soviet hard currency expenditures.

One implication of the high priority given to foreign automotive technology is that evidence of technology transfer-induced changes may be more pronounced in this sector than in others. However, as research by Antony Sutton and others has shown,[5] many Soviet industries have benefitted from Western technology transfers. Moreover, the experience of the automotive industry does appear to be representative of a Soviet pattern for using foreign technology that is characterized by the concentration of purchases of foreign technology in large, new, "showcase" projects. This pattern has been evident in the Soviet chemical, metal-working and other industries. The large scale of automotive technology transfer in both periods makes it a useful case study because it highlights the differences and continuities of the Soviet approach to economic ties with the West.

INITIAL PLANNING AND PURCHASE OF TECHNOLOGY FOR GAZ

On May 31, 1929, the Ford Motor Company signed a contract with the Soviet Supreme Economic Council (VSNKh) to assist in the construction of an automobile plant at Nizhni-Novgorod (renamed Gorkii in 1932). The initial agreement provided for Ford assistance in building a factory to produce annually about 100,000 vehicles of two types: a passenger car modeled after the Ford Model A (the Soviet version was called GAZ-A) and a light truck modeled after the Ford Model AA (the Soviet GAZ-AA).[6] The 1929 contract was followed by supplementary agreements with Ford to increase the capacity of the plant and by contracts with other Western firms providing for their assistance in various specialized operations

116

at the plant. Western assistance to the automotive industry was intended to coincide with the First Five-Year Plan. More passive ties with Ford continued into the Second Five-Year Plan.

The signing of a contract with Ford culminated a debate among Soviet planners, that had continued for several years. The major questions in the debate were whether the Soviet Union needed a mass-production automotive industry, what the scale of domestic production should be, what types of production facilities and automobiles were needed, and who should supply the automobile-manufacturing technology. These were controversial questions for Soviet planners in the 1920s. Some economists questioned the cost-effectiveness of domestic automobile production altogether, and at least one important study concluded that, under Soviet conditions, the Russian horse and cart was a more efficient mode of transportation than the American automobile.[7] Others accepted the need for automobiles, but believed that the Soviet economy had quite limited needs which could be met primarily by imports of finished automobiles. Still others believed that the creation of an indigenous automotive industry must take place gradually, beginning with small-scale production which would meet the immediate needs of the economy.[8]

While the importance of a domestic automotive industry to a rapidly industrializing country may appear self-evident in retrospect, a number of Soviet planners had reservations about the capacity of the Soviet economy, with virtually no automobile-manufacturing experience and little of the necessary infrastructure, to begin "automobilization" on a massive scale. In particular, the paucity of good roads and the absence of complementary industries were noted by opponents as major barriers to mass production of automobiles in Soviet Russia. Moreover, there appeared to be a considerable gap between the two sides of the debate in their perceptions of what the pace of Soviet industrialization would be. Indeed, probably few of the participants anticipated the rapid pace of industrialization that was to be mandated by the First Five-Year Plan.

The debates over Soviet automotive needs continued until the eve of the First Five-Year Plan. VSNKh's announcement on December 19, 1928, that negotiations were being conducted with two large U.S. firms, Ford and General Motors, concerning the construction of a large, mass-production automobile plant in Soviet Russia brought a rather abrupt end to the debates. The decision to select a large U.S. firm appears to have been grounded in the common Soviet belief that U.S. manufacturing techniques represented the latest word in world industrial technology. In addition, given the ambitious goals of the First Five-Year Plan, it was apparent that only the major U.S. firms had experience in the scale of production which would be needed in the Soviet Union.

The enormity of the Soviet automobile industry's task can readily be illustrated by comparing output levels at the beginning of the First Five-Year Plan with the goals set by Soviet planners. In 1928, only 841 automobiles were produced in the Soviet Union. The goal for the last year of the First Five-Year Plan (1932) was 300,000.[9] Approximately one-tenth of that goal was achieved, with production devoted almost exclusively to trucks. Annual production was a little over 200,000 on the eve of the war, with trucks accounting for about 90 percent of output. (See Appendix C.) This number was far short of Soviet wartime needs; those needs had to be met by large shipments of trucks under the U.S.-Soviet Lend Lease agreement. The gap between the plan figures and accomplishments suggests the kind of pressure felt by Soviet planners to expand automobile production rapidly.

Several factors dictated the ultimate choice of Ford as a supplier of technology. Soviet authorities were favorably impressed with the performance of imported Ford vehicles, which at that time comprised the bulk of the small Soviet automobile park. Ford's Model A passenger cars and Model AA trucks were light, rugged and relative inexpensive and simple to mass produce. Their roadability under difficult Soviet conditions was considered excellent.[10] In addition, Henry Ford's production techniques had a special mystique in Soviet political and technical circles.[11] The Soviet term "fordizatsiia" ("Fordization") became synonomous with modernization in the 1920s. Finally, Henry Ford appeared to be more favorably disposed than many Western industrial leaders toward the transfer of modern technology to Soviet Russia.[12]

Soviet leaders first signaled their interest in an active commercial relationship with Ford in 1926, when the Government invited Ford to send a delegation to Soviet Russia. Ford accepted the invitation and sent a group of engineers to recommend to the Soviet Government ways to rationalize the

repair and servicing of Ford tractors being used in
Soviet Russia. They were also asked by the Soviet
Government to consider building a tractor factory
in Soviet Russia, apparently on a concession basis.
The delegation's report to Ford presented a negative
appraisal of conditions in Soviet industry, comment-
ing in particular on poor management and labor discipline, absence of servicing and repair facilities,
and a poor supply system. With regard to a possible
concession, the delegation found several reasons
why Ford should not become involved. All concessions, they reported, operated under fear of expro-
priation without adequate compensation. They also
noted that interference by political commissars in
Soviet factories was commonplace, and that Western
patent rights were not being respected.[13]

Curiously, one of the infringements against
Western property rights noted by the delegation was
against a Ford product, the Fordson tractor. They
found that the Soviets with considerable difficulty
had begun to reproduce the Fordson at the Krasnyi
Putilovits Tractor Plant. This had been accomplished
by disassembling an imported tractor and making
drawings of all the parts. Soviet engineers had
also attempted to copy equipment and production techniques employed at Ford's Highland Park tractor plant,
apparently by studying written descriptions and drawings of the latter.[14] This approach to borrowing
Ford's technology had not been successful. Charles
Sorenson, chief Ford engineer and leader of a subsequent delegation to the Soviet Union in 1929
(after the contract had been concluded), noted two
general problems with tractor production at the
Soviet plant. First, while Soviet engineers could
copy the parts, they knew nothing of specifications
for the materials used in their production. Consequently, the end product had inferior parts. Secondly,
Sorenson observed serious shortcomings in the organization and management of the plant. "Anything that
meant mass production," he noted, "seemed to have
the Russians stumped."[15]

Such experiences in copying foreign technology
impressed many Soviet observers with the need to
seek more active technology transfer arrangements
with Western firms. In contemplating the kind of
assistance which the Soviet Union would need in
building an automotive plant, one Soviet specialist
noted:

Copying foreign automobile models will enable
us to avoid many "childhood diseases" and will

reduce the cost of starting up production.
The main problem lies not in the design of the
automobile: one can draw very beautiful designs
on paper. The main problem is to skillfully
adapt the design to production and to organize
the production efficiently. Clearly, by relying on foreign experience we will achieve our
desired results more quickly and more cheaply.
That is why, during the first stage of developing production, we must take the best which is
available abroad--automobile designs together
with the experience of producing automobiles.[16]

Not surprisingly, Ford rejected the Soviet proposal to build a tractor plant in the Soviet Union
on a concession basis. The next major contact
between Soviet representatives and Ford came in 1928,
when a Soviet delegation went to Detroit with a proposal that Ford assist in building an automobile
factory. As with many other key projects of the
First Five-Year Plan, negotiations with Ford were
conducted from the Soviet side by a delegation
headed by representatives of VSNKh, rather than the
Foreign Trade Commissariat. The importance attached
to the Ford negotiations by the Soviet Government
was signified by the appointment of a high-level
official, Valerii I. Meshlauk, Vice-Chairman of
VSNKh, to negotiate and sign the contract. Meshlauk
and other Soviet negotiators had extended stays in
the United States, visiting Ford facilities and the
plants of other potential suppliers to GAZ.
The problems which Soviet industry had experienced in the attempts to copy Ford's tractor technology and Ford's refusal to accept a tractor concession in the Soviet Union undoubtedly influenced
Soviet negotiating strategy on the proposed automobile factory. To build a large automobile factory,
the Soviet Government clearly needed a technology
transfer mechanism that would insure a more active
exchange with Ford technical personnel and that
would provide adequate incentives to induce Ford
participation. The presented a proposal in 1928 which
combined the central elements of a technical assistance
agreement with a Soviet commitment to purchase a large
number of Ford vehicles. At first, Soviet officials
proposed a plant with an annual capacity of 25,000
vehicles when working one shift, or 50,000 when working two. Ford rejected this proposal on the grounds
that it was too small to interest him. After prolonged negotiations, during which Soviet negotiators
increased the proposed capacity to 100,000, the two

sides reached agreement.

The Ford arrangement with the Soviet Government was typical of the technical assistance contracts and is generally cited in the Soviet literature as one of the more successful agreements with Western firms.[17] Indeed, it was a well-conceived device for transferring technology to a country that lacked the economic and technical infrastructure needed for such a massive undertaking. Ford, in collaboration with other Western firms which assisted in construction and setting up certain parts of the production facilities, took part in every phase of the creation of the plant, from design to start-up of production. Ford sold much of the necessary machinery and equipment to the Soviet Government, supervised its installation at GAZ and provided training for Soviet workers and engineers, both in the United States and in the Soviet Union.

The contract with Ford provided for Soviet automobile production to start up in phases. Initially, the Soviets merely assembled the vehicles from parts produced by Ford in the United States. For this purpose, there were two assembly plants—one at the Gorkii site and the other in Moscow. The Moscow plant, called the Kim Works, was an unused railroad shop, which the Soviets, with Ford's assistance, converted to auto production. The Moscow plant assembled the first vehicles, while the Gorkii plant gradually phased in production of various parts. After the first year, bodies, fenders, hoods, and all sheet-metal parts were to be produced. Over the next four years, fittings, engines, axles, instruments, batteries, and electrical equipment would be phased in, so that after five years, GAZ would be working at capacity and producing most of the parts needed for the two vehicles it would produce. The major incentive in the contract for Ford was a Soviet commitment to buy 72,000 Ford vehicles (cars, trucks and equivalent parts) during this phase. GAZ would also use Ford-made parts exclusively for repairs.[18]

The contract provided for active Ford assistance at GAZ to continue for four years—until the start-up of production. Ford committed itself to a more passive technological exchange for another five years. Soviet officials attempted to insure that GAZ, once in operation, would represent the latest word in Western technology. The agreement not only required Ford to place all of its patents at the disposal of GAZ, but further required that any innovations or improvements which were introduced in Ford automobiles during the life of the contract (nine years)

121

were to be made available to the Soviet plant.[19]
Ford apparently took this stipulation seriously.
For example, Ford offered to help the Soviets introduce its new V-8 engine, probably the most important
Ford innovation during the life of the contract, at
GAZ.[20] (The new engine was still on Ford's drawing
boards when the contract was signed.) The Soviets
declined, preferring to produce the simpler and
proven Model A. In 1932, when production of the
Model A was just underway at GAZ, Ford discontinued
its production and put the V-8 engine into production in the United States. Soviet specialists noted
the development, pointing out that they had the option
to acquire the new technology, but did not do so during the life of the contract.[21]

Ford was not a general consultant for the entire
Gorkii plant. Soviet engineers and managers jealously
guarded their prerogative in matters of design and
selection of machinery. For example, when GAZ engineers believed that technology superior to Ford's was
available, they purchased it from other firms in the
West.[22] In other cases, they rejected what they
considered "too specialized machinery," apparently
motivated by the belief that, under Soviet conditions,
more labor-intensive operations would be efficient.[23]
The Soviet Government also signed contracts with other
Western firms to perform specialized tasks in building and equipping GAZ. Contracts were signed with
companies such as Timken-Detroit Axle Co., Brown
Lipe Gear Co., and Austin Company.[24] The Austin
Company, which had built several U.S. automobile
plants (including Ford plants), played a particularly
important role in the construction of GAZ. Austin
signed a contract with the Soviet Government in
August 1929 to help design and to provide advice
during the construction of the buildings housing the
factory. This was to be completed not later than
the fall of 1931 and would accommodate a revised
planned capacity of 120,000 vehicles.[25] Austin was
paid $250,000 for drafting the project and received
additional payments for technical assistance during
construction.[26]

ABSORPTION OF WESTERN TECHNOLOGY FOR GAZ

After Soviet officials had signed contracts
with the most important Western suppliers, the planning and designing of GAZ proceeded in several stages.
Initial planning was done in the Soviet Union, where
general plan directives were translated into concrete

122

goals for GAZ. The plan worked out at this stage
was very general and had little influence on the
final shape and organization of GAZ.

After the preliminary plans were completed, the
major part of the planning and design work began in
the United States. A Soviet Government commission,
led by S. S. Dybets, head of Avtostroi,[27] went to the
United States to work primarily with the Ford Motor
Company in Detroit and the Austin Company in Cleveland.
Most of their work was completed in one and a half
years (1929-1930). Ford engineers worked with their
Soviet counterparts on designs for all of the production processes and assisted in selecting machinery
and equipment. Ford also provided the Soviet engineers complete opportunity to study production techniques at its own plants and the plants of many of
its suppliers. At the same time, the Austin Company,
working with five Avtostroi engineers, provided a
general plan for most of the construction work.
Designs for roads, railroads, the water system, the
main production facilities and many of the auxiliary
shops were done in Cleveland.

After the U.S. designs were completed, Soviet
officials decided to have parts of the plant rede-
signed in Germany, where Soviet engineers found that
German-built metal structures could be substituted
for parts of Austin's designs. It was decided that
purchasing these structures in Germany would be less
expensive than manufacturing them in the Soviet
Union. Finally, minor parts of the design work were
carried out entirely by Soviet specialists, working
in the Soviet Union. The Soviet-designed parts of
GAZ included the heat and energy systems, a number
of auxiliary shops, warehouses and living quarters
for workers.[28]

The living quarters were an integral part of the
overall design. A unique feature of the Gorkii
plant was the combined construction of the factory
and an entire new city to provide housing and services for the factory's employees. The Soviets chose
not to locate the factory in a large metropolitan
area, where workers and an urban infrastructure would
already be in place. The plant was actually constructed
outside of Gorkii (then Nizhni-Novgorod) where no infrastructure existed. Although construction of auxiliary facilities required additional allocation of
scarce capital resources, Soviet planners seemed
determined to create a completely modern island within the backward Soviet economy. This pattern was
copied for future "avtogiganty"--VAZ and KamAZ.

It was in the project planning and design stage

123

that Western companies played a central and probably indispensable role in supplying technology to GAZ. Because they had no experience in mass production of automobiles, Soviet engineers could not have proceeded without the basic designs for buildings, production processes and vehicles provided by foreign suppliers. Nevertheless, Soviet engineers did not play a passive role during the project planning stage. Soviet specialists not only designed some of the auxiliary facilities for GAZ, but also had the ultimate authority and responsibility to approve or reject every detail of the designs provided by foreign firms. They rejected some foreign designs and when possible actively adapted foreign designs to Soviet conditions.

The roles of Ford, Austin and other Western companies at GAZ can best be described as technical or engineering consultants. In each phase of the technology transfer process, Western specialists were advisors to Soviet directors, rather than supervisors of the ongoing work. No Western firm had the role of general contractor or general consultant for the project. Soviet officials dealt with each Western firm individually. Moreover, the skills which Western firms transferred to Soviet specialists were essentially engineering rather than managerial in nature. The distinction between engineering and managerial assistance proved to be an important one because the absence of foreign management participation limited the role of foreign companies during the absorption phase. They had no overall responsibility, either for the construction of GAZ or for its operation after startup. The limitations in the role of Western firms contributed to numerous problems during the absorption phase.

The problems began almost immediately during construction, which began in 1929, shortly after the Ford contract was signed. Roads were not completed in time to service the construction project, thus delaying deliveries. The excavation work was poorly planned. Quarters for the workers were not finished soon enough and were poor in quality. This contributed to another problem--the inability of the project managers to attract and keep trained construction workers--which was so severe that it received the attention of the Communist Party Central Committee. The Party leadership decreed that Avtostroi, along with several other selected construction organizations, be accorded the highest priority in allocation of labor supplies.29 There were also insufficient building materials and other supplies.

In explaining the problems experienced during
construction, Soviet engineers from Avtostroi later
noted several defects in the planning and organization
of the work. The major mistake, they claimed, was
beginning the preliminary construction work without
complete design and planning data. Indeed, construction began at the project while Austin and Soviet
engineers were just beginning their design work.
Some Soviet observers later blamed the Austin Company
for delays in the design work. However, the Soviet
engineers who participated in the project maintained
that the design work in the United States proceeded
at a satisfactory pace, and attributed the problems
to the Soviet decision to begin preliminary construction work "prematurely" and "blindly." Work at the
project was further complicated because plans for
GAZ were revised, increasing both the planned output
of the plant and the number of living quarters. In
general, the Soviet engineers found that "the construction of GAZ was actually carried out without a
plan for organizing the construction work." Although
individual parts of the project were well planned,
"there was no integrated, unified organizational idea."
The project's Soviet engineers intimated that more
active foreign participation in the construction
work would have been very useful. "Having learned
much from the Americans about project planning,"
they concluded, "we must also learn how to properly
organize construction...."[30]
     One result of the poor planning and organiza-
tional work was a considerable overexpenditure of
time and money. Although planners had allocated
some "reserves" to the construction project, they
found that the builders still had inadequate inputs
to meet their needs. An example of how materials
inputs could have been saved is provided by Soviet
adaptation of the American building designs. The
U.S.-designed structures were found to be too capital-
intensive, calling for a considerable overuse of
building materials, such as cement, which were in
short supply in the Soviet Union. Soviet engineers
claimed that by redesigning some features, they
built lighter and less expensive, but completely
functional structures. If they had had more time
to adapt the facilities to Soviet conditions, they
maintained, their savings would have been much
greater. In general, they concluded that with proper
organization "the amount of money and human and
material resources spent on construction could have
been considerably reduced."[31]
     A second result was that the plant was not truly

completed on time. Although the builders, with
great fanfare, nominally met their deadline for com-
pletion--January 1, 1932--there were many important
details which were not ready. This adversely affected
GAZ during the startup and early operation of the
facilities.32 In January 1932, when Soviet officials
inspected the production facilities, they found poor
and incompleted work in a number of shops. Installation of some of the equipment, particularly in the
foundry, had not been completed. Some of the shops
could not make use of foreign workers who had come
with deliveries of machinery in order to assemble
them. This contributed to a very slow mastery of
the foreign equipment. Shortcomings were also noted
in transportation, feeding of workers and construction
of living quarters.33

     More significantly, Soviet officials found no
plan for organizing production. Interplant deliveries
of materials and parts were not coordinated properly,
and machinery and workers were idle much of the time.
On April 2, 1932, the Communist Party Central Committee issued a special decree criticizing the management of GAZ:

        With the available technical equipment, the
        shops of the plant have the capacity not only
        to fulfill but to overfulfill the designated
        programs for production. However, the plant
        at present has stopped production, primarily
        because of completely unsatisfactory manage-
        ment...34

The decree blamed GAZ's managerial problems on "complete absence of unified management, substitution
of party officials for economic directors, presence
of anti-specialist attitudes and badgering of
administrative-technical personnel."35 As during
the construction phase, the absence of Western management assistance undoubtedly contributed to the
plant's managerial problems. By 1932, only three
Ford specialists remained as instructors at GAZ.36
Thus, after only three years, the involvement of
Ford technicians at Gorkii had virtually ended.

     Another critical problem at GAZ was providing
adequate supplies of materials and parts to the production facilities. Initially, many of the supplies
were imported, but this was both expensive and at
odds with the Soviet goal of establishing a self-
sufficient automotive industry. Despite great
difficulties, GAZ managers had achieved their goal
by 1934 of independence from foreign suppliers: all

126

parts and materials were supplied internally.[37]
During the early planning for mass automobile production, Soviet specialists had taken note of the
importance of an extensive supply network to the U.S.
automotive industry and had proposed a drastic expansion of complementary industries in the Soviet
Union to accommodate the future needs of GAZ and
other plants.[38] In part, this was accomplished.
Soviet production of metals, glass, rubber and other
material inputs expanded rapidly. However, these
were frequently of poor quality and, especially in
the early years, seldom delivered to GAZ in sufficient quantities.

The production of parts and components for GAZ
was accomplished in a different manner than in the
U.S. automotive industry. While Ford and other U.S.
factories purchases these from supplier factories
and concentrated on the production of finished
vehicles, GAZ produced most of them at its own
facilities. A Soviet study of productivity in
Soviet industry found that in 1937, the average
Soviet automotive worker produced only 12.6 percent
as many vehicles as the average U.S. worker of 1929.
This difference was attributed partially to the comparatively large percentage of truck produced in the
Soviet Union (passenger cars were only a minor part
of Soviet output). However, the difference in
worker productivity was explained largely as a function of the large percentage of production at Soviet
automotive factories devoted to spare parts and
components--about 30 percent of total output. At
Soviet automotive plants in 1937, it was found that
about one-half of all workers were employed in
auxiliary shops.[39] GAZ, for example, produced all
of the castings and forged parts needed for its
vehicles, while Ford's River Rouge Plant produced
only a small percentage. In addition, GAZ produced
all of the main components, many spare parts and
even some machine-tools which it needed.[40] This was
a sharp departure from the system of subcontracting
that had developed in Western, especially American,
automobile industries. GAZ's high degree of vertical integration, which was necessitated by the absence
of complementary industries in the Soviet Union,
became a distinctive feature of the Soviet automotive industry.

The shortage of skilled workers was also a
serious problem during the early days of GAZ's
operation. An integral part of the Ford contract
was Ford's agreement to train Soviet workers and
technicians, both in the Soviet Union and the United

States. Altogether, about 250 Soviet specialists
went to Detroit.[41] Ford also sent about twenty engineers and foremen to the Soviet Union (for six-month
periods) to train Soviet workers. However, the training was rapidly phased out as the factory neared completion. Thus, training was limited to a small number of people and was short in duration. The results
of using a relatively untrained work force to run the
modern machinery at GAZ was predictable. "In the
first half of 1932 alone," a Soviet observer noted,
"323 new machine tools broke down at the Gorky Motor
Works because the workers did not know how to handle
them correctly."[42]

To allow for the paucity of skilled labor (and
the relative abundance of unskilled labor), GAZ officials had more adaptations in Ford's original designs
for the production processes. In adapting Ford's
designs, the dual technology approach which typified
many Western-assisted projects during the First Five-
Year Plan[43] was applied at GAZ. However, the adoption
of more labor-intensive processes was mostly limited
to auxiliary processes. The basic production processes were modern and capital-intensive. Indeed, GAZ's
engineers maintained that, in many respects, their
plant was technologically superior to Ford's River
Rouge Plant, which was generally considered to be the
most advanced in the West. The Soviet engineers
claimed that GAZ was more carefully planned, had more
modern machinery and was more automated than the Ford
Plant. This was particularly true of the foundry and
forge at GAZ, for which the Soviets had obtained more
advanced equipment than existed at Ford's plant. (To
accommodate the larger output of these shops, GAZ engineers had purchased machinery from Western metallurgical firms.) GAZ's assembly line, on the other hand,
was practically identical to Ford's.[44] Of the basic
production processes, only GAZ's mechanical department had been equipped with less capital-intensive
machinery than Ford. GAZ engineers decided that
much of the very specialized machinery in Ford's
mechanical department, while appropriate for the
Ford plant's huge output, could not be justified for
GAZ's smaller capacity. In this case, the Soviet
engineers claimed considerable savings as a result
of their choice of less capital-intensive machinery.[45]

The relatively extensive adaptations made
by GAZ technicians, both in the Western designs
for the buildings at GAZ and in the designs for the
production processes illustrate the active role of
Soviet specialists in the technology transfer
process. Despite their inexperience in automobile

manufacturing, the Soviet directors of the project
did not limit themselves to mere copying of Ford's
River Rouge Plant. They assumed overall responsibility for each stage of the technology transfer
process and showed no compunction in rejecting or
changing proposals offered by their foreign counterparts. The one exception was Ford's vehicle designs
which were accepted with little, if any, adaptation.
Essentially, GAZ began to reproduce Ford's Model A
and Model AA in the Soviet Union.

Thus, Western firms played a carefully delimited
(if critically important) role during the early stages
of transferring technology to GAZ, and, shortly after
startup, their ties to GAZ were virtually terminated.
By limiting the participation of Western firms,
Soviet officials undoubtedly exacerbated the difficulties of absorbing technology which could be expected under even the best conditions. "The mastering of the modern technology of large-scale industrial production," acknowledged some of GAZ's engineers in 1932, "is for us the result of a persistent
and difficult struggle."[46]

There were two tangible consequences of the
problems experienced in absorbing Western technology
at GAZ. First, production was interrupted numerous
times during the first few years of operation, and
the plant was unable to even come close to meeting
its production goals. Only a few thousand vehicles
were produced in 1932, and GAZ reached its capacity
output much more slowly than anticipated. The
Soviet Government had to continue importing vehicles
for a short time, and thereafter continued to experience a shortage of vehicles in the domestic economy.

Secondly, GAZ was apparently unable to attain
the quality of production that existed in Ford's
plants, even for the relatively simple and already
technologically dated vehicles that it was producing.
Ford's chief engineer Charles Sorenson relates that
some of Ford's staff had been critical of the transfer of automotive technology to the Soviet Union,
fearing that Ford was building up competition for
its own factories and its subsidiaries in Europe.
In fact, few of GAZ's products were exported in the
pre-War period. Sorenson heard of only a few which
had been exported to Turkey. Ford purchased one of
these and had it shipped to the United States for
study of its construction. Ford's engineers found
that "It was a pretty poor reproduction of Model A."[47]

The Ford-Soviet and related contracts of GAZ
were relatively active technology transfer mechanisms,
in that they provided frequent and specific

communications between Soviet engineers and their
Western counterparts. However, the effectiveness
of the arrangement was limited by the provision
for an abrupt cutoff of commercial ties with Ford,
and with Western industry in general. Soviet economic independence involved not only an end to
imports of materials and parts but also substantial
isolation from technological developments in the
Western automotive industry. Between the termination
of the Ford contract and the mid-1960s, the Soviet
automotive industry's technological ties to the
West consisted of only sporadic and relatively
passive technology transfer mechanisms.

Not only was GAZ relatively isolated from
Western technological developments, it did not
devote sufficient attention and resources to gen-
erating technological progress domestically. Research
and development expenditures in the Soviet automotive industry were kept to a minimum. Moreover,
much of the R&D work was carried out not at the
factory, but at the ministry level in the Scientific Automotive Institute (NAMI--<u>Nauchnyi Avtomotornyi
Institut</u>).[48] NAMI was the target of frequent criticism by engineers at Soviet automotive factories for
carrying out research that was irrelevant to their
production needs. They maintained that NAMI's
staff was spending too much time and resources on
esoteric research and not enough on the development of new products and processes. Some Soviet
engineers proposed improving the industry R & D
effort by redirecting NAMI's activities, locating
more of the R & D work at the factory level, and by
increasing expenditures on R & D. One Soviet automotive specialist proposed spending not less than
eight to ten percent of the value of the industry's
output on R & D.[49]   (There is no evidence that he
was taken seriously by Soviet planners.)

Some Soviet specialists warned that the lack
of attention to domestic R & D would result in
technological retardation of the Soviet automotive
industry. For example, E. A. Chudakov, a prominent
Soviet automotive engineer and member of the Soviet
Academy of Sciences, noted that Western methods of
producing automobiles were constantly changing,
resulting in more efficient production and improved
vehicles. In Ford's plant, he wrote, over 4,000
changes in production techniques were introduced
in 1929 and 1930 alone. Chudakov believed that
Soviet industry could maintain this pace of technological progress only by spending funds on research
and development:

130

Thus, mere copying of foreign production, although it might be the most rational approach at present, is in practice impossible and dooms us to falling immediately behind the general tempo of production abord. Parallel with the development of production, it is necessary to establish at the factory a research organization for improving production and making it more efficient.[50]

The subsequent retardation of technological change in the Soviet automotive industry suggests that Chudakov's advice was not accepted. Chudakov noted in 1936 that the GAZ-AA truck had already fallen behind the technological levels of comparable Western models. The GAZ-AA, he wrote, "is not the most modern model and has a comparatively weak engine. The most modern trucks of this tonnage have better dynamic qualities."[51] Chudakov's approach, while it was undoubtedly ideal from the Soviet engineer's viewpoint, could not be accommodated to the overall needs of the Soviet economy during the period of rapid industrialization. The economic development strategy of the first two five-year plans placed priority on maximizing physical output, not on improving quality. For automobile production, maximization of output was particularly important because of the extremely small existing automobile park in the Soviet Union, the importance of the automobile to other sectors of the economy, and the high cost of importing them. To expand the production of automobiles at the necessary rate, the Soviet planners had to concentrate scarce capital on tooling up on the basis of existing technology and mass-producing a few standardized vehicles--primarily trucks. With this goal in mind, research and development and retooling for new models had to be considered a luxury. Likewise, continuing contacts with the West were considered too costly, both in economic and political terms.

While technological progress at GAZ was slow in the 1930s, at least some attempts were made to improve its major products, the GAZ-A and GAZ-AA. In 1936, the GAZ-M-1 replaced GAZ-A, and, in 1938, the GAZ-MM replaced GAZ-AA. These model changes may have been introduced to take advantage of Ford's commitment, under the 1929 contract, to provide data on the technological innovations which it introduced over a nine-year period. Despite this passive technological exchange with Ford, the model change-overs were not very successful. The new models

131

represented only minor changes over the original ones.
Ford's V-8 engine and other major innovations were
not incorporated in the model changes. (The V-8 was
not introduced in Soviet automobiles until the 1950s.)
The GAZ-MM truck had a slightly more powerful engine
than the GAZ-AA, weighed the same, had the same maximum speed, and, like the GAZ-AA, had a maximum load
capacity of one and one-half tons. The GAZ-M-1 had
a slightly more powerful engine and was capable of
slightly higher speeds than the Model A, but was
heavier.[52] In fact, the performance of the GAZ-M-1
under the poor road conditions which predominated in
the Soviet Union was found to be inferior to the
Model A:

> ...We frequently came into conflict with the
> wishes of some automobile organizations in
> outlying districts to exchange the GAZ-M-1 for
> the old GAZ-A, production of which had long
> since stopped. Their preference was due to
> the fact that the GAZ-A was better adapted to
> movement on poor roads than the GAZ-M-1, even
> though the latter was adapted to higher class
> roads and was more expensive.[53]

In retooling for the new models, Soviet officials
chose not to rely on active foreign technical assistance. The installation of new machinery and equipment (a second conveyor line was added for the
GAZ-M-1) was accomplished without the help of foreign
specialists.[54] However, the start-up of the M-1 conveyor was accompanied by considerable difficulties.
In 1937, it was reported idle thirty-five percent
of the time.[55] Over a year and a half after startup of production of the M-1, GAZ had failed to attain
the previous daily production figures for the older
model.[56]
During the interim period, the most successful
examples of innovation at GAZ probably occurred
during World War II. Once again, Soviet officials
relied primarily on passive mechanisms for absorbing
Western technology. At the beginning of the war,
work had begun on developing new designs for trucks.
The most promising of the new designs was the GAZ-51,
which was to replace the MM and become the most
widely used medium-sized truck in the post-war
economy. During the war, GAZ acquired, tested and
studied American, English and German, as well as
domestic vehicles. According to A. A. Lipgart the
chief designer at GAZ during this period, GAZ accumulated valuable information in this manner, allowing

its designers to radically revise designs for both GAZ-51 and another truck model, the GAZ-63.[57] By most assessments, these vehicles represented a notable qualitative jump in comparison with pre-war models.[58]

Lipgart provides insights into why passive technology borrowing worked during World War II, whereas it had been unsuccessful before:

> The establishment at the plant of a strong staff of designers and the experience which we accumulated permitted us to confidently work on the creation of new types of special vehicles, which until then were completely unknown to us. The work on military projects had a highly beneficial influence on the entire design-experimental staff. We began to feel our strength, became bolder, and lost the last traces of our "awe" of foreign technology.[59]

It is clear from this description of wartime work at GAZ that its importance to the war effort gave it a much higher priority, in terms of allocation of R & D funds, personnel and other inputs. By concentrating high quality technological resources at GAZ, Soviet automotive officials were able to overcome the difficulties normally associated with passive technology borrowing. The result was considerable spinoffs to the civilian automotive industry. However, the extraordinary measures taken during the war to promote technological progress at GAZ were not feasible, either before or after the war.

NOTES

1. Hereafter, the three projects will be identified by their Russian abbreviations: GAZ (Gor'kovskii Avtomobil'nyi Zavod), VAZ (Volzhskii Avtomobil'nyi Zavod), and KamAZ (Kamskii Avtomobil'nyi Zavod).

2. D. D. Mishustin, Vneshniaia torgovlia i industrializatsiia SSSR (Moscow, Mezhdunarodnaia kniga, 1935), p. 174. Mishustin's figures apparently include only the cost of imported machinery and equipment. Wages and expenses of Western specialists who assisted at GAZ and payments for unassembled automobiles shipped by Ford to GAZ may not be included. A Ford official later estimated that

133

Ford had done over $40 million in business with the
Soviet Union, a figure which presumably includes
sales of automobile parts and payments for technical
assistance. See Charles E. Sorenson (with Samuel
T. Williams), My Forty Years with Ford (New York:
W. W. Norton and Company, Inc., 1956), p. 193.

3. Imogene U. Edwards, "Automotive Trends in
the U.S.S.R.," in U.S. Congress, Joint Economic
Committee, Soviet Economic Prospects for the Seventies. Joint Committee Print (Washington, D.C.:
Government Printing Office, June 27, 1973), p. 296.
4. Chase World Information Corporation. Kamaz,
the Billion Dollar Beginning, (New York, 1974).
5. Antony C. Sutton, Western Technology and
Soviet Economic Development, Vol. I: 1917-1930
(Stanford: Hoover Institution Publications, 1968).
6. Details of the contract are provided in
Amtorg Trading Corporation, Economic Review of the
Soviet Union, July 1, 1929, pp. 230-31.
7. Cited by M. L. Sorokin, Za avtomobilizatsiiu
SSSR (Moscow: Moskovskii rabochii, 1928), p. 42.
8. The debates are described in B. V. Lavrosvkii,
Tsifry i fakty za 15 let po avtostroenii v SSSR
(Moscow: Gosudarstvennoe aviatsionnoe i avtotraktornoe
izdatel'stvo, 1932), p. 27.
9. Grigorii T. Grinko, The Five-Year Plan of
the Soviet Union: A Political Interpretation (New
York: International Publishers, 1930), p. 104.
10. M. Sorokin, "Ob avtomobilizatsii Soiuza,"
Ekonomicheskoe obozrenie, July, 1929, p. 95.
11. Maurice Hindus, "Henry Ford Conquers Russia,"
The Outlook, June 29, 1927), 280-83.
12. See, "Why I am Helping Russian Industry,"
Henry Ford interviewed by William A. McGarry,
Nation's Business, June, 1930, pp. 20-23.
13. Ford Motor Company. Report of the Ford
Delegation to Russia and the U.S.S.R. (Hoover
Institution Microfilms, 1926). See, also, Allan
Nevins and Frank Ernest Hill, Ford, Expansion and
Challenge, Vol. II: 1915-1933 (New York: Charles
Schribners Sons, 1957), pp. 674-77.
14. Nevins and Hill, 676-77 and Charles E.
Sorenson, (with Samuel T. Williams), My Forty Years
with Ford (New York: W. W. Norton and Company,
Inc., 1956, p. 203.
15. Sorenson, p. 203.
16. Sorokin, Za avtomobilizatsiiu, p. 85.
17. L. Mertts et al., "GAZ i Ford," Planovoe
khoziaistvo, No. 6-7, 1932, p. 258, and V. Kasianenko,
How Soviet Economy Won Technical Independence
(Moscow: Progress Publishers, 1966), p. 141.

18. Nevins and Hill, p. 677.

19. Amtorg, July 1, 1929, p. 230.

20. Sorenson, p. 198.

21. N. Osinskii, "Novyi Ford v Amerikanskoi i nashei obstanovke," Za rulem, no. 9-10, May 1932, p. 9.

22. Mertts et al., p. 239.

23. David Granick, "Organization and Technology in Soviet Metalworking: Some Conditioning Factors," American Economic Review, XLVII (May, 1957), 632.

24. Sutton, Vol. I, p. 248.

25. Amtorg Trading Corporation, Economic Review of the Soviet Union, November 15, 1929, p. 378.

26. Sutton, Vol. I, p. 248.

27. Avtostroi was the domestic construction organization which had overall responsibility for building GAZ.

28. Details of the planning and design stage are provided in M. V. Vavilov et al., Avtostroi analiz organizatsii stroitel'stva Gor'kovskogo Avtozavoda im. t. Molotova (Moscow: Glavnaia redaktsiia stroitel'noi literatury, 1934), pp. 27-28.

29. M. P. Kim et al., Industrializatsiia SSSR, 1929-1932 gg. (Moscow: Izdatel'stvo Nauka, 1970), p. 267.

30. Vavilov et al., pp. 30, 33, 87.

31. Ibid., pp. 4, 29, 30, 85.

32. Ibid., p. 4.

33. B. V. Lavrovskii, pp. 34-35.

34. Ibid.

35. Ibid., p. 35.

36. Mertts et al., p. 259.

37. Sutton, Vol. I, p. 247.

38. Sorokin, "Ob avtomobilizatsii," pp. 98-100.

39. P. A. Khromov, Proizvoditel'nost' truda v promyshlennosti SSSR (Moscow: Gosplanizdat, 1940), p. 200.

40. Mertts et al., pp. 246-55.

41. Ibid., p. 259.

42. V. Kasyanenko, How Soviet Economy Won Technical Independence (Moscow: Progress Publishers, 1966), p. 98.

43. Supra, pp. 62-63.

44. Mertts et al., pp. 246-56.

45. Ibid., pp. 254-55.

46. Ibid., p. 240.

47. Sorenson, p. 207.

48. Between 1930 and 1936, the Institute was called the Scientific Auto-Tractor Institute (Nauchnyi Avtotraktornyi Institut, or NATI). In 1936, NATI was split into two institutes, with one

specializing in tractors and the other (NAMI), in
automobiles.

49. Lavrovskii, p. 54. See also, Evgenii
Alekseevich Chudakov, Razvitie avtomobilestroeniia
v SSSR (Moscow: Gosplanizdat, 1948), pp. 20-23.
50. E. A. Chudakov, "Problemy avtotransporta,"
Sotsialisticheskaia rekonstrucktsiia i nauka,
No. 2-3, 1931, p. 154.
51. E. A. Chudakov, "Razvitie dinamicheskikh
kachestv avtomobilia," Sotsialisticheskaia
rekonstrucktsiia i nauka, No. 3, 1936. p. 34.
52. Chudakov, Razvitie, pp. 56-57.
53. Ibid., p. 24.
54. Polina Aleshina, et al., Gor'kovskii
Avtomobil'nyi (Moscow: Profizdat, 1964), p. 86.
55. Antony C. Sutton, Western Technology and
Soviet Economic Development Vol. II, 1930-1945
(Stanford: Hoover Institution Press, 1971), p. 182.
56. Ibid., p. 324.
57. A. A. Lipgart, "Razvitie konstruktsii
avtomobilei zavoda im. V. M. Molotova," in Akademiia
nauk, SSSR, Institut Mashinovedeniia, Voprosy
mashinovedeniia: sbornik statei posviashchennyi
shestideciatiletiu Akademika E. A. Chudakova
(Moscow: Izdatel'stvo Akademii Nauk SSSR, 1950),
p. 105.
58. While Lipgart represents the GAZ-51 and GAZ-
63 as composites of the best Western and Soviet
designs, Antony Sutton maintains that they "were
almost exact duplications of U.S. Army World War II
vehicles." Sutton, II, p. 198.) Whichever version
is accurate, the new truck designs represented
an unusually successful example of passive technology
borrowing.
59. Lipgart, p. 105.

6. Western Technology Transfer to the Soviet Automotive Industry: The Volga Automobile Plant and the Kama River Truck Plant

THE LEGACY OF THE STALINIST ECONOMIC GROWTH STRATEGY

In view of the priorities of Soviet economic planning during rapid industrialization, the performance of the Soviet automotive industry in the Stalinist period must be considered a partial success. A mass production industry was established in an extremely short period of time. While the ambitious output goals of the economic planners were not met, the level of production rose at an impressive rate, reaching a pre-war peak in 1938 when over 211,000 vehicles were produced. (After falling rapidly during World War II, Soviet production surpassed its pre-war peak in 1949 and grew moderately--with an annual average growth rate of less than five percent--until the mid-1960s.) (See Appendix C.) The volume of Soviet automobile production sufficed to meet many of the needs of the economy. The industry also attained a reasonably high level of technology in the pre-war period, although it proved incapable of keeping pace with the automotive industries in the West. Perhaps most importantly, from the vantage point of the political leadership, it was a self-contained industry, which, in peace time, did not rely on imports of vehicles from the West and did not require active Western technical assistance.

However, the structure and technological level of the Soviet automotive industry were not suitable for the needs of an increasingly complex post-Stalinist Soviet economy. Predictably, the Soviet emphasis on maximizing output on the basis of a given technology and the drive to isolate Soviet industry from the West resulted in a backward, stagnant industry. The technological lag behind the Western automotive industry began to widen rapidly

137

in the post-war period. Reliance on passive technology borrowing created a greater need for domestic
R & D expenditures. However, with the exception of
the high priority it received during the war, the
Soviet automotive industry did not receive adequate
technological resources.

Efforts to spur technological progress have been
thwarted not only by the Stalinist growth strategy
and the industry's isolation from technological
developments in the West. Organizational problems,
particularly the high degree of vertical integration
in Soviet automotive plants and departmental barriers
among the various ministries associated with automobile production, are partially responsible for its
backwardness. On the model of GAZ, each major Soviet
automobile factory was established as an unspecialized, complete-cycle operation, with its own forging
and casting shops, machine shops and assembly lines.[1]
In addition, they manufacture machine tools, spare
parts and various other items. This integrated
structure was a natural result of the absence of
specialized, complementary factories in the Soviet
economy and the unreliability of deliveries from
other industries. However, numerous problems have
been associated with the organizational structure of
Soviet automotive enterprises.[2] Such enterprises
tend to be less efficient because they cannot attain
economies of scale. The existence of numerous
autonomous automotive plants makes it difficult
to standardize parts and components for various
models. Moreover, the unspecialized plants cannot
devote sufficient attention to improving designs for
the great variety of items which they manufacture.
The small, self-contained R & D facilities at each
of the plants tend to duplicate each other's efforts
and, in general, are inadequate for keeping abreast
of new technological developments.

Another set of problems in the Soviet automotive
industry results from the "narrow departmental"
approach (i.e., preoccupation with meeting output
goals rather than the ultimate performance of the
product) to production and distribution of vehicles.
Since Soviet consumers (both individuals and industrial enterprises) have relatively little choice
when buying a vehicle, Soviet automotive plans are
not subjected to the discipline of "consumer
sovereignty." Thus, the Soviet automotive industry has not had adequate incentives to produce high
quality vehicles. Nor has it borne the responsibility for servicing its products or supplying
adequate spare parts to repair shops. It also has

not responded adequately to demand for a greater
variety of vehicles.[3]

The state of the Soviet automotive industry,
particularly its technological retardation, became
increasingly evident to Soviet specialists, who in
the post-Stalinist era, began to voice publicly
their criticisms:

Against a background of rapid growth of other
branches of machine building, the backwardness
(of the automobile industry) becomes even
clearer; gradually the situation of the automobile industry has come to be characterized
by the very unpleasant word, stagnation.[4]

A 1958 U.S. study of the Soviet automotive industry
reached the same conclusion:

Although long hailed as the technologically
most advanced branch of Soviet machine building, the automobile industry has been losing
ground steadily. This decline has been
characterized by increasingly obsolescent
technology, inefficient organization of labor,
and inferior products.[5]

Among the major reasons cited by the latter study
for the technological obsolescence of the Soviet
automotive industry were: lack of incentives for
innovations; infrequency of model changes; problems
in obtaining modern inputs from suppliers; the relatively small scale of Soviet production; lack of
exchange of information among Soviet plants and
duplication of effort in research and development;
and the relatively little use made of foreign
developments.[6]

The Soviet political leadership also began to
acknowledge the problems of the automotive industry.
In a speech to the 22nd Party Congress, Nikita
Khrushchev singled out the Moscow Likhachev Automobile Factory as an example of how slowly new technology was introduced to Soviet industry.[7] According
to Khrushchev, the factory was producing four-ton
trucks which had been put into production fourteen
years earlier and had had no significant improvements
during that period. Substantial resources and time
(about six years) had been spent to design and
organize production of a better truck, but no
progress had been made.

Khrushchev himself bore responsibility for
continuing the Stalinist neglect of the Soviet

passenger car industry. On a number of occasions,
he expressed his disdain for widespread private
ownership of cars in the West and advocated further
development of mass transit and car rentals as an
alternative for the Soviet Union.

In a 1965 speech to the State Planning Committee,
Khrushchev's successor as Premier, Alexei Kosygin
criticized the previous leadership for stubbornly
adhering to the idea that the Soviet Union did not
need to develop production of passenger cars on a
large scale.[8] Kosygin suggested that the new leadership would change this approach. In the same speech,
Kosygin criticized the automobile industry for
manufacturing obsolete trucks which did not meet
the needs of the Soviet economy. He claimed that
Western manufacturers had long ago ceased production
of some types of trucks still being produced in the
Soviet Union. He expressed pessimism about the Soviet
automobile industry's ability to improve the situation: "We are reconstructing ZIL and GAZ for output
of vehicles with greater capacity, but I am not certain that everything has been done properly."[9] One
of the vehicles to which Kosygin referred was the
GAZ-51, production of which had begun in 1946.
Replacement of the GAZ-51 by a more modern vehicle
had been scheduled originally in 1963,[10] but was
not accomplished until 1975. Thus, the GAZ-51 was
in production for almost 30 years. Even then, its
replacement, the GAZ-52, was not given a new engine
and apparently will not have one until a new engine
plant is built.[11]

Kosygin's 1965 speech reflected an awareness
on the part of the new leadership of two elements
in the stagnation of the Soviet automotive industry.
Not only was it falling behind Western industry
technologically--a state of affairs that had been
recognized by Khrushchev--but it was also failing
to meet the growing and changing needs of the Soviet
economy. These needs include satisfying consumer
demands as well as modernizing the freight transportation system.

To meet these needs, the current Soviet leadership initiated a comprehensive program to expand
and modernize the automotive industry. The new
program combines a major increase in investment with
potentially important organizational changes and
efforts to strengthen the industry's ties to Western
firms. Thus, during the Eighth Five-Year Plan
(1966-1970), the allocation of investment for the
automotive industry increased by 220 percent.[12] The
industry continued to be accorded high priority

during the Ninth Five-Year Plan. While the construction of two new plants--the Volga Automobile
Plant (VAZ) and the Kama River Truck Plant (KamAZ)--
was the major new development, a number of existing
plants have also been expanded and re-equipped. In
addition, considerable resources have been allocated
to the development of specialized plants supplying
the major automobile factories. The major organizational change was the establishment of large production associations throughout the industry. Most
of the major plants, including VAZ and KamAZ, are
now organized as production associations.

The industry's new international orientation
has been characterized both by large-scale imports
of technology for VAZ, KamAZ and other plants and
by expanded exports of automobiles. Automobiles
have become the Soviet Union's leading manufactured
goods export item.[13] Although most automobile
exports go to Eastern Europe and less developed
countries, Soviet automotive industry officials
are attempting to expand exports to Western industrial countries.

THE VOLGA AUTOMOBILE PLANT

Within four months after Kosygin's 1965 speech
to Gosplan, the State Committee for Science and
Technology signed a protocol for scientific and
technical cooperation with the Italian automobile
manufacturer FIAT (Fabbrica Italiana Automobili
Torino). This type of agreement was unique in
1965, but has since become a commonly used Soviet
device for initiating long-term contacts with
Western firms. The protocol led to discussions
between FIAT and Soviet automotive officials which
culminated in the signing of a contract on August 15,
1966, providing for FIAT assistance in the construction of a massive new passengar car factory
in Tol'iatti, the Volga Automobile Plant (VAZ).

Initial Planning and Purchase of Technology

The FIAT contract followed a long debate among
Soviet automotive officials over Soviet needs for
modern passenger cars. Khrushchev's dislike for
widespread private ownership of cars had not been
shared by many industry officials.[14] In the late
1950s and early 1960s, a substantial lobby developed
in the automotive industry, advocating a transition
to mass production of inexpensive, small cars.

Existing Soviet passenger cars were criticized by some Soviet engineers as being obsolete and wasteful of resources. A half-hearted attempt to produce a new small car began with the startup of production of the "Zaporozhets" in 1962. However, the Zaporozhets (which is still being produced) has proved to be an unsuccessful venture, both in terms of its ability to incorporate the latest technology and its appeal to the Soviet consumer. Its lack of success, apparently a result of inadequate experience and opposition from those who supported Khrushchev's position, probably contributed directly to the decision to seek foreign help in building a new small car factory.

The idea of a new Western-assisted automobile plant received impetus from Khrushchev's successors, Brezhnev and Kosygin, who appeared to have a better understanding of the extraordinary appeal to automobiles to the Soviet consumer. (Soviet researchers have found that the average citizen desired a passenger car above all other consumer goods.)[15] Initially, production plans could only meet the needs of relatively well-to-do Soviet citizens. The cost of the new Zhiguli--the passenger car produced at Tol'iatti--is prohibitive for most Soviet citizens, and the waiting lists are still long. While long-run production plans suggest an effort to provide passenger cars for a wider spectrum of the population, it is unlikely that cars will be available for most Soviet citizens in the near future. Nevertheless, the rapid expansion of production of private passenger cars at VAZ is an integral part of the new leadership's efforts to provide quality consumer goods as incentives for Soviet citizens.

Negotiations between FIAT and Soviet officials had actually begun in 1962, when the two sides held extensive talks about FIAT's possible participation in the construction of tractor and automobile manufacturing facilities in the Soviet Union. These early negotiations did not result in any signed agreements. Between 1962 and 1965, there were forty-six Soviet trade and technological visits to Italy and at least two personal meetings between Kosygin and the president of FIAT, Vitorrio Valletta.[16] The 1965 and 1966 agreements were the outcome of these prolonged negotiations.

The scientific and technical cooperation agreement proved to be an important first step toward the final contract and, from the Soviet perspective, was a very useful mechanism for learning about FIAT's

R & D activities, production techniques and finished
products:

> This agreement gave Soviet specialists the
> opportunity, to the extent that it was neces-
> sary, to become acquainted with the firm's
> work experience--its achievements in the field
> of automobile production and also its plans
> for the future, especially the development of
> variants of the FIAT-124 small car, which the
> firm was preparing to mass produce.[17]

Thus, it appears that the scientific and technical
cooperation agreement, itself, provided the basis
for a relatively active technology exchange before
a commercial contract was signed. The benefits which
accrued to Soviet participants in the exchange with
FIAT were undoubtedly instrumental in establishing the scientific and technical cooperation agreement as a fixture in Soviet economic and technological relations with the West.
   The Soviet Government also seriously considered
the French firm Renault as a major source of technology for VAZ. Like FIAT, Renault had some experience in selling machinery and equipment to the Soviet
automotive industry. Both companies had also been
successful in building subsidiary plants in other
countries. Renault, while it did not win the VAZ
contract, also signed a scientific and technical
cooperation agreement with SCST (in 1966) and began
to play a major role in expansion and modernization
of other parts of the Soviet automotive industry.
It was later to sign a major contract to provide
assistance in building a part of the Kama River Truck
Plant.[18]
   In choosing between the two West European firms,
a major consideration was undoubtedly the favorable
credit terms offered by the Italian official export
credit agency, Istituto Mobiliare Italiano. A
credit of approximately $322 million was extended
to cover ninety percent of the cost of imported
machinery and equipment. The loan was to be repaid
over eight and one-half years from delivery dates,
at an interest rate of 5.6 percent. The soft terms
of the credit (Soviet officials acknowledged that
they were better than the Soviet Union had received
before)[19] attest to the fact that the Soviet side
negotiated skillfully on credit matters.
   Another important element of the negotiations
concerned the vehicle which would be produced in
the Soviet Union. Soviet negotiators had reservations

about the adaptability of the FIAT-124 to harsh Soviet road and climate conditions. They persuaded FIAT to render assistance in making numerous adaptations in the vehicle design.

The credit terms, vehicle design and other matters were settled at the final negotiations in Italy between February and May 1966. The Soviet Union was represented at the negotiations by a high-level delegation headed by A. M. Tarasov, Minister of the Automotive Industry. High-ranking officials from the Ministry of Foreign Trade, Gosplan, SCST and the Foreign Trade Bank also participated.

Under the contract for VAZ, FIAT agreed to assist in building a factory to produce 600,000 passenger cars.[20] FIAT assumed the role of general consultant for the entire project and participated in each phase of the transfer of technology. FIAT agreed to provide designs for the production process, to specify what machinery and equipment should be purchased (and who the Western manufacturers were), and to train Soviet specialists in the operation of the production processes. FIAT sold to the Soviets the manufacturing rights for the FIAT-124, the prototype for the vehicles produced at VAZ, and agreed to assist in adapting the vehicle to Soviet operating conditions. Finally, FIAT agreed to supervise the assembly and installation of all imported equipment and to assure its successful operation.

FIAT's role at VAZ has frequently been characterized as "general contractor." In Western industrial parlance, this term often connotes a firm which carries out the actual construction of a plant—a role which Soviet construction organizations executed. FIAT's role in providing technical advice and assistance for the entire project is perhaps better termed "general consultant." As a general consultant, FIAT, not only sold equipment and licenses to the Soviet plant, but also acted as a consultant for other Soviet purchases in the West. Thus, a large percentage of the Western machinery installed in VAZ was produced by other Western manufacturers on a subcontract basis for FIAT. FIAT specialists selected and purchased the equipment and supplied it to the Soviet plant. FIAT also acquired licenses from vendor firms and sold them to the Soviets. The assembly and installation of all Western machinery and equipment was supervised by FIAT, and Soviet manufactured materials were sent to FIAT's factory in Turin to be tested for quality control. The degree of FIAT's involvement at VAZ exceeded that of Ford's at GAZ and is unparalleled in relations between the Soviet and Western automotive industries. A similar foreign involvement was considered but could not be arranged in the construction of KamAZ.

Absorption of Technology at VAZ

When the contract with FIAT was signed in 1966, only the broad parameters of the project had been defined: the plant would produce 600,000 vehicles (the planned capacity was soon revised upward to 660,000); VAZ vehicles would be based on the FIAT-124 prototype; and all of the basic production processes would be concentrated on one site in Tol'iatti. The location of VAZ had been the subject of con- siderable debate among Soviet planners. Some plan- ners wanted to disperse it by building smaller factories in several towns. This variant lost out because of the leadership's insistence on starting up production as soon as possible. It was decided that an early startup could best be accomplished by building the entire plant at one location.[21]

One consequence of the decision to concentrate production of VAZ at one site was a degree of verti- cal integration which many planners had hoped to avoid. The Tol'iatti plant combined all of the basic production processes--casting, forging, stamp- ing and pressing, engine production, assembly and tooling--in addition to production of some spare parts and components. Nevertheless, the planners for VAZ did depart from the traditional organization of Soviet automotive plants by immediately beginning to develop an extensive system of vendor plants to supply most of the parts and components to Tol'iatti.

In designing the production facilities at VAZ, there was relatively little need for any fundamental adaptation of Western designs. For example, there was no dual technology strategy, as there had been at GAZ in the 1930s. In view of the labor shortage in the Soviet Union, Soviet planners were interested in maximizing labor productivity in both basic and auxiliary production processes. Indeed, this was a major motivation for seeking Western technological assistance. In the post-war Western automotive industries, research and development had been directed toward developing labor-saving technologies. A variety of special tooling and equipment had been introduced, replacing labor-intensive with capital- intensive processes. Generally speaking, the Soviet automotive industry had not developed similar tech- nologies; it had specialized in the large-scale pro- duction of general purpose machinery. Thus, when

faced with the task of equipping a giant new automobile plant with the latest labor-saving technologies, Soviet planners were forced to turn to the West.

Of critical importance to the success of VAZ
was FIAT's assistance in production engineering.
Although Soviet engineers had had extensive experience in automobile production, their isolation from
Western technological developments had resulted in
general unfamiliarity with the most modern production processes. Without FIAT's assistance, Soviet
engineers would have had great difficulty in choosing among alternative Western processes and inte-
grating them into an efficient automobile-manufacturing
operation.

VAZ's first products were three modified ver-
sions fo FIAT vehicles: a standard sedan (VAZ-2101)
and a station wagon (VAZ-2102), based on the FIAT-124
prototype, and a luxury sedan (VAZ-2103), which is
similar to the FIAT-125. The cars are named the
"Zhiguli" in the Soviet Union and the "Lada" for
export. FIAT's engineers were forced to make extensive modifications in order to make the vehicle
suitable for Soviet road and weather conditions.
The body, chassis, suspension system, and numerous
parts were strengthened, and the ground clearance
was raised from 140 millimeters to 175 millimeters.
Many changes were made to adapt the vehicle to the
extremely low temperatures of some regions of the
Soviet Union: a larger battery, a sealed radiator
with anti-freeze to withstand temperatures as low
as minus forty degrees centigrade, and changes in
various mechanical parts. Gas tanks were enlarged
because of the small number of service stations in
the Soviet Union. In the end, sixty-five percent
of the parts were different from the standard FIAT-
124.[22] The modifications made the Soviet vehicle
twenty-seven kilograms heavier than the FIAT-124, but
Soviet engineers claimed superior performance for the
Zhiguli--a maximum speed of 140 kilometers per hour
(against 134 for the FIAT-124) and fuel consumption
of eight-nine liters per 100 kilometers (against ten
liters per 100 kilometers for the Italian car).[23]

The Kuibyshev Hydraulic Construction Organization
(Kuibyshevgidrostroi) was chosen as general contractor for construction of the production facilities,
living quarters and other municipal buildings at
Tol'iatti. It supervised the work of numerous construction organizations from several different
ministries. The buildings at Tol'iatti were designed
by Soviet engineers, who consulted with FIAT technicians to coordinate architectural designs with the

layout of the production process. The buildings
were designed so that the plant's capacity could be
expanded up to thirty percent in the future without
major additional construction.[24]

The most striking aspect of the absorption of
technology at VAZ was the rapid pace at which it was
to be accomplished. The 1966 agreement foresaw
production of the first automobiles in 1969 and
attainment of capacity production in 1972. To
achieve these goals, Soviet directors of the project insisted that planning go forward in parallel
with construction. Thus, construction of the project began soon after the contract was signed and
before complete designs for the production processes
were completed. Although Soviet engineers claimed
that this was the first time that the parallel planning and construction method had been used,[25] it
bore a remarkable similarity to the approach employed
in the construction of GAZ.

The purpose of appointing a Soviet general contractor was to avoid interindustry supply problems
which frequently plague Soviet construction projects.
However, the rapid pace of construction exacerbated
the problem of coordinating inputs of materials,
machines and workers for such a large project. Many
of the problems encountered during the construction
of VAZ were associated with what proved to be un-
realistic goals for starting up production. Suppliers of vital materials such as cement, bricks
and pre-cast ferro-concrete, were unable to meet
the rigid delivery schedules. Construction or
expansion of the factories which were to supply
building materials fell behind schedule. The construction of living quarters and other social facilities for workers was also delayed because workers
were diverted to construction of the plant. There
was also a shortage of skilled construction workers,
and the recruitment of young, inexperienced workers
sometimes resulted in a lack of labor discipline and
rapid labor turnover.[26]

These problems led to an early administrative
change at the project. For the first time in Soviet
practice, the general directorship of the future
plant functioned not only as the initiator of orders
for equipment of the plant, but as an organization
with full responsibility for finishing the construction on time. This responsibility and the
corresponding authority gave the general director
of VAZ the ability to actively influence the design
and construction process. The usual Soviet practice
is to delegate this authority to the construction

147

firm which serves as general contractor. However,
at the VAZ project, a skeleton staff, composed of
some of the mangerial and technical personnel of
the future plant, began to operate long before the
startup of production. In addition the VAZ management was permitted to establish representative offices
in Moscow and Turin. The independence given to VAZ's
representatives in Turin was unprecendented in Soviet
practice:

> ...These representatives, especially the dele-
> gation in Turin, had broad powers to act on
> behalf of the general director and therefore
> could insure a high degree of operational
> effectiveness in carrying out decisions.

> The technical delegation in Turin took part in
> the development of the project design and,
> together with representatives of the Ministry
> of Foreign Trade, in the purchase of equipment.
> They made important decisions in Turin without
> coordinating them with Moscow.[27]

Another response to the construction delays at
VAZ was the assignment by the Party and government
hierarchy of the highest priority to deliveries
to the project:

> The Central Committee and the government
> rendered the widest support for the construction
> of the plant. VAZ's orders were fulfilled very
> quickly. Cargos bound for the All-Union shock
> work construction project were given the "green
> light."[28]

The training of production workers was also a
major undertaking during and after construction.
Only ten percent of the workforce at VAZ had previously worked in the automotive industry.[29] Training for production workers and technicians began
as soon as construction was underway. Training
took place at other Soviet automotive factories,
at VAZ, and in foreign factories. The large role
of FIAT and other foreign firms in training Soviet
workers and specialists is illustrated by the enor-
mous (by Soviet standards) exchange of personnel.
About 2,500 Western specialists traveled to Tol'iatti,
including 1,500 from FIAT.[30] (This number compares
with a few dozen Western specialists at GAZ in the
1930s.) At the same time, over 2,500 Soviet technicians went to Italy (about ten times the number of

148

Soviet personnel who traveled to the U.S. in the earlier period).

Construction delays and other problems set back the startup of VAZ considerably. Whereas startup had been planned for 1969, actual serial production began in August 1970. The 1972 goal for capacity production was only half fulfilled (322,900 vehicles). The projected 660,000 capacity was attained in 1975. During the startup period, FIAT maintained an active presence at Tol'iatti. In addition to its obligations to insure the successful startup of the production processes and to instruct Soviet specialists in the operation of machinery, FIAT also provided many of the components for the first vehicles assembled at VAZ. Its engineers were also busy in Turin, checking the quality of various materials supplied to VAZ by Soviet vendor plants. FIAT had guaranteed the quality of VAZ vehicles only if materials used in its production met FIAT's quality specifications.[31]

Perhaps the central problem for VAZ, both during construction and operation of the plant was (and remains) the unreliability of the Soviet supply system. The problem of obtaining supplies in sufficient quantities and qualities and according to rigid schedules has traditionally plagued Soviet automotive plants. However, two aspects of VAZ operations exacerbated the supply problem. First, the advanced technological level of the Zhiguli required VAZ's suppliers to begin production of some new materials and components which had never been produced in the Soviet Union. Secondly, the rapid expansion of Soviet automobile production brought on by the startup of VAZ simply made it impossible for the traditional supply system to keep pace. By 1975, VAZ was producing almost one-half of all Soviet passenger cars.

Soviet planners did not ignore the supply needs of VAZ. Indeed, they departed from the traditional pattern of the Soviet automotive industry by placing high priority on development of a system of vendor plants. A large network of suppliers--much more extensive than for previous Soviet automobile plants-- has been developed for VAZ. Two-thirds of all the parts and materials for the Zhiguli come from other plants,[32] many of which are newly constructed or modernized with the assistance of Western firms. Among the new vendor plants built with Western assistance are: a rubber fittings plant at Balakovo, built with assistance of Pirelli of Italy; plants for making oil and air filters and upholstery

materials, purchased from Japanese firms; a plant
for car seats purchased from West Germany; a plant
for oil seals at Kursk; and an anti-friction bearing
plant at Vologda.[33] In addition, many parts and
components are being supplied by East European countries. Poland and Yugoslavia, which produce FIAT-
designed cars, are major suppliers, while Bulgaria
and Hungary also supply some parts.

Moreover, Soviet domestic suppliers have
apparently been directed to give the highest priority to supplying VAZ. One example is the development of special lubricants and coolants needed for
the Zhiguli. After discovering that Soviet production of these vital supplies was at a technological
level of the 1920s or 1930s, a major effort was
undertaken to meet VAZ's needs. This effort began
with a meeting at the SCST, chaired by SCST's
Chairman V. A. Kirillin and attended by high-level
officials from various ministries. It was decided
to reorganize a Kiev research institute and recruit
highly qualified specialists to develop the new
materials. This was accomplished to the satisfac-
tion of VAZ engineers.[34] Another example was the
diversion of supplies intended for other parts of
the automotive industry to VAZ. The Dnepropetrovsk
Tire Factory, which formerly produced tires for the
Zaporozhets, was directed to supply tires to VAZ,
creating severe shortages of tires for Zaporozhets-
owners.[35]

Despite such efforts, VAZ's supply problems
have not been solved. Shortcomings in the supply
system have generated two deleterious effects on
the plant's operations: shortages of various
inputs make it difficult to meet output goals, and
defective materials and components reduce the quality and reliability of the finished vehicles. Moreover, the management of VAZ is more reluctant to
introduce improvements in the Zhiguli which might
further disrupt supply schedules. Thus, in 1975,
VAZ's general manager, A. Z. Zhitkov, complained
of the tendency of Soviet suppliers to "lower the
technical level of equipment offered to us," which,
he said, "is a retreat by some branches associated
with us from positions already won."[36] He asserted
that VAZ's ability to improve the Zhiguli depended
on improving the quality of machinery and materials
supplied to the plant.

One possible approach to solving the supply
problem is suggested by Soviet negotiations with
the U.S. firm Bendix Corporation for assistance in
building a new plant for production of spark plugs

in the Soviet Union. The negotiations, which are
now underway, concern an arrangement under which
Bendix would provide machinery, equipment and technical assistance for a plant which would produce
50 to 75 million spark plugs each year. Three-
fourths of the plugs, which would carry the Bendix
trademark, would be sold in the Soviet market, and
the remainder would be marketed abroad by Bendix.
While Soviet officials would have managerial control,
Bendix personnel would be on site to monitor quality
control, determine the type of spark plugs produced
for export and advise on any decisions involving
further investment.[37] If signed, the agreement might
be a precedent for future Soviet industrial cooperation agreements, permitting greater involvement by
Western firms in Soviet industry. Such arrangements
could also help to solve the supply and quality control problems in the Soviet automotive industry.

VAZ's management has shown an awareness of the
need for continued technological progress that is
uncharacteristic of past Soviet industry officials.
One result has been continued purchases of foreign
technology. In 1975-1976, for example, processing
equipment was purchased from West German and Japanese
firms, and a license to manufacture a new automatic
ignition device was purchased from a French subsidiary
of Bendix Corporation.[38] A Soviet economist, E. B.
Golland, has suggested that it is time to formulate
a complete program for reconstruction and modernization of VAZ.[39] He noted that the world level of
automobile manufacturing technology is progressing
at an extremely rapid rate and that VAZ's machinery
and equipment are already becoming obsolete and worn
out. Golland recommended that VAZ's managers pro-
ceed on two fronts--creation of a domestic industry
capable of producing modern automobile manufacturing
machinery and equipment and purchase of foreign
equipment and licenses.

The Soviet Union has also maintained a relatively
permanent working relationship with FIAT. Unlike
the traditional Soviet agreements with Western firms,
which terminated when a project was completed,
Soviet-FIAT ties remain close under the framework
of the 1965 scientific and technical cooperation
agreement. The original five-year agreement has
been renewed twice, in 1970 and 1975, and has led to
FIAT involvement in Soviet tractor production and in
other areas. Moreover, consideration has been given
to a new contract for FIAT assistance in expanding
the capacity of the Tol'iatti plant to perhaps twice
its present size,[40] although FIAT's willingness to

expand the capacity of a potential competitor is
questionable. Soviet officials are clearly interested in maintaining this relationship. One VAZ
engineer, citing the development of new equipment
at FIAT's Italian plant, remarked: "This experience
cannot be ignored; we must simply use the established
U.S.S.R.-Italy channel more actively and on a large
scale."[41]

VAZ officials have also made efforts to improve
the R & D base of the Soviet automotive industry.
According to its engineers, VAZ R & D facilities
are better equipped than other Soviet automotive
plants, but still understaffed. They have complained that the ministry's central research institutes are inadequate to meet their needs and have
proposed the establishment of a complex scientific-
research and design center at VAZ.[42] Such facilities
are particularly important if VAZ is to achieve its
goal of continuously modernizing its product. It
plans to produce a new basic model every five years
and to improve the Zhiguli even more often.

One of the major incentives for VAZ managers
to maintain a rapid pace of technological progress
is the need to remain competitive on international
markets.[43] VAZ is departing from traditional Soviet
practice by earmarking a large part (thirty percent)
of its production for foreign sales. Most of its
foreign sales have gone to Eastern Europe, but an
effort is underway to market a significant number
of Ladas in Western Europe and North America. Ladas
and other Soviet cars, particularly the Moskvich,
are exported by Avtoeksport, which has invested in
foreign-based joint stock companies to market these
vehicles in the West. They provide the advertising
and after-sales servicing which are necessary to
promote sales in Western countries. Avtoeksport
owns shares in nine Western companies: Ferchimex,
Nafta-B and Scaldia-Volga (in Belgium); Keteko
(Cameroon); Konela (Finland); Konela Norge Bil
(Norway); Matreco Bil (Sweden); UMO (United Kingdom);
and WAATECO (Nigeria).[44]

Several aspects of VAZ operations described
above--development of an extensive network of
suppliers, attention to technological progress, and
a strong international orientation--represent a
sharp departure from past practices in the Soviet
automotive industry. They also bear striking resemblance to current practices in Western industry.
There are other elements of similarity in the management and organization of VAZ and Western plants.
For example, managers at VAZ boast of a new

independence and accountability in decision making.
This apparently applies to the plant's director,
as well as his subordinates at VAZ and at subsidiary
plants. Another innovation is a wage system which
is designed to provide incentives for improving
quality and increasing labor productivity, rather
than merely increasing physical output. The VAZ
wage system is based on hourly labor wages (as
opposed to the piece rate system used in most of
Soviet industry) with supplements for professional
skills, attainment of normed assignments and increases in productivity. Both the style of management and the wage system at VAZ are claimed to be
more appropriate for a modern, technologically
progressive enterprise.[45] Elements of the VAZ
management system have been copied by a number of
other Soviet enterprises. However, there is reportedly considerable opposition among many Soviet
managers who are tied to traditional modes of
enterprise management.[46]

Perhaps the most striking innovation at VAZ
is its consumer orientation. In 1972, VAZ introduced a "company system" for servicing its cars--an
important first in the Soviet automotive industry.[47]
The system, which apparently is patterned after
Western practice, includes pre-sale preparation,
technical maintenance, and warranty and general
repairs. For the first time, the Soviet automobile
purchaser receives a service booklet which describes
maintenance schedules and entitles the owner to free
warranty repairs for a year or 20,000 kilometers.
This system marks a dramatic change from traditional
practice in Soviet automobile plants, where responsibility for their products ends as soon as the
vehicles are shipped to the consumer.[48]

The purpose of the company system is to correct
a chronic problem of Soviet car owners--inadequate
servicing facilities and a lack of spare parts. A
large spare parts production department has been put
into operation at Tol'iatti, and a nationwide network of auto centers is being developed. Construction of the centers did not keep pace with VAZ's output, however. Thirty-three such centers were planned
by the end of 1973, but only one-third were completed
on schedule.[49] Western firms are playing an important role in equipping these centers. The service
network, along with the production facilities at
Tol'iatti, suppliers of some parts and components,
engineering and design sections, and training
facilities, are all supervised by the production
association AvtoVAZ.

The FIAT-Soviet contract did not provide explicitly for FIAT assistance in managerial and organizational matters. However, the VAZ innovations in this realm appear to be largely a byproduct of FIAT's technical assistance. The exchange of personnel with FIAT included future managers of VAZ, as well as engineers and workers. For example A. K. Osipov, Chief of the Administration of Labor Organization and Wages at VAZ, spent a year and a half at FIAT's Turin plant and intimates that this experience was instrumental in formulating VAZ's wage system.[50] While there is no evidence that VAZ is merely imitating FIAT's system of management, some aspects of VAZ's management have undoubtedly been influenced by the prolonged contacts with FIAT. This may have been one of the most important elements of Western technology transfer to VAZ.

THE KAMA RIVER TRUCK PLANT

The Kama River Truck Plant is being built to boost rapidly the production of trucks in order to provide a more balanced freight transport system for the Soviet economy. The project will bring about another massive infusion of Western automotive technology to complement VAZ's contributions to technological progress in passenger car production. KamAZ is being built at Naberezhnye Chelny (in the Tatar Autonomous Soviet Socialist Republic) with a capacity to produce 150,000 heavy-duty, three-axle trucks and 250,000 diesel truck engines a year. Western technology transfers consist primarily of machinery and equipment shipments and production engineering assistance for various parts of the complex. Soviet hard currency payments to the numerous Western firms providing assistance are estimated to total over $1 billion.

Initial Planning and Purchase of Technology

Soviet planners have long recognized the need for expanded production of trucks to complement their rail and marine transport systems. The present Soviet truck park is considered inadequate, both in terms of numbers and technological sophistication. Perhaps equally important is the shortage of specialized vehicles for the many different jobs required of truck transport in a modern economy. One glaring deficiency recognized in the early and mid-1960s was the shortage of heavy-duty trucks with

large-load capacities which can be operated on poor
Soviet roads. KamAZ's products are designed primarily to solve this problem. KamAZ trucks when
loaded do not exceed six metric tons per axle,
and consequently can be operated on all Soviet roads,
including those without good foundations (the vast
majority of Soviet roads). Because they have three
axles, they can carry more cargo than most existing
Soviet trucks of their class.

However, KamAZ will not meet the needs for
other types of vehicles. For example, there will
still be an unsatisfied need for various types of
specialized trucks, such as off-road vehicles for
construction sites, small panel trucks, insulated
trucks, trucks with refrigeration units and tank
trucks.[51] Even more important is a steadily growing
need for trucks with a high cargo-carrying capacity
(six to ten metric tons per axle) to be used on the
small Soviet network of first-class roads.[52] KamAZ
trucks will not be the most efficient vehicles for
inter-city transport on these roads, which will
become increasingly important in the future. The
needs for such vehicles will presumably be met by
further expansion of existing facilities and construction of new truck plants. Thus, the construction of KamAZ represents only one step in the
expansion and modernization of Soviet truck production.

Development of KamAZ trucks began in 1968,
and the Central Committee Politburo approved the
project in September 1969. One month later, the
Soviet press announced that construction had begun
with 2000 workers on site.[53] By the time that the
Soviet leadership officially announced plans to
build KamAZ at the 24th Party Contress in 1971,
Soviet representatives had already visited a number
of Western automobile manufacturers in an effort to
find a Western company which would undertake the role
of general consultant for the project (the same role
which FIAT had played at VAZ). FIAT, Ford, Daimler-
Benz, Toyota, Renault, Volkswagen, British Leyland,
Mack Trucks and others were approached, and, for a
variety of reasons, all rejected the offer.

Ford, after announcing in 1970 that it would
become a general consultant, decided against
involvement when the Department of Defense opposed
the transaction. Mack Trucks, after signing a letter
of intent, encountered problems in obtaining export
licenses from the U.S. Government and also had
second thoughts about taking on a job as large as
KamAZ. Daimler-Benz had problems in settling the

terms for the sale of licenses to the Soviet Union.
(For example, Soviet officials balked at a clause
prohibiting the export of KamAZ trucks to the West.)
In addition, all of the Western firms were influenced
by problems that had been encountered by FIAT in its
role as general consultant for VAZ.[54]

Faced with the unwillingness of Western firms to
undertake the job, KamAZ's managers were forced to
do it themselves. To assist the project's directors
in Naberezhnye Chelny, the Kama River Purchasing
Commission (Kamatorg), with permanent offices in New
York and Paris, was established in 1973. The
commission's purpose is to search for the best
Western technology and to select Western consultants
for individual parts of the project. Kamatorg has
coordinated the activities of various Soviet specialists engaged in checking out machinery before
it is shipped to the Soviet Union or being trained
by Western firms which have signed contracts to
supply technology to KamAZ. In 1974, Kamatorg was
reported to be supervising ninety Soviet specialists,
based in Pittsburgh, and thirty-five in Paris.[55]
Two foreign trade organizations of the Ministry of
Foreign Trade, Avtopromimport and Metallurgimport,
assisted Kamatorg in concluding most of the contracts.

Contracts were signed with dozens of Western
firms. The largest were with the Swindell-Dressler
Company (U.S.), for technical assistance with KamAZ's
foundry; Renault, for assistance with the engine
plant; and Liebherr Verzahnungstechnik, GmbH (West
Germany), for assistance with the transmission
plant.[56] The total value of all KamAZ contracts
exceeded $1 billion, one-fifth the estimated cost
for the entire project. To finance the purchases,
Soviet officials made extensive use of Western
official and private credits, including one of
the first credits extended by the U.S. Export-
Import Bank to the Soviet Union. Of the major
Western participants, only one, Renault, had previously signed a scientific and technical cooperation agreement with SCST. Soviet officials apparently
urged some of the other major suppliers to sign such
agreements, but were unsuccessful.[57]

Absorption of Technology at KamAZ

Before the details of the KamAZ project had
been made public, Soviet officials had already made
important decisions on the location of the plant
and the design of future KamAZ vehicles. The
Naberezhnye Chelny site was selected and approved

by the Party's Politburo in 1969. The site was
found to be ideal for a number of reasons--proximity
to other major automotive plants, access to transportation facilities, availability of hydroelectric
power, and the existence of underemployed manpower
in the surrounding, largely agricultural districts.[58]
However, the choice of Naberezhnye Chelny was made
only after extensive debate over whether to concentrate the entire KamAZ complex at one site or to
build parts of the plant elsewhere.[59] Opposition
to the decision to locate the entire plant at
Naberezhnye Chelny was strongest among economists
at Gosplan, who argued that truck production should
be more dispersed, along the lines of the U.S.
automotive industry. Specifically, they advocated
placing only the plant for production of diesel
engines in Naberezhnye Chelny, while locating the
main truck plant in another city in Siberia and
plants for various parts and components in other
cities. A major argument for this approach was
that the more dispersed industry would assist in
providing employment for the surplus labor existing in various small cities. This "American"
approach was successfully opposed by proponents of
a single complex in Naberezhnye Chelny. The
victors, led by engineers from the automotive and
construction ministries, were successful in con-
vincing the Party leadership that Naberezhnye
Chelny would be the most efficient location for
the entire plant.

The location debate paralleled the earlier
debate over the location of VAZ. As at VAZ, a
major consideration for those responsible for building the plant was undoubtedly the very tight deadline set for completion of construction. The
startup of production was planned for 1974. Like
VAZ (and, in the First Five-Year Plan, GAZ), the
builders were required to construct both the production facilities and an entire new city in a very
short time.

Another important decision concerned the design
of the KamAZ vehicles. It was decided that KamAZ
trucks and diesel engines should be designed by
Soviet engineers without assistance from the West.
Although Soviet officials initially were inclined
to seek assistance in building a new engine through
a licensing arrangement with a Western firm, they
decided that their own engineers at the Yaroslavl'
Engine Plant could provide a better design.[60]
This was a surprising decision in view of the difficulties previously experienced by the Soviet

automotive industry in producing high performance
diesel engines. In the end, Yaroslavl's designs
for KamAZ apparently proved unsatisfactory because,
in 1972, Soviet officials enlisted the help of
Renault to make improvements in the engines.[61]
The results of the collaboration with Renault are
V-form engines of 180, 210 and 260 horsepower, which
Soviet specialists maintain are substantial improvements over existing Soviet engines. The engines
will be used in three basic variants of KamAZ
trucks, which will be produced at the following
rates when capacity output is reached:

1. Truck with standard body (stake and plat-
    form) which also can pull a trailer, com-
    bined capacity up to sixteen tons (30,000
    per year), and a variant with an extended
    chassis (25,000 per year);
2. Truck tractor for pulling semi-trailer up
    to twenty tons capacity (55,000 per year);
3. Dump truck with seven ton capacity (40,000
    per year).[62]

The absence of a general consultant for KamAZ
made it necessary to divide the task of designing
the production facilities among numerous domestic
and foreign firms. About seventy Soviet organizations, headed by the design organization Giproavto-
prom, provided designs for the architecture (which
was the primary responsibility of Promstroiproekt),
the heating, water, electrical and transportation
systems, and other parts of the complex. Foreign
firms provided designs for some of the major production processes. The process of coordinating
these designs and blending the various technologies
from the West and the Soviet Union into a con-
sistent, integrated manufacturing system was
accompanied by numerous problems.
A dramatic example of this kind of problem
surfaced in a dispute between Soviet officials and
representatives of Swindell-Dressler. In 1973,
Soviet officials publicly charged that Swindell-
Dressler had not provided designs for the foundry
on time. Swindell-Dressler spokesmen acknowledged
some delay, but complained that they had not been
given sufficient information about related machinery
supplied by other firms or about the buildings in
which the foundry was to be housed.[63] They explained
that completion of some aspects of the designs
required the integration of machinery from various
suppliers, and that some of the machinery had not

yet been purchased by Soviet importers. Swindell-
Dressler's task was further complicated by the
initial reluctance of Soviet officials to allow
foreign engineers adequate access to the construction site. As a result, Western machinery was
sometimes delivered, but would not fit into buildings that had already been constructed, necessitat-
ing modifications in the building. In other cases,
machinery purchased from one supplier did not meet
the specifications required by machinery and equipment supplied by other firms. The job of coordinating the infusion of foreign technology, one of the
most difficult tasks in any technology transfer,
had been a vital part of FIAT's assistance at VAZ.

One of the reasons cited by Swindell-Dressler
officials for the delays in providing designs for
the foundry was the active and frequently critical
participation of Soviet engineers in the design
phase. (A rotating team of seventy Soviet engineers
was assigned to the firm's headquarters in Pittsburgh to oversee the engineering and design work.)
After working about a year, Swindell-Dressler's
engineers presented the first draft of the foundry
(about 500 drawings indicating the various layout
details and a list of equipment that would be
recommended for purchase) to their Soviet counterparts. According to Swindell-Dressler's project
director, the Soviet engineers were very critical
of this draft:

> We were constantly challenged by the Russian
> engineering team who often insisted on two,
> three or four alternate layouts so that they
> could select what appears to be the best of
> all worlds. This, of course, added enormously
> to the amount of work in hammering out the
> preliminary design.[64]

As at GAZ and VAZ, the Soviet project directors
attempted to speed the construction of KamAZ by
starting construction "in parallel" with the design
stage (i.e., before complete designs were available).
The rapid tempo of construction created problems for
both domestic and foreign firms. Thus, the director
of Promstroiproekt noted that complexities stemming
from the need "to issue blueprints on important
projects not having the final engineering plans,
as well as precise basic data on industrial equipment."[65] Likewise, Swindell-Dressler engineers
found that they were locked into previous decisions
that had already determined the exact exterior

dimensions of the building in which the foundry was to be housed. This resulted in what was described as "a rather crowded foundry according to American standards."[66]

The rapid pace of construction also created considerable difficulty in obtaining adequate supplies of building materials and labor for the project. The general contractor for the construction project, Kamgesenergostroi (Kama Hydroelectric Power Plant Construction Trust), was criticized repeatedly for failure to meet scheduled completion dates for various parts of the complex. Representatives of the construction firm attributed the delays to shortages of skilled manpower, the slow delivery of materials and building structures to the project and the slow delivery of technical documentation.[67] In particular, the shortage of skilled construction workers and rapid labor turnover have plagued the project.[68] The resultant delays have escalated the costs of construction. For example, large quantities of equipment were delivered before there was space where it could be installed. Consequently, large sums were spent on construction of auxiliary buildings for storing the incoming equipment.[69] In another case, designs for some of the main buildings had to be changed because of delays. When the prefabricated partitions called for in the architectural designs were not delivered on time, more costly brick partitions were substituted. The brick partitions were not only expensive, but defeated the purpose of the original design--to avoid permanent internal walls so machinery could be modernized, rearranged or replaced when necessary.[70]

Construction delays set back the startup of KamAZ for two years. When the Soviet press originally announced the beginning of construction in late 1969, the projected date for startup was 1974. However, by the end of 1974, only the main buildings had been erected, and installation of equipment had just begun. The first vehicles were produced in February 1976 and output expanded slowly thereafter. Only 5,000 were produced in 1976, and 22,000 in 1977.

Confronted with such delays, Soviet officials have shown a keen awareness of the shortcomings of the KamAZ construction project. M. Troitskii, Party regional secretary in the province where KamAZ is located, identified the major problem in the construction of KamAZ as the absence of a "systems approach." Troitskii indicated that large numbers of sophisticated machines have been brought to KamAZ without careful planning on how the different parts of the plant fit together. "In short," he concluded, "for projects such as KamAZ, what is needed is not simply many machines and mechanisms, but systems of complementary machines."[71] This is precisely the job that a general consultant would do. After the experience of KamAZ, Kamatorg officials have publicly indicated that they prefer Western general consultants for future large projects.[72]

In reaction to the chronic delays of Soviet construction projects, innovations were introduced in KamAZ's supply system. In 1970, the State Supply Committee (Gossnab) created a special regional agency, Kamsnab, to coordinate incoming supplies from various ministries.[73] The creation of a special supply agency (the first time this had been done in Soviet industry) was supposed to obviate the need for construction firms working at KamAZ to secure their own supplies of materials directly from other factories or through the inadequate supply-and-sales bases near the remote construction site. Kamsnab continues to coordinate the supply system, both for the remaining construction and for the production process at KamAZ. In creating a special supply agency. Soviet officials undoubtedly hoped that it would serve to prod suppliers to meet rigid schedules for deliveries. As was the case at VAZ, suppliers have been urged to assign the highest priority to meeting KamAZ's needs.

Despite these efforts, the supply system has functioned poorly, both during the construction phase and during the early operation of the plant. Soviet observers have expressed their concern that many of the 300 subcontractors for KamAZ, which are to supply various parts, components and materials for KamAZ trucks are not being modernized and expanded rapidly enough. They are apprehensive about both the quantity and quality of inputs which will be delivered to KamAZ. Before the start of production, KamAZ's management was reportedly renting helicopters and airplanes to deliver supplies to the plant after startup.[74]

Soviet officials anticipate that KamAZ, when operating at full capacity, will bring a major technological advance to Soviet truck production. They claim that KamAZ production processes represent a much greater degree of automation and mechanization than other Soviet truck plants and will foster significant increases in labor productivity. Western businessmen who have visited KamAZ seem to agree with KamAZ promises to be a modern facility. In choosing among the available foreign technologies,

Soviet engineers generally followed the example of
VAZ: they selected the latest technologies available in the West. However, in at least one case--
the selection of equipment for the foundry--they
appeared to follow a more conservative approach,
which reflected the influence of traditional practices in Soviet industry. KamAZ engineers did not
consistently select the best labor-saving machinery
for the foundry, showing a preference in many
instances for manual controls over automated controls.
In parts of the foundry where automation is being
used, they have stationed workers to monitor the
automated operations. This practice led one
Western observer to conclude that KamAZ officials
were overmanning job stations at the foundry and
not placing great emphasis on maximizing output
per manhour.[75] However, other descriptions of the
production processes by both Soviet and Western
observers suggest that this conservative approach
may not be typical. At least in terms of hardware,
there is evidence that KamAZ has generally accumulated the most modern processes.

   The decision to concentrate the entire KamAZ
complex at one site also appears to reflect a conservative or traditional Soviet approach to industrial organization. KamAZ is a highly integrated
complex, comprising six major production plants
(engine, gear and transmission; foundry; assembly;
pressing and stamping; forge; and tooling and repair);
extensive support facilities, and housing for a
labor force of 80,000.[76] Soviet attitudes toward
this concentrated variant for KamAZ appear ambivalent.
On the one hand, it appears to contravene the thinking of many Soviet automotive and general machine-
building specialists about the need to build highly
specialized and decentralized plants.[77] Moreover,
as noted above, the location of the complex was a
controversial decision, which was opposed by many
Soviet planners. Even the proponents of the vic-
torious concentrated variant acknowledge that the
decentralized or "cooperative" approach may be more
appropriate in some cases:

   Of course, the KamAZ experience is not the only
   possible solution of such problems. A detailed
   study of all of the factors of production in
   the conditions of our country, allows us to
   decide in each concrete case which is the more
   advantageous--concentration or cooperation...[78]

In rebuilding and modernizing the Moscow Motor Works

(ZIL), which has been carried out at about the same
time as the construction of KamAZ, Soviet officials
decided to follow the decentralized approach, dis-
persing the basic production processes of the plant
in various suburbs of Moscow.

On the other hand, KamAZ officials believe that
the establishment of such a large, concentrated
plant at a single location can also provide a basis
for efficient specialization within the complex.
They anticipate that the long production runs of the
individual plants of KamAZ will facilitate the
achievement of significant economies of scale. At
the same time, the organization of the complex as
a production association, with a single general
director, is expected to avoid some of the uncer-
tainties of the supply system. To secure supplies
of materials and parts produced outside the complex,
KamAZ's management hopes to benefit from the continuing expansion and modernization of supplier
plants in the automotive and other ministries,
although this development is proceeding more slowly
than planned. Like VAZ, KamAZ will be supplied
by numerous Soviet enterprises, as well as plants
in Eastern Europe (Hungary, Poland, Bulgaria and
Czechoslovakia).

Soviet officials have placed high priority on
developing a new style of management at KamAZ which
they hope will insure efficient production and
maintenance of a rapid pace of technological progress.
In formulating the management system to be used at
the complex, KamAZ officials have studied intensively
new developments in Western management science,
particularly the applications of systems analysis,
mathematical modeling and computer science. Soviet
specialists have acknowledged the influence of
Western management science, but emphasize that the
"mechanical transfer" of Western techniques to the
Soviet economy is neither feasible, nor desirable.[79]
They emphasize that KamAZ's management system will
reflect the best of both Western and Soviet practices. Thus, B. Z. Mil'ner, a researcher at the
Institute for the Study of the U.S.A. and Canada
in Moscow and one of the top Soviet management
specialists, noted that KamAZ's managers will use
"the leading domestic and foreign experience in
organizing the management of the big production
complex."[80]

For the most part, KamAZ has not benefitted
directly, through active technology transfer
mechanisms, from Western management practices.
The directors of KamAZ have not had as great an

opportunity as their counterparts at VAZ to study
extensively and at first hand the managerial
operations of the Western firms supplying technology to the project. This is due in part to the
absence at KamAZ of the kind of close, long-term
personnel interactions which characterized VAZ's
relationship with FIAT. The smaller scale of
personnel exchanges between KamAZ (which is substantially larger than VAZ) and Western firms
illustrates this point. During the early construction phase of KamAZ, few if any Western specialists
were allowed to visit the KamAZ site. At the peak
of the construction and installation work, only
200-250 Western specialists were at the site.

To compensate for the relatively small degree
of active borrowing of Western management techniques, Soviet specialists have devoted considerable
efforts to borrowing through passive mechanisms.
Specifically, they have organized the study of
Western management science at several research
institutes, the most import of which is the Institute for the Study of the U.S.A. and Canada, headed
by G. Arbatov. A number of workers at the Institute worked jointly with large numbers of specialists
from KamAZ and several other new Soviet enterprises
to find applications of Western techniques for Soviet
industry. Thus, Mil'ner and other management specialists at the Institute, actively participated in
the planning of KamAZ's management structure.[81]

Although KamAZ's management system is still
evolving, some of the central elements have been
described in the Soviet press.[82] They include a
new role for the general director of the plant.
The first director, L. B. Vasiliev reportedly has
had a greater degree of authority and independence
than the traditional Soviet manager. For example,
his strong intervention was reportedly instrumental
in solving disputes with Western suppliers during
the construction phase.[83] His role after startup
is also intended to be different. He will concentrate on long-term problems and on problems relating to coordination of the different parts of the
complex. Day-to-day functional operations will be
the primary job of his subordinate executive
director.

KamAZ is to devote a major effort to research
and development. In Arbatov's words:

A special research and development service, new
in our industry, has been introduced at KamAZ;
its tasks include working out perspective

designs for the main products of the plant,
developing technology and quality, standardization, and collecting scientific-technical
information. The service will include a strong
engineering center providing an experimental-
production base for the development and introduction of new technology.[84]

Another proposed innovation at KamAZ is a
fuller integration of the plant's computer center
with management functions. Soviet specialists note
that, in the past, computer centers in Soviet industry have worked in isolation from the managerial
staff of the enterprise. Their work has frequently
been either irrelevant, or, at best, limited to
automation of routine calculations at the plant.[85]
KamAZ's management is reportedly developing a computer center which will work on more complicated
managerial functions. Equipment imported from
International Business Machines will be used in the
center. The IBM computer systems will perform not
only routine tasks such as monitoring of production
processes and inventory control, but also production
reporting and production planning functions.[86]
KamAZ is also following VAZ's lead in establishing closer ties with the end-users of its
products and in placing heavy emphasis on the quality of its output. The executive director will be
in charge of sections responsible for contracts,
analysis of relations with consumers, export deliveries, special orders, and a spare parts center.
KamAZ is also assuming the responsibility for
servicing its vehicles. A network of service
stations and repair plants, similar to the VAZ
system, is to be built at locations throughout the
country.
The organization and management of KamAZ will
have uniquely Soviet features, and the enterprise
will have to function in an economic system which
is still bound by traditional Soviet practices.
However, the influence of Western management science
on the organizational structure which is being
developed at KamAZ is apparent.[87] The long-run
success of the absorption of Western production
technology at KamAZ will depend in part on the skill
with which its directors learn Western management
techniques and adapt them to the Soviet industrial
environment.

NOTES:

1. Barney K. Schwalberg, "The Soviet Automotive Industry, A Current Assessment," Automotive Industries, CXVIII, (January 1, 1958), 69.

2. Evgenii Alekseevich Chudakov, Razvitie avtomobilestroeniia v SSSR (Moscow: Gosplanizdat, 1942), pp. 82-83; and William P. Baxter, "The Soviet Passenger Car Industry," Survey, IXX, (Summer 1973), 228.

3. A. Aganbegyan, "Evaluate According to the Final Results," Trud, July 26, 1977, p. 2 (Translated in Joint Publications Research Service, 69714, Translations on USSR Economic Affairs, No. 799, August 31, 1977, pp. 59-60.

4. Promyshlenno-ekonomicheskaia gazeta, November 14, 1956, cited by Schwalberg, p. 69.

5. Schwalberg, pp. 60-61.

6. Ibid., passim.

7. N. S. Khrushchev, XXII S"ezd Kommunisticheskoi Partii Sovetskogo Soiuza, stenograficheskii otchet, October 17-31, 1961 (Moscow: Gosudarstvennoe izdatel'stvo politicheskoi literatury, 1962), p. 62.

8. A. N. Kosygin, "Povyshenie nauchnoi obosnovannosti planov--vashneishaia zadacha plannovykh organov," Planovoe khoziaistvo, April, 1965, p. 6.

9. Ibid., pp. 9-10.

10. Imogene U. Edwards, "Automotive Trends in the U.S.S.R.," U.S. Congress, Joint Economic Committee, Joint Committee Print in Soviet Economic Prospects for the Seventies, (Washington, D.C.: Government Printing Office, June 27, 1973), p. 306.

11. Izvestiia, December 7, 1974, p. 3 (Translated in The Current Digest of the Soviet Press, XXVI (January 1, 1975), 15.

12. S. Matveev, "Perspektivy razvitiia avtomobil'noi promyshlennosti v novom piatiletii," Planovoe khoziaistvo, July, 1966, p. 28.

13. Paul Ericson, "Soviet Efforts to Increase Exports of Manufactured Products to the West," in U.S. Congress, Joint Economic Committee, Soviet Economy in a New Perspective, Joint Committee Print (Washington, D.C.: Government Printing Office, October 14, 1976), p. 722.

14. V. Papkovskii, "Kakogo tipa legkovye avtomobili nam nuzhny," Kommunist, XXXVI, no. 14, 1959, pp. 126-28.

15. U. A. Zamozikin, L. N. Zhilina, and N. I. Frolova, "Sdvigi v massovom potreblenii i lichnost'," Voprosy filosofii, VI (June, 1969), p. 33.

16. U.S. Congress, House of Representatives, Committee on Banking and Currency, Subcommittee on International Trade, The FIAT-Soviet Auto Plant and Communist Economic Reforms, Committee Print (Washington, D.C.: Government Printing Office, March 1, 1967), p. 4.

17. V. N. Sushkov, "Sotrudnichestvo s firmoi 'FIAT' rasshiriaetsia," interview in Vneshniai torgovlia, No. 8, 1966, p. 44.

18. Michele Boumsell and Nicolas Simon, "L'Evolution de la Cooperation Franco-Sovietique dans l'Industrie Automobile," Le Courier des Pays de l'Est, No. 192, January 1976, pp. E-29-37.

19. Sushkov, p. 44.

20. Some of the details of this contract are provided in V. Buffa, "Economic and Commercial Cooperation Between East and West," Draft of a speech, November 3, 1973, provided by the Italian Embassy, Washington, D.C. (Buffa was in charge of FIAT's operations at Tol'iatti.) See also, U.S. Congress, FIAT-Soviet, passim.

21. Aron Katsenelinboigen, "Soviet Science and the Economists/Planners," (paper presented at the Workshop on Soviet Science and Technology sponsored by George Washington University and the National Science Foundation, Airlie House, Virginia, November 18-21, 1976).

22. Buffa.

23. V. Soloviev, Za rulem, no. 6, 1968, pp. 6-7.

24. P. M. Katsura and M. N. Meshcheriakova, Novye formy organizatsii promyshlennogo proizvodstva (Opyt VAZa) (Moscow: Izdatel'stvo "Ekonomika", 1974), pp. 23.

25. Ibid., p. 7.

26. Radio Liberty, "Soviet Popular Car Industry's Slow Start," January 26, 1971.

27. B. M. Katsman, "Glavnyi vyigrysh--vremia," Ekonomika i organizatsiia promyshlennogo proizvodstva, no. 1, 1976, pp. 65-66.

28. Ibid., p. 68.

29. Katsura and Meshcheriakova, p. 8.

30. Buffa.

31. "Organizatsiia nauchno-issledovatel'skikh razrabotok na VAZe," Ekonomika i organizatsiia promyshlennogo proizvodstva, no. 1, 1976, pp. 159-61.

32. Izvestiia, December 18, 1974, p. 3.

33. Edwards, p. 296.

34. "Organizatsiia nauchno-issledovatel'skikh," p. 159.

35. Radio Liberty, "Why the Volga Automobile Plant's Production Schedule has been Disrupted," November 8, 1972.

36. Pravda, August 28, 1975, p. 2.
37. V. N. Sushkov, "O torgovo-ekonomicheskom sotrudnichestve s kapitalisticheskimi stranami v stroitel'stve v SSSR krupnykh promyshlennykh ob"ektov," Vneshniaia torgovlia, No. 2, 1976, p. 11; and "Bendix breaks ground in trade with Russia, Business Week, January 31, 1977, p. 49.
38. Business International, Eastern Europe Report, September 19, 1975, p. 266; January 9, 1976, p. 5; May 14, 1975, p. 151.
39. E. B. Golland, "Tekhnicheskaia osnova vysokoi proizvoditel'nosti truda," Ekonomika i organizatsiia promyshlennogo proizvodstva, No. 1, 1975, pp. 84-86.
40. Edwards, p. 296.
41. "Organizatsiia nauchno-issledovatel'skikh," p. 162.
42. Ibid., passim.
43. Ibid., pp. 163, 181.
44. U.S. Central Intelligence Agency, Soviet Commercial Operations in the West (ER 77-10486), Washington, D.C., September 1977, p. 25.
45. VAZ's management system is described in Katsura and Meshcheriakova, and in Ekonomika i organizatsiia promyshlennogo proizvodstva, no. 1, 1976, pp. 47-210, passim.
46. N. Mironov and N. Petrov, "Universitety avtograda," Pravda, May 6, 1976, p. 2.
47. Izvestiia, December 18, 1974, p. 3.
48. A. Aganbegyan, p. 63.
49. Andreas Tenson, "Too Few Service Stations for Soviet Cars," Radio Liberty Dispatch, August 20, 1974.
50. "VAZ--shkola upravleniia," Ekonomika i organizatsiia promyshlennogo proizvodstva, No. 1, 1976, pp. 116-17.
51. E. Trubitsyn, "Motor Transport in the New Conditions," Ekonomicheskaia gazeta, no. 47, November 1974, p. 8. (Translated in Current Digest of the Soviet Press, XXVII, no. 16, May 14, 1975.)
52. D. Velikanov, "Needs of National Economy in Technical Progress in Development of Motor Transport Facilities," Avtomobil'nyy transport, no. 11, November 1974 (Translated by Joint Publications Research Service, USSR Trade and Services, no. 845, March 21, 1975, pp. 25-26.)
53. Trud, October 11, 1969.
54. Chase World Information Corporation, KamAZ, the Billion Dollar Beginning, New York, 1974, pp. 4-5. Harlan S. Finer, Howard Gobstein and George D. Holliday, "KamAZ: U.S. Technology Transfer to the

Soviet Union," Technology Transfer and U.S. Foreign
Policy, ed. by Henry R. Nau, (New York: Praeger
Publishers, 1976), pp. 87-119.
    55. Chase, p. 5.
    56. For a list of other important contracts, see
Chase, pp. 7-21.
    57. For example, Donald E. Stingel, then Execu-
tive Vice President of Swindell-Dressler Company,
stated that his company declined such an offer.
Remarks at George Washington University, Washington,
D.C., on February 25, 1975.
    58. Chase, pp. 49-53.
    59. M. Troitskii, "Na novom etape," Novyi mir,
No. 1, January 1975, pp. 170-71 and 178-79.
    60. L. Bliakhman, "Glavnyi vyigrysh--vremia;
zametki o problemakh uskoreniia nauchno-tekhnicheskogo progressa," Neva, no. 1, 1973, p. 173.
    61. Edwards, p. 309.
    62. Ibid., p. 305.
    63. Stingel.
    64. Jack H. Schaum, "Kamaz Foundry...U.S.A. on
Display," Modern Casting, March 1976, p. 44.
    65. Stroitel'naia gazeta, August 31, 1975, p. 3.
    66. Schaum, p. 44.
    67. Sotsialisticheskaia industriia, March 26,
1975, p. 2.
    68. Pravda, December 9, 1972, p. 2.
    69. Pravda, December 26, 1974, p. 2.
    70. Stroitel'naia gazeta, August 31, 1975, p. 3.
    71. Troitskii, p. 177.
    72. Eastwest Markets, January 27, 1975, p. 11.
    73. G. V. Plekhanov, "New System for the Organi-
zation of Supply Operations in the Construction Industry," Material'no-tekhnicheskoe snabzhenie, No.
5, May 1977, pp. 26-32. (Translated in JPRC 69346,
Translations on USSR Trade and Services, 1032,
July 1, 1977.)
    74. Pravda, December 27, 1974, p. 2.
    75. Schaum, p. 46.
    76. Edwards, p. 305.
    77. Supra, pp. 126-127. See also: B. V. Vlasov
et al., Ekonomicheskie problemy proizvodstva
avtomobilei (Moscow: Izdatel'stvo "Nashinostroenie,"
1971).
    78. Troitskii, p. 178.
    79. G. Arbatov, "Proektirovanie organizatsii
krupnykh proizvodstvenno-khoziaistvennykh kompleksov
i upravleniia imi," Planovoe khoziaistvo, May 1975,
p. 18.
    80. B. Mil'ner, "On the Organization of Manage-
ment," Kommunist, no. 3, February, 1975 (Translated

in Joint Publications Research Service, 64452,
April 1, 1975, p. 50.)

81. Arbatov, p. 22; and B. Z. Mil'ner, ed.,
Organizatsionnye struktury upravleniia proizvodstvom
(Moscow: Izdatel'stvo "Ekonomika," 1975), p. 136.

82. Arbatov, pp. 22-27, and Mil'ner, Organizatsionnye struktury, pp. 136-46.

83. Herbert E. Meyer, "A Plant that Could Change
the Shape of Soviet Industry," Fortune, November,
1974, pp. 153-56.

84. Arbatov, p. 23.

85. Ibid., pp. 25-26.

86. Personal letter from International Business
Machines. See also, Chase, pp. 81-88.

87. Nicholas Simon, "L'organisation du complexe
automobile "KamAZ": un nouveau style de management
Sovietique," Le courier des pays de l'est, No. 205,
March 1977, p. 28.

7. Conclusions

In the introduction to this study, three broad questions were posed about the Soviet experience in borrowing technology from the West during two periods, 1928-1937 and 1966-1975. First, what has been the role of Western technology in Soviet economic development? The answer to this question was intended to help explain Soviet motivations for borrowing Western technology and to provide a basis for discussing the prospects for future Soviet commercial and technological relations with the West. Second, how does the Soviet experience as a recipient of foreign technology compare with the experiences of other countries. This question was directed primarily toward explaining the impact of Soviet attitudes and institutions on the technology transfer process. A final question, central to this study, was to define the basic Soviet orientation or policy toward the international economy in general and Western technology in particular. Three hypotheses were outlined as possible explanations of the expansion of Soviet commercial and technological ties to the West since the 1960s. A part of the last question was to determine whether Soviet policy in this area has undergone a significant change.

The three questions are interrelated. Thus, this study suggests that changing Soviet institutional arrangements and attitudes are evidence of a gradual but fundamental change in Soviet policy toward economic and technological ties with the West. It also suggests that a new Soviet economic growth strategy requires an enhanced role for technological progress in general and for Western technology in particular. One of the implications of the new growth strategy is that Soviet technological ties to the West are likely to endure. All of these

questions are controversial and perhaps defy definitive answers. However, the general analysis of
Western technology transfer to the Soviet Union and
the case study do provide evidence which sheds light
on each of them.

THE ROLE OF WESTERN TECHNOLOGY IN SOVIET ECONOMIC
DEVELOPMENT

Most Western assessments conclude that Western
technology has made an important contribution to
Soviet economic and technological progress. This
conclusion is generally supported by the evidence
presented both in the general analysis in Chapter 3
and in the case study. The importation of Western
mass-production techniques played a crucially
important role at the beginning of Soviet rapid
industrialization. In the 1960s and 1970s, Western
labor-saving technology has been assigned an important role in the modernization of many Soviet industries. The transition from an extensive to an
intensive growth strategy necessitates a prominent
role for foreign technology On the other hand,
during the long interim period (roughly from the
mid-1930s to the mid-1960s) Soviet economic growth
was extensive: it resulted primarily from increased
inputs of capital and labor, rather than technological progress. The strategy of Soviet planners
was to expand industrial production as rapidly as
possible with the technological base created during
the First Five-Year Plan. After the initial infusion
of Western technology, relatively few resources were
devoted either to domestic research and development
at the enterprise level or to the absorption of
foreign technology. Consequently, Western technology
played a relatively small role in Soviet economic
growth during the interim period.
    This general pattern was observed in the case
study of Western technology transfer to the Soviet
automotive industry. The first Soviet mass-production
automobile plant was established at Gorkii with
assistance from Ford and other Western firms. After
termination of the technical assistance agreements,
GAZ developed as the linchpin of an independent
Soviet automotive industry. With great difficulty,
Soviet economic planners substituted domestic production for all of the inputs for GAZ that had
initially been imported from Western firms. More
importantly, technological ties between GAZ and
foreign automotive firms were minimized. GAZ's

isolation from the West (and the low priority assigned to domestic efforts to maintain technological progress) soon resulted in the obsolescence of both the products and production processes at the Soviet plant.

In the 1960s and 1970s, Soviet planners have undertaken an extensive expansion and modernization of the automotive industry, with large-scale Western assistance at VAZ, KamAZ and, to a lesser extent, at other automotive enterprises. This effort, involving major expenditures of domestic resources and hard currency, illustrates the reversal of the traditional priorities of Soviet economic planners. At VAZ and KamAZ, for example, technological progress and quality of output, rather than increases in the volume of output, are emphasized. The new growth strategy is reflected in several aspects of the operations of these plants—the long-term technological ties between VAZ and FIAT; the large research and development facilities at both plants; their consumer orientation; and their interest in export markets.

While Soviet observers tend to downplay the overall contribution of Western technology to the Soviet economy, they acknowledge substantial Western contributions at each of the three projects in the case study. Thus, GAZ was cited as one of the most successful examples of Western technical assistance during the First Five-Year Plan, and VAZ and KamAZ are credited with achieving major technological gains as a result of cooperation with Western firms. The contribution of Western technology to these projects consisted not only of designs for automobiles and new production processes. Of more importance was the transfer of technological knowhow needed to mass produce automobiles efficiently. Without this vital contribution, the Soviet automotive industry could not have met its output goals. In addition, at VAZ and KamAZ, Soviet specialists are attempting to borrow Western managerial knowhow needed to operate the large production facilities efficiently while achieving additional goals, such as maintaining a rapid pace of technological progress and meeting the special needs of consumers in both the domestic and foreign markets.

The Soviet automotive industry, like most other Soviet civilian industries, has not been a technologically dynamic one. Most major innovations in automotive production techniques and product designs have come from abroad. This is not an unusual phenomenon. All industrial countries borrow heavily from the technical achievements of others. For

173

example, during the first three decades of the
Twentieth Century, many of the innovations in automobile manufacturing came from the United States.
Since then, perhaps a majority of the major inventions and innovations in the industry originated
in Europe. Nevertheless, the United States, Europe
and, in recent times, Japan have maintained relatively
dynamic automotive industries by borrowing heavily
from technologies created abroad. Indeed, the ability to borrow effectively appears to be positively
related to the level of technological progress
already achieved. In other words, technologically
advanced countries tend to be more effective bor-
rowers than technologically backward countries.
Thus, the lack of domestic invention or first-time
innovation does not necessarily condemn a country
to technological backwardness. What is important
is the ability to absorb technology rapidly and
efficiently, and to adapt it to the special needs
of domestic or foreign markets. The ability to
use foreign technology effectively and creatively
has been a key to industrial progress in a number
of Western countries, most notably Japan.

In the general analysis of Western technology
transfer to the Soviet Union, the keen Soviet
interest in Japan's experience as a technology
borrower was noted. Japan's success in using foreign technology to spur domestic economic growth
and to produce manufactured products that are competitive on foreign markets appears to hold a
special attraction for some Soviet economic planners.
VAZ, for example, appears to represent a Soviet
attempt to imitate the pattern of international
technological exchange which is epitomized in Japan's
foreign trade and is reflected to some extent in the
trade of other Western industrial countries. Thus,
imports of Western technology for VAZ have been
followed by exports of a substantial portion of VAZ's
output to foreign, including Western, markets. The
need to compete on Western markets has, in turn,
provided a stimulus for further technological progress at VAZ. To maintain the necessary pace of
technological change, VAZ's managers are attempting
simultaneously to spur domestic innovation and to
continue importing new generations of Western technology. The result of this approach is continuing
ties to the West--both to Western suppliers of
technology and to Western markets for the Lada. The
contrast between the role of Western technology at
GAZ and VAZ is striking. While a single large infusion of Western technology sufficed to meet the

174

goals set by Stalinist planners for GAZ, VAZ requires
continual imports of technology to meet its goals.
The success of the new strategy has thus far been
limited. VAZ's export products have captured only
a small portion of Western markets, and its ability
to maintain the rapid pace of technological progress
of Western firms remains to be proven. VAZ's success
in following the example of Japanese firms will be
tested seriously as it attempts to match the achievements of Western firms in meeting new safety, fuel
efficiency and pollution control standards now being
established by Western governments.

THE IMPACT OF SOVIET ATTITUDES AND INSTITUTIONS ON
THE TECHNOLOGY TRANSFER PROCESS

     How does the Soviet experience in borrowing
foreign technology compare with the experiences of
other countries? What has been the impact of Soviet
attitudes and institutions on the technology transfer process? The case study provides considerable
evidence that Soviet absorption of foreign technology
has been slow and inefficient by comparison with
Western industrial countries. To some extent, this
phenomenon has resulted from economic and technological conditions which the Soviet Union shares with
less developed countries--inadequate economic infrastructure; paucity of trained workers, engineers
and managers; insufficient domestic research and
development capabilities; and underdevelopment of
crucial complementary industries. Like many other
countries, the Soviet Union has also experienced
difficulties in financing technology imports and has
accumulated substantial hard currency debts. In
short, the Soviet Union has not had many of the
necessary preconditions for successful technology
borrowing. Naturally, the absence of these preconditions was more pronounced in the Soviet Union
of the 1930s than of today, but, to some extent,
shortcomings persist.
     More importantly, the évidence presented in
this study suggests that many of the barriers to
effective absorption of foreign technology have been
associated with uniquely Soviet institutions and
attitudes. For example, the Soviet Government's
insistence on maintaining full control over domestic
economic activities has precluded foreign direct
investment in the Soviet economy. Moreover, Soviet
leaders have been reluctant to allow extensive interaction between Soviet and foreign industrial specialists.

These attitudes were institutionalized in the form
of the Ministry of Foreign Trade's strict monopoly
over foreign economic activities and reliance on
passive technology transfer mechanisms, characterized
by short-term contractual arrangements with little
exchange of personnel. These institutions, which
predominated in the interim period, had a number of
political and economic origins. Specifically, they
were useful in minimizing the political and economic
costs generally associated with technology transfer.
Thus, the use of passive technology transfer mechanisms helped to insulate Soviet citizens from the
potentially dangerous (from a political standpoint)
interaction with foreigners. The foreign trade
monopoly enabled the government to ration limited
hard currency reserves.

The political and economic costs associated
with importing Western technology were important
motivating factors in the drastic cutback of Soviet
economic and technological ties with the West in the
1930s. This study provides evidence that a third,
frequently overlooked, factor--the somewhat naive
views of the Soviet political elite toward technological matters--was also important. Soviet political
leaders tended to underestimate the technological
dynamism of the Western economies and the difficulties of importing Western technologies and apply-
ing them to Soviet economic needs. They also tended
to overestimate the capacity of the Soviet economy
to achieve technological progress independently.
Thus, there was some anticipation among the political elite that the initial infusion of Western technology during the First Five-Year Plan would allow
Soviet industry to catch up with the technological
level of the West in a short period of time. This,
it was suggested, would be a point of departure, at
which the rate of Soviet technological progress
would begin to surpass that of the West. Such attitudes fostered the strategy of relying on only
occasional, passive technology borrowing. Evidence
presented in the case study suggests that these
views on technology were not shared by many Soviet
engineers. The latter tended to have a higher esti-
mation of Western technological prowess and a greater
understanding of the difficulties associated with
domestic technological progress. The attitudes of
the technical elite were reflected in a number of
initiatives: the decision to manufacture the simpler
Model A, rather than Ford's new V-8 engine; the
resistance of Soviet managers and engineers to the
decision to stop importing Western machinery; the

176

complaints of Soviet engineers about the obsolescence of the Soviet automotive industry; and the calls for improvement of domestic research and development efforts.

The case study concentrates on three relatively active technology transfer mechanisms, but also provides examples of attempts to borrow Western technology through passive mechanisms. Among the latter were the copying of the Fordson tractor in the 1920s, the model changes at GAZ in the late 1930s, and the designing of new trucks during World War II. Only the wartime attempt proved very successful, largely because of the extraordinary technological resources which were apparently concentrated at GAZ during the war. GAZ's high-priority as a military enterprise gave it access to the kinds of inputs, especially highly skilled engineers, which it needed to effect technological change without active Western assistance. In general, however, the case study suggests that passive mechanisms have been slow and ineffective means of borrowing foreign technology.

In the construction of GAZ, VAZ and KamAZ, Soviet officials employed more active mechanisms, although these arrangements also limited the role of foreign firms to a greater extent than is common in the West. At each of the projects, the Soviet technology recipients encountered two sets of problems: problems associated with the recipient's interface with foreign firms and those involving the project's interface with the rest of the domestic economy. The utilization of active mechanisms was designed to minimize the problems associated with the first interface. Nevertheless, these problems were formidable, especially at GAZ and KamAZ. Several key shortcomings in the contractual arrangements at these two projects accounted for many of the problems. The personnel exchanges were relatively small-scale (by comparison with VAZ). Ties to foreign firms were relatively short-term, particularly at GAZ, where there was an abrupt cutoff of active ties to Ford and other Western firms immediately after startup of production. Finally, at both GAZ and KamAZ, there was no Western general consultant to provide assistance in the overall design of the project and to coordinate the inputs of various Western firms. The technology transfer mechanism used at VAZ was more active in these three regards: personnel exchanges were considerably larger; longer term relations were established with FIAT (formal ties began before the construction of the project and continue today); and FIAT served as a

general consultant for the project. In this respect,
KamAZ represents a Soviet step back from more active
ties to Western firms. However, it is important to
note that Soviet officials preferred a FIAT-type
contract for KamAZ, but could not persuade Western
firms to undertake the job.

The problems associated with the second interface (between the technology recipients and other
domestic economic institutions) were serious at
all of the projects studied. These problems were
naturally most severe at GAZ because of the underdeveloped economic and technological infrastructure
in the Soviet Union during the First Five-Year Plan.
In addition, GAZ was required to absorb general, as
well as system-specific and firm specific automotive
manufacturing technologies from the West. The
Soviet Union simply had no experience in the mass
production of automobiles prior to GAZ. GAZ's
problems in absorbing Western technologies were
exacerbated by management problems (little effort
was made to learn Western management techniques),
the lack of R & D facilities at the plant, and the
discontinuation of active ties with Western industry.
GAZ's vertically integrated structure appears to
have been necessary in the absence of important complementary industries. However, such a structure
also generated difficulties because it necessitated
numerous adaptations of the more decentralized
Western automotive manufacturing processes.

VAZ and KamAZ, despite the long previous Soviet
experience in automotive manufacturing, have also
experienced considerable problems in their interaction with other parts of the economy. In particular, such problems have been manifest in the
operations of the supply systems for the two projects, both during construction and after startup.
Supplies from other Soviet enterprises have been
inadequate in quantity and quality, resulting in
delays in startup, slow achievement of capacity output, and products with substandard parts. Because
model changes and technological improvements require
changes in many parts and components, deficiencies
in the supply system create a serious obstacle to
technological progress at VAZ and KamAZ.

To some extent, supply problems were anticipated
by the decisions to build VAZ and KamAZ as highly
integrated plants and to establish them as production
associations with control over some of their suppliers.
The decisions to concentrate each of the plants at a
single site were controversial ones. In retrospect,
it appears that their vertical structure has not

solved their supply problems. Indeed, during the
construction stage of the two plants, supply problems appear to have been made worse because the huge
facilities were located in somewhat remote areas,
at considerable distances from supply sources. In
addition, both sites had inadequate labor supplies,
and Soviet authorities had great difficulty in
attracting skilled workers from other parts of the
country. In both cases, the construction and equipping of several smaller plants, instead of a single
concentrated one, might have been easier to manage.
In addition, the imported Western technology
probably would have been better suited for more
decentralized plants, and the problems of coordinating and blending Western and Soviet technological
inputs might have been minimized.

  VAZ and KamAZ have departed from the model of
GAZ and other traditional Soviet plants in several
ways. They are devoting substantial resources to
the establishment of R & D facilities at the plants.
VAZ has established, and KamAZ is planning a network
of stations to ameliorate the chronic service
problems of Soviet automobile users. VAZ is also
making a major effort to penetrate foreign, including Western, markets. Both enterprises have established new management structures which appear to
be heavily influenced by Western management science.
Such innovations have the potential to improve substantially the technological performance of the
Soviet automotive industry. However, the success
of VAZ and KamAZ will depend largely on improvements
in the general Soviet industrial environment in
which they operate.

  In describing Soviet techniques for borrowing
foreign technology, the case study tends to emphasize
problems and shortcomings encountered by the Soviet
recipients. This discussion would not be balanced
without acknowledging the considerable Soviet
achievements in mastering foreign technology. Thus,
each of the projects represented a major technological jump for the Soviet automotive industry. GAZ
and VAZ achieved capacity production (albeit later
than planned) and made substantial contributions
to the Soviet economy. There is little doubt that
KamAZ will do likewise. VAZ and KamAZ may also
serve as models for Soviet industry and contribute
to an improvement in Soviet managerial practices.
Moreover, Soviet officials have achieved important
economic goals while maintaining an unprecedented
degree of control over the technology transfer
process.

These achievements highlight the paradox
described in the introduction to this study. In
view of the many shortcomings in the Soviet absorption of foreign technology, how has the Soviet
Union succeeded in absorbing Western technology on
such a large scale? Why has Western technology
contributed so heavily to Soviet economic development? The case study suggests two explanations
of this apparent paradox. First, the performance of
Soviet techniques and institutions for borrowing
foreign technology has not been uniformly poor.
At times, they have operated reasonably well, particularly in the early stages of the technology transfer process. During the two periods which are the
focus of this study, Soviet officials have retreated
from their reliance on passive mechanisms and strict
control by the foreign trade monopoly. GAZ, VAZ and
KamAZ represent relatively active technology transfer mechanisms by Soviet standards, although they
too presented institutional barriers to effective
absorption of Western technology. One of the primary benefits of the Soviet institutional flexibility, particularly in the current period, has been
a closer, longer-term interaction of Soviet end-
users with foreign firms. Such interaction has
facilitated the transfer of engineering knowhow and,
particularly at VAZ, management skills. In addition,
it has allowed Soviet industrial specialists to
participate actively in the selection and adaptation
of Western technologies. Active Soviet involvement
in the process appears to have contributed to the
transfer of technologies which have been appropriate
to the Soviet industrial environment.

A second and perhaps more important explanation
is the high priority that has been assigned to key
projects using Western technology. The case study
presents evidence that at GAZ, VAZ and KamAZ Soviet
authorities directed designers, builders and suppliers to give first priority to completing the
projects. In some cases, supplies intended for
other parts of the economy were diverted to the
Western-assisted projects. Each of the projects
attracted some of the best technological resources,
such as high-quality materials and talented engineers
and managers. Substantial resources were also allocated to important suppliers. In short, inefficiencies in the technology transfer process have
been compensated for by larger-than-planned expenditures of Soviet domestic resources. This pattern
suggests that the alternative costs of acquiring
foreign technology have been high. Each of the

180

projects was costly not only in terms of labor, capital and material resources, but also in time. Each began production much later than planned. Thus, the case study suggests that the slowness with which foreign technologies are absorbed may be an important contributing factor to the technological lag between Soviet civilian industries and their Western counterparts.

The recognition by many Soviet planners that the absorption of foreign technology has been slow and inefficient has provided a strong incentive to improve the process. While concentration of resources on a few technology transfer projects has resulted in notable successes, such an approach cannot be used to modernize the Soviet economy simultaneously on a wide front. Moreover, the accelerating speed of technological change in many industries makes it imperative that the technology transfer process operate more rapidly. Recognition of these factors has led to Soviet discussion of, and experimentation with, more active technology transfer mechanisms. The Soviet experience in borrowing Western automotive technology in the 1960s and 1970s provides evidence of movement away from the traditional approach and toward what was termed in Chapter 4 the "alternative industrial cooperation model" of technology transfer.

BASIC SOVIET ORIENTATION TO THE INTERNATIONAL ECONOMY

How can one best characterize the basic Soviet orientation or policy toward economic and technological relations with the West? In the introduction, three hypotheses, culled from the Western and Soviet literature on this subject, were identified:

HYPOTHESIS I: The recent upsurge in Soviet trade with the West is part of a cyclical pattern that is observable in the past, most recently during the First Five-Year Plan. Economic historians have pointed to similar periods in pre-Revolutionary Russia, such as the era of Peter the Great and the 1890s and early 1900s. Soviet economic planners follow a strategy of importing as much Western technology as they need to modernize the economy and then cutting off or cutting back to a minimum economic ties with the West. Thus, they pursue a deliberate policy of autarky or economic self-sufficiency, interrupted by occasional

181

expedient resorts to borrowing foreign technology in order to catch up with the West.

HYPOTHESIS II: Soviet leaders have a fundamentally different orientation to the international economy today. Autarky or self-
sufficiency was the goal of Soviet foreign
economic policy during the 1930s (and during
certain Tsarist periods). However, the current
leadership has rejected this strategy in favor
of a policy of technological interdependence
or "interrelatedness" with the West. The new
policy portends continued and deeper commercial
and technological ties with the West.

HYPOTHESIS III: The Soviet Union pursued a
goal of economic and technological independence
in the pre-War period in order to protect itself against a "hostile capitalist encirclement." It has not followed a policy of autarky,
but has consistently encouraged trade with all
countries. Commercial relations with the West
were poor in the 1930s and in the early post-
War period because of trade restrictions and
other hostile actions by Western governments
and capitalist companies and bankers. Trade
relations also worsened because of the international economic situation. The recent upsurge in Soviet trade with the West is explained
by a repudiation by current Western governments
of their old policies.

The evidence presented in this study supports the
acceptance of Hypothesis II and the rejection of the
antithetical Hypothesis I as the closest approxima-
tion of Soviet policy toward economic and technological relations with the West. Some elements of
Hypothesis III are also supported by the evidence.
However, its overall emphasis on the continuity of
Soviet policy in the Stalinist and post-Stalinist
eras is not supported.
     The acceptance of the second hypothesis and the
rejection of the first follows from the foregoing
discussion of the role of Western technology in
Soviet economic development and the evolution of
Soviet institutions and attitudes related to the
technology transfer process. Thus, the exigencies
of a new economic growth strategy dictate a greater
role in Soviet economic growth for technology in
general and for Western technology in particular.
Since the extensive growth pattern of the Stalinist

182

economic model is no longer appropriate for Soviet
conditions, a return to a policy of economic and
technological independence from the West appears
to be precluded. Moreover, the Soviet political
leadership, as evidenced by their statements and
actions, now realize the benefits of continuous
technological exchange with the West and, conversely,
the costs of technological isolationism. Their
attitudes are in sharp contrast to those of the
Stalinist political leadership. The development of
new elite attitudes has been paralleled by the
development of new institutions which promote closer,
longer-term interaction between Soviet enterprises
and Western firms. The new industrial cooperation
arrangements favored by the Soviet leadership represent a major departure from the passive mechanisms
used during the interim period and are more active
than those employed temporarily during the First
Five-Year Plan.

Elements of the third hypothesis are supported
by the evidence presented in this study and elsewhere. The hypothesis provides at least partial
insights into Soviet policy toward economic and
technological relations with the West. Thus, Soviet
suspicions of the motives of Western governments and
firms undoubtedly tempered the Soviet Government's
enthusiamsm for closer commercial ties. In addition,
it is reasonable to assume that trade and credit
restrictions imposed by Western governments has had
a restrictive effect on economic and technological
relations. Moreover, the importance of purely
economic factors (such as the adverse shift in
Soviet terms of trade and growing Soviet indebtedness)
in the timing of the drastic cutback of Soviet technology imports in the 1930s must be acknowledged.

Nevertheless, Hypothesis III is, for several
reasons, an unsatisfactory description of Soviet
policy. Central to the hypothesis is the assumption
that the cutback in economic and technological relations with the West was unpremeditated and was
merely a reaction to external phenomena which were
beyond the control of Soviet policy makers. This
assumption is contradicted by the frequently expressed
(both before and after the cutback) predilection of
Soviet political leaders for a policy of economic
and technological independence. Moreover, the attri-
bution of Stalin's isolationist policy to worsening
Soviet diplomatic relations is belied by the timing
of the cutback: at the end of the First Five-Year
Plan, relations with Germany remained close, if
uneasy, and relations with the United States were

actually improving. Likewise, trade and credit restrictions did not suddenly worsen at that time. (The United States established diplomatic relations with the Soviet Union in 1933, and most-favored-nation tariff treatment was extended to Soviet exports. In 1934, the U.S. Export-Import Bank was established for the primary purpose of granting credits to facilitate U.S.-Soviet trade, although it was not to be used for that purpose until 1973.) In both the pre-war and post-war periods, the Soviet Government has always succeeded in establishing close ties with Western firms when it chose to do so. For example, Ford and other Western firms showed no compunction in providing assistance to GAZ during the First Five-Year Plan, and formal, though unutilized, ties with Ford continued after the First Five-Year Plan. In the 1960s, when credit restrictions and export controls discouraged U.S. firms from taking an active role at VAZ, Soviet authorities found willing partners in Western Europe.

Thus, the general analysis of Western technology transfer to the Soviet Union and the case study support the view that the Soviet approach to economic and technological relations with the West is undergoing a gradual but definitive change. The essence of the Stalinist policy of economic and technological independence was a refusal to rely on imports from the West of either goods or technology which were critical for the most important branches of the economy. Under this policy, the large-scale borrowing of Western technology was a temporary measure, to be discontinued at the earliest possible moment. This is the policy which led to an abrupt cutback of foreign economic and technological relations after the First Five-Year Plan. The policy was reflected in the technology transfer mechanism employed at GAZ, which provided for a complete cutoff of active ties to Western industry after the plant began operation.

The traditional Stalinist strategy is yielding to a new policy of technological interdependence with the West. The new policy implies an acceptance of the need to continuously import technology in order to maintain the pace of technological progress which exists in the rest of the industrial world. Under present Soviet conditions, technological interdependence also implies a need to export technology-intensive manufactured goods to world markets. Such exports are important both to pay for technology imports and to provide a competitive stimulus to domestic technological progress.

The choice among the three hypotheses about Soviet
foreign economic and technological relations is important both for determing the historical record and for
drawing implications for future Soviet policy. Thus,
the conclusion that Soviet leaders have adopted a new
policy of technological interdependence suggests that
they have reassessed the costs and benefits of the
Stalinist approach. Adoption of the new policy implies that Soviet political leaders are willing to
accept greater political and economic costs in order
to reap the benefits of expanded commercial relations
with the West.

Naturally, there is some level of costs, particularly in the political realm, which Soviet leaders
would find unacceptable. If the international or
domestic political situation were perceived by the
leadership to be extremely threatening, a more isolationist posture might be adopted. This study suggests
not that another curtailment of economic and technological ties with the West is impossible, but that
such an initiative would be very costly. Moreover,
it is suggested that Soviet policy makers understand
the costs of technological isolationism much more
clearly today than in the 1930s.

In describing the attitudes of Soviet policy
makers, it is important to acknowledge that differences
of opinion exist within the political and technical
elites and among other "interest groups" in Soviet
politics. While this study has emphasized what
appears to be the predominant views of Soviet policy
makers toward commercial relations with the West, it
does provide examples of disagreement. A more detailed
identification of opposing points of view within the
Soviet hierarchy on this policy issue is outside the
scope of this study. However, further research in
this area could add greatly to our understanding of
the basic Soviet orientation to the international
economy. Central to such research should be a discussion of alternative Soviet policy proposals. Do
opponents of the current leadership approach believe
that technological independence is feasible? Could
the relatively rich technological resources of the
Soviet military be substituted for Western technology
imports? Would a more comprehensive integration of
the economic and technological resources of the Council of Mutual Economic Assistance obviate the need
for Soviet technological interdependence with the
West? An understanding of different Soviet proposals
for solving the problems of insuring domestic technological progress would provide a better basis for
judging the stability of the current leadership's
policy.

Appendixes

APPENDIX A

WESTERN COMPANIES HAVING COOPERATION
AGREEMENTS WITH THE SOVIET STATE COMMITTEE
FOR SCIENCE AND TECHNOLOGY

Western Country	Company
United States	Abbott Laboratories
	Allis-Chalmers
	American Can Co.
	American Home Products
	Armco Steel
	Arthur Andersen
	Bechtel Corp.
	Bendix Corp.
	Boeing Co.
	Bristol-Myers
	Brown & Root
	Burroughs Corp.
	Coca-Cola
	Colgate-Palmolive
	Control Data Corp.
	Corning International
	Deere & Co.
	Dresser Industries
	FMC Corp.
	General Electric
	General Dynamics
	Gould, Inc.
	Gulf Oil
	H. H. Robertson Co.
	Hewlett-Packard
	ITT Corporation
	Industrial Nucleonics
	International Harvester
	International Paper
	Kaiser Industries
	Litton Industries
	Lockheed
	R. J. Reynolds Industries
	Rohm & Haas
	Stanford Research Institute
	Singer Co.
	Sperry Rand
	Standard Oil of Indiana
	Union Oil Products
	Union Carbide

*Through mid-1976.

Western Country	Company
United States	Varian Associates
	Louis Berger, Inc.
	McKinsey & Co.
	Monsanto
	Norton Simon
	Occidental Petroleum
	Pepsico Inc.
	Pfizer International, Inc.
	Phillip Morris
	Phillips Petroleum
	Raymond Loewy
	Reichold Chemicals
	Revlon International
West Germany	Schering AB
	Werkzeugmaschinen-Fabrik Gildemeister
	Runrkohle AG
	Krupp
	Lurgi-Gessellschaften
	Otto Wolff AG
	Robert Bosch
	Daimler-Benz
	AEG-Telefunken
	Kimsch
	Thyssen-Roehenwerke
	Bayer
	Siemens
	Hoeschst
	Degussa
	Henkel
	BASF
	Hemscheidt
Austria	Schoeller Bleckmann Stahlwerke
	Voest
	Manfred Swarovaki GMBH
Italy	Pirelli-Dunlop
	Sina Viscosa
	Metenco
	Liquichimica
	Finmeccanica
	Monticatini Edison
	E.N.I.
	Pressindustria
	FIAT

Western Country	Company
Canada	Polysar Ltd.
	Canadian Broadcasting Co.
Netherlands	Synres Nederland Sigma
	Verenigde Machinefabrieken
	AKZO NV
Switzerland	Durisol AG
Belgium	Picanol
United Kingdom	Marconi Ltd.
	Dunlop-Pirelli
	Lucas Industries
	Rank Xerox
	Rolls Royce
	Beecham Group
	Shell Oil
Sweden	Volvo
	LKB Producter
	Sandvik
Japan	Mitsubishi
	Mitsui
	Tokyo Boeki
	Mayekawa
	Teijin Co.
	C. Itoh Co.
Finland	W. Rosenlew
France	Moet Hennessy
	Renault

Source: Lawrence H. Theriot, "U.S. Governmental and Private Industry Cooperation with the Soviet Union in the Fields of Science and Technology," in Soviet Economy in a New Perspective, U.S. Congress, Joint Economic Committee, Joint Committee Print (Washington, D.C.: Government Printing Office, October 14, 1976), pp. 763-66. The list of foreign companies was derived from published sources and is not complete. Several companies have been added to Theriot's original list.

APPENDIX B

MAJOR SOVIET COMPENSATION PROJECTS, 1976

Partner/Country	Project	Value (millions)	Soviet Product Payment
France	Gas field equipment	$250.0	Natural gas
Austria	Large diameter pipe	400.0	Do.
Italy	do	190.0	Do.
Finland	Pipe	NA	Do.
West Germany	Large diameter pipe	1,500.0	Do.
France, Austria, West Germany	Large diameter pipe and equipment	900.0	Do.
Japan	Forestry handling equipment	163.0	Timber products
Do.	Wood chip plant	45.0	Wood chips and pulp
Do.	Forestry handling equipment	500.0	Timber products
France	Pulp paper complex	60.0	Wood pulp
United Kingdom	Shoes	3.2	Food products, toys
West Germany	Polyethylene plant	39.0	Polyethylene
Do.	do	61.0	Do.
France	Styrene/polystyrene	100.0	Polystyrene
Italy	Chemical plants (7)	600.0	Ammonia
United Kingdom/United States	Polyethylene plant	50.0	Polyethylene
France	Ammonia plants (4)	220.0	Ammonia
Italy	Chemical plants (6)	670.0	Chemical products

APPENDIX B (cont.)

MAJOR SOVIET COMPENSATION PROJECTS, 1976

Partner/Country	Project	Value (millions)	Soviet Product Payment
United States	Ammonia plants (4)	200.0+	Ammonia
Do.	Fertilizer storage and handling facilities	100.0	Do.
France	Ammonia pipeline	200.0	Ammonia
United States	do	100.0	Do.
Italy	Surface active detergent plant	NA	Organic chemicals, surface active detergents
Do.	Polypropylene	100–130.0	Chemical intermediates
United States	Equipment, cola concentrates	NA	Vodka
Japan	Oil exploration	150–250.0	Oil and gas
Italy	Large diameter pipe	1,500.0	Scrap metal, coal, iron ore
Japan	Coal Development equipment	450.0	Coal
West Germany	Steel complex	1,200.0	Pellets, steel products
France	Aluminum refinery	1,000.0	Aluminum
West Germany	Ethylene, oxide/glycol plant	80.0	Related products

APPENDIX B (cont.)

MAJOR SOVIET COMPENSATION PROJECTS, 1976

Source: Central Intelligence Agency, cited in Maureen R. Smith, "Industrial Coopera-
tion Agreements: Soviet Experience and Practice." In Joint Economic Committee,
Soviet Economy in a New Perspective, Joint Committee Print (Washington, D.C.:
Government Printing Office, October 14, 1976, p. 773.

APPENDIX C

SOVIET AUTOMOBILE PRODUCTION

Year	Total	Trucks	Passenger Cars	Buses
1924	10	10	--	--
1925	116	116	--	--
1926	366	366	--	--
1927	478	475	3	--
1928	841	740	50	51
1929	1,712	1,471	156	85
1930	4,226	4,019	160	47
1931	4,005	3,915	--	90
1932	23,879	23,748	34	97
1933	49,710	39,101	10,259	350
1934	72,437	54,572	17,110	755
1935	96,716	76,854	18,969	893
1936	136,488	131,546	3,679	1,263
1937	199,857	180,339	18,250	1,268
1938	211,114	182,373	26,986	1,755
1939	201,687	178,769	19,647	3,271
1940	145,390	135,958	5,511	3,921
1945	74,657	68,548	4,995	1,114
1946	102,171	94,572	6,289	1,310
1947	132,968	121,248	9,622	2,098
1948	197,056	173,908	20,175	2,973
1949	275,992	226,854	45,661	3,477
1950	362,895	294,402	64,554	3,939
1951	288,683	229,777	53,646	5,260
1952	307,936	243,465	59,663	4,808
1953	354,175	270,667	77,380	6,128
1954	403,873	300,613	94,728	8,532
1955	445,268	328,047	107,806	9,415
1956	464,632	356,415	97,792	10,425
1957	495,408	369,504	113,588	12,316
1958	511,074	374,900	122,191	13,983
1959	494,994	351,373	124,519	19,102
1960	523,591	362,008	138,822	22,761
1961	555,330	381,617	148,914	24,799
1962	577,480	382,355	165,945	29,180
1963	587,012	382,220	173,122	31,670
1964	603,084	385,006	185,159	32,919
1965	616,312	379,630	201,175	35,507
1966	675,211	407,633	230,251	37,327
1967	728,751	437,350	251,441	39,960
1968	800,836	478,147	280,332	42,357
1969	844,186	504,529	293,558	46,099

SOVIET AUTOMOBILE PRODUCTION

Year	Total	Trucks	Passenger Cars	Buses
1970	916,118	524,507	344,248	47,363
1971	1,142,607	564,250	529,041	49,316
1972*	1,378,800	596,800	730,100	51,900
1973	1,602,200	629,500	916,700	56,000
1974	1,846,000	666,000	1,119,000	61,000
1975	1,964,000	696,000	1,201,000	67,000

*1972-1975 figures are rounded

Source: U.S.S.R. Sovet Ministrov. Tsentral'noe Statisticheskoe Upravlenie. Promyshlennost' SSSR (1964); Narodnoe khoziaistvo SSSR 1927-1972 gg. (1972); Narodnoe khoziaistvo SSSR v 1975 g. (1976). Moscow: Statistika.

APPENDIX D

SOVIET EXPORTS OF AUTOMOBILES, 1966-1976

Year	Trucks	Passenger Cars	Buses	Total
1966	29,700	66,500	1,400	97,600
1967	33,800	68,900	1,600	104,300
1968	29,100	82,300	1,200	112,600
1969	31,500	73,800	1,100	106,400
1970	34,900	83,800	1,400	119,700
1971	31,700	149,700	2,200	183,600
1972	35,600	194,900	1,300	231,800
1973	34,300	237,500	2,000	273,800
1974	32,500	287,300	2,300	322,100
1975	33,500	295,600	2,000	331,100
1976	31,900	344,700	2,100	378,700

Source: U.S.S.R. Ministerstvo Vneshnei Torgovli, Vneshniaia torgovlia za god, statisticheskii obzor. Moscow: Vneshtorgizdat.

Bibliography

SELECTED BIBLIOGRAPHY

<u>Technology Transfer: Technology and
Economic Growth (General)</u>

Balasubramanyam, V. N. <u>International Transfer of
Technology to India</u>. New York: Praeger, 1973.
Baranson, Jack. <u>Automotive Industries in Developing
Countries</u>. Baltimore: The Johns Hopkins Press,
1969.
_____ . <u>Industrial Technologies for Developing
Economies</u>. New York: Frederick A. Praeger,
Publishers, 1969.
Basche, James R., Jr., and Duerr, Michael G. <u>Inter-
national Transfer of Technology: A Worldwide
Survey of Chief Executives</u>. New York: The
Conference Board, 1975.
Caves, Richard E., and Uekusa, Masu. <u>Industrial
Organization in Japan</u>. Washington, D.C.: The
Brookings Institution, 1976.
Crain, Ben. "The Regulation of Direct Foreign Invest-
ment in Australia, Canada, France, Japan and
Mexico." Unpublished report, Library of
Congress, Congressional Research Service, 74-52E,
February 28, 1974.
Denison, Edward F. <u>Accounting for United States
Economic Growth, 1929-1969</u>. Washington, D.C.:
The Brookings Institution, 1974.
_____ . <u>The Sources of Economic Growth in the
United States and the Alternatives Before Us</u>.
New York: Committee for Economic Development,
1962.
_____ . Assisted by Jean-Pierre Pouillier. <u>Why
Growth Rates Differ: Postwar Experience in
Nine Western Countries</u>. Washington, D.C.:
The Brookings Institution, 1967.
Dunning, John H. "Technology, United States Invest-
ment and European Economic Growth." <u>The Inter-
national Corporation, A Symposium</u>. Edited
by Charles P. Kindleberger. Cambridge, Mass.:
The M.I.T. Press, 1970.
Gabriel, Peter P. <u>The International Transfer of
Corporate Skills: Management Contracts in
Less Developed Countries</u>. Boston: Harvard
University Press, 1967.
Gomulka, Stanislaw. <u>Inventive Activity, Diffusion
and the Stages of Economic Growth</u>. Denmark:
Aarhus, 1971.
Gruber, William H., and Marquis, Donald G., eds.
<u>Factors in the Transfer of Technology</u>. Cambridge,
Mass.: The M.I.T. Press, 1969.

Hu, Y. S. The Impact of U.S. Investment in Europe:
    A Case Study of the Automotive and Computer
    Industries. New York: Praeger Publishers, 1973.
Hufbauer, G. C. Synthetic Materials and the Theory
    of International Trade. Cambridge, Mass.:
    Harvard University Press, 1966.
Humphrey, Thomas M. "Changing Views of Comparative
    Advantage." Federal Reserve Bank of Richmond:
    Monthly Review, LVIII (July, 1972), 9-15.
India. National Council of Applied Economic Research.
    Foreign Technology and Investment (A Study of
    their Role in India's Industrialization).
    New Delhi, June 1971.
Jackson, Sarah. Economically Appropriate Technologies
    for Developing Countries. Washington, D.C.:
    Overseas Development Council, 1972.
Johnson, Harry G. Technology and Economic Inter-
    dependence. New York: St. Martin's Press,
    1975.
Keesing, D. B. "Labor Skills and Comparative Advan-
    tage." American Economic Review, LVI (May, 1966),
    249-58.
Komzin, B. "Iaponskii put' nauchno-tekhnicheskogo
    razvitiia." Mirovaia ekonomika i mezhdunarodnye
    otnosheniia, June, 1973.
Langrish, L., et al. Wealth from Knowledge: A Study
    of Innovation in Industry. London: MacMillan,
    1972.
Layton, Christopher; Harlow, Christopher; and
    DeHoughton, Charles. Ten Innovations: An
    International Study on Technological Development
    and the Use of Qualified Scientists and Engineers
    in Ten Industries. New York: Crane, Russak
    & Company, Inc., 1972.
Mansfield, Edwin. Technological Change. New York:
    W. W. Norton & Company, Inc., 1971.
_____. "Technology and Technological Change."
    Economic Analysis and the Multinational Enter-
    prise. Edited by John H. Dunning. London:
    George Allen & Unwin Ltd., 1974.
Mason, R. Hal. "The Selection of Technology: A
    Continuing Dilemma." Columbia Journal of World
    Business, IX (summer, 1974), 29-34.
Morrall, John F. III. Human Capital, Technology, and
    the Role of the United States in International
    Trade. Gainesville, Fla.: University of
    Florida Press, 1972.
Nau, Henry R. Technology Transfer and U.S. Foreign
    Policy. New York: Praeger Publishers, 1976.
Nelson, Richard R.; Peck, Merton J.; and Kalachek,
    Edward D. Technology, Economic Growth and

Public Policy. Washington, D.C.: The Brookings
Institution, 1967.
Obminskii, E. "Rynok tekhnologii i razvivaiushchiecia
strany." Mirovaia ekonomika i mezhdunarodnye
otnosheniia, September, 1975, pp. 40-50.
Organisation for Economic Co-operation and Development.
The Conditions for Success in Technological Inno-
vation. Paris, 1971.
_____. Gaps in Technology: Analytical Report.
Paris, 1970.
_____. Science, Economic Growth and Government
Policy, by Christopher Freeman, M. Raymond
Poignant, and Ingvar Svennilson. Paris, 1963.
_____. The Transfer of Technology, by Edward P.
Hawthorne, Paris, 1971.
Ozawa. Terutomo. Japan's Technological Challenge
to the West, 1950-1974: Motivation and
Accomplishment. Cambridge, Mass.: The M.I.T.
Press, 1974.
Posner, Michael. "International Trade and Technical
Changes." Oxford Economic Papers, XIII
(October, 1961), 323-41.
Quinn, James Brian. "Technology Transfer by Multi-
national Companies." Harvard Business Review,
XLVII (November-December, 1969), 160-61.
Rodriguez, Carlos Alfredo. "Trade in Technological
Knowledge and the National Advantage,"
Journal of Political Economy, LXXXIII (February,
1975), 121-35.
Rosenberg, Nathan, ed. The Economics of Technological
Change: Selected Readings. Baltimore: Penguin
Books, 1971.
Servan-Schreiber, J. J. The American Challenge.
New York: Atheneum, 1968.
Solo, Robert A., and Rogers, Everett M. Inducing
Technological Change for Economic Growth and
Development. n.p.: Michigan State University
Press, 1972.
Solow, Robert. "Technical Change and the Aggregate
Production Function." Review of Economics and
Statistics, XXXIX (August, 1957), 312-20.
Spencer, Daniel Lloyd. Technology Gap in Perspective:
Strategy of International Technology Transfer.
New York: Spartan Books, 1970.
_____, and Woroniak, Alexander. "The Feasibility
of Developing Transfer of Technology Functions."
Kyklos, XX, No. 2, 1967, 431-59.
_____. The Transfer of Technology to Developing
Countries. New York: Praeger, 1967.
Teece, David J. The Multinational Corporation and
the Resource Cost of International Technology

Transfer. Cambridge, Mass.: Ballinger Pub-
lishing Company, 1976.
Tilton, John E. International Diffusion of Technology:
The Case of Semi-conductors. Washington, D.C.:
The Brookings Institution, 1971.
Tsurumi, Yoshihiro. "Technology Transfer and Foreign
Trade: The Case of Japan, 1950-1966." Unpub-
lished Ph.D. dissertation, Harvard University,
1968.
"UNCTAD: The Transfer of Technology." Journal of
World Trade Law, IV (September-October, 1970),
692-718.
United Nations. Conference on Trade and Development.
Secretariat. Guidelines for the Study of the
Transfer of Technology to Developing Countries.
New York, 1972.
_____. Restrictive Business Practices. (TD/B/C2/
104). New York, 1971.
_____. Department of Economic and Social Affairs.
The Acquisition of Technology from Multinational
Corporations by Developing Countries. (ST/ESA/
12). New York, 1974.
_____. Transport Modes and Technologies for
Development. (ST/ECA/127). New York, 1970.
_____. Industrial Development Organization.
Establishment and Development of Automotive
Industries in Developing Countries. Report and
proceedings of seminar held in Karlovy Vary,
Czechoslovakia, February 24-March 14, 1969,
Part I: Report of the Seminar. New York, 1970.
_____. Institute for Training and Research.
International Transfer of Automotive Technology
to Developing Countries, by Jack Baranson.
UNITAR Research Reports, no. 8. New York, 1971.
_____. The International Transfer of Commercial
Technology to Developing Countries, by Walter A.
Chudson. UNITAR Research Reports, no. 13.
New York, 1971.
_____. The Transfer of Technology and the Factor
Proportions Problem: The Phillipines and
Mexico, by R. Hal Mason. UNITAR Research
Reports, no. 10. New York, 1971.
U.S. Congress. House. Committee on International
Relations. Subcommittee on International
Security and Scientific Affairs. International
Transfer of Technology: An Agenda of National
Security Issues. Committee Print. Washington,
D.C.: Government Printing Office, February 13,
1978.
_____. Science and Technology in the Department
of State: Bringing Technical Content Into

Diplomatic Policy and Operations, by Franklin P.
Huddle. Committee Print. Washington, D.C.:
Government Printing Office, June 1975.
_____. Committee on Science and Technology.
Science Policy, A Working Glossary, by Franklin
P. Huddle. Committee Print. Washington, D.C.:
Government Printing Office, March 1976.
_____. Joint Economic Committee. Subcommittee on
Economic Growth. Technology, Economic Growth
and International Competitiveness, by Robert
Gilpen. Joint Committee Print. Washington,
D.C.: Government Printing Office, July 9, 1975.
U.S. Department of Defense. Office of the Director
of Defense Research and Engineering. Defense
Science Board Task Force on Export of U.S.
Technology. An Analysis of Export Control of
U.S. Technology--A DOD Perspective, Washington,
D.C., February 4, 1976.
Vaitsos, Constantine V. "Strategic Choices in the
Commercialization of Technology: The Point of
View of Developing Countries." Social Science
Journal, XXV, No. 3, 1973, 370-86.
Vernon, Raymond. "International Investment and
International Trade in the Product Cycle."
Quarterly Journal of Economics, LXXX (May, 1966),
190-207.
_____, ed. The Technology Factor in International
Trade. New York: National Bureau for Economic
Research, 1970. (Distributed by Columbia
University Press.)
Wells, Louis T., Jr., ed. The Product Life Cycle
and International Trade. Boston: Harvard
University Press, 1972.
Williams, B. R., ed. Science and Technology in
Economic Growth. Proceedings of a Conference
held by the International Economic Association
at St. Anton, Austria. New York: John Wiley
& Sons, 1973.
Wionczek, Miguel S. "Changing Attitudes in the
Developing World." Intereconomics, No. 1,
1973, p. 6-8.

Soviet Domestic Economic and
Technological Development

Afanas'ev, Viktor Grigor'evich. Nauchno-tekhnicheskaia
revoliutsiia, upravlenie, obrazovanie. Moscow:
Izdatel'stvo politicheskoi literatury, 1972.
Amann, R. Soviet Science Policy: Some Strategies
for the Seventies. Centre for Russian and East
European Studies, University of Birmingham.

Discussion paper no. 8, Series RC/C8. Birming-
ham, England, July 1972.
Amann, R.; Cooper, Julian; and Davies, Bob. "No
Change on the Eastern Front." New Scientist,
LXXVI (November 24, 1977), 477-80.
Armstrong, John A. The European Administrative Elite.
Princeton: Princeton University Press, 1973.
Bailes, Kendall E. "The Politics of Technology:
Stalin and Technocratic Thinking Among Soviet
Engineers." American Historical Review, LXXIX
(April, 1974), 445-69.
Baibakov, N. K., ed. Gosudarstvennyi piatletnii plan
razvitiia narodnogo khoziaistva SSSR na 1971-
1975 godu. Moscow: Izdatel'stvo politcheskoi
literatury, 1972.
Balz, M. W. Invention and Innovation Under Soviet
Law: A Comparative Analysis. Toronto and
London: Lexington Books, D. C. Heath, 1975.
Bergson, Abram. Economic Trends in the Soviet
Union. Cambridge, Mass.: Harvard University
Press, 1963.
_____. Soviet Post-War Economic Development.
Stockholm: Almqvist & Siksell International,
1974.
_____. "Toward a New Growth Model." Problems
of Communism, March-April, 1973, pp. 1-9.
Berliner, Joseph. "The Economics of Overtaking and
Surpassing." Industrialization in Two Systems:
Essays in Honor of Alexander Gerschenkron.
Edited by Henry Rosovsky. New York: John
Wiley & Sons, Inc., 1966, pp. 159-185.
_____. The Innovation Decision in Soviet Industry.
Cambridge, Mass.: The M.I.T. Press, 1976.
Bliakhman, L. "Glavnyi vyigrysh--vremia: zametki o
problemakh uskoreniia nauchno-tekhnicheskogo
progress." Neva, no. 1, 1973, pp. 173-81.
Bogushevskii, Vladimir Sergeevich, ed. Sovetskaia
promyshlennost' v tret'em reshaiushchem godu
piatletki. Moscow: Izdatel'stvo VSNKh SSSR,
1931.
Boncher, William H. "Innovation and Technical Adap-
tation in the Russian Economy: The Growth in
Unit Power of the Russian Mainline Freight
Locomotive." Unpublished Ph.D. dissertation,
Indiana University, 1976.
Boretsky, Michael. "Comparative Progress in Tech-
nology, Productivity, and Economic Efficiency:
U.S.S.R. Versus U.S.A." U.S. Congress. Joint
Economic Committee. New Directions in the Soviet
Economy. Part II-A: Economic Performance.
Joint Committee Print. Washington, D.C.:
Government Printing Office, 1966, pp. 133-256.

Burks, R. V. "Technology and Political Change in
     Eastern Europe." Change in Communist Systems.
     Edited by Chalmers Johnson. Stanford: Stanford
     University Press, 1970, pp. 265-311.
Cohn, Stanley H. "The Soviet Path to Economic
     Growth: A Comparative Analysis." Review of
     Income and Wealth, March, 1976, pp. 49-59.
Cooper, J. M. The Concept of the Scientific and
     Technical Revolution in Soviet Theory. Center
     for Russian and East European Studies, Birming-
     ham University. Discussion paper No. 9, Series
     RC/C. Birmingham, England, 1973.
Danilovtsev, P., and Kanygin, Iu. Ot laboratorii
     do zavoda. Novosibirsk: Zapadno-Sibirskoe
     knizhnoe izdatel'stvo, 1971.
Dobb, Maurice. Soviet Economic Development Since
     1917. London: Routledge and Kegan Paul Ltd.,
     1948.
Dodge, Norton T. "Trends in Labor Productivity in
     the Soviet Tractor Industry: A Case Study in
     Industrial Development." Unpublished Ph.D.
     dissertation, Harvard University, 1960.
Erlich, Alexander. The Soviet Industrialization Debate,
     1924-1928. Cambridge, Mass.: Harvard University
     Press, 1960.
Fallenbuchl, Zbigniew M., ed. Economic Development
     in the Soviet Union and Eastern Europe, Volume
     I: Reforms, Technology and Income Distribution.
     New York: Praeger Publishers, 1975.
Fleron, Frederic J., Jr., ed. Technology and Commu-
     nist Culture: The Socio-Cultural Impact of
     Technology under Socialism. New York: Praeger
     Publishers, 1977.
Gerschenkron, Alexander. Economic Backwardness in
     Historical Perspective. New York: Praeger,
     1962.
Granick, David. "On Patterns of Technological
     Choice in Soviet Industry." American Economic
     Review, LII (May, 1962), 149-57.
_____. Soviet Introduction of New Technology: A
     Depiction of the Process. Prepared for the
     Defense Advanced Research Projects Agency.
     Stanford Research Institute, Strategic Studies
     Center. SRI Project 2625. January 1975.
_____. Soviet Metal-Fabricating and Economic
     Development: Practice versus Policy. Madison:
     University of Wisconsin Press, 1967.
Grossman, Gregory. "Scarce Capital and Soviet
     Doctrine." Quarterly Journal of Economics,
     LXVII (August, 1953).
Gvishiani, D. Organisation and Management: A

Sociological Analysis of Western Theories.
    Moscow: Progress Publishers, 1972.
Hardt, John P., and Modig, Carl. "Stalinist Indus-
    trial Development in Soviet Russia." The
    Soviet Union: a Half Century of Communism.
    Edited by Kurt London. Baltimore: The Johns
    Hopkins Press, 1968.
Khavin, Abram Fishelevich. Kratkiy ocherk istorii
    industrializatsii SSSR. Moscow: Izdatel'stvo
    politicheskoi literatury, 1962.
Kheinman, S. A. "Mashinostroenie: perspektivy i
    reservy." Ekonomika i organizatsiia
    promyshlennogo proizvodstva, November-December,
    1974, pp. 37-62.
Kim, M. P. et al., eds. Industrializatsiia SSSR,
    1929-1932 gg., dokumenty i materialy. Moscow:
    Izdatel'stvo Nauka, 1970.
McKay, John P. Pioneers for Profit: Foreign
    Entrepreneurship and Russian Industrialization,
    1885-1913. Chicago: The University of Chicago
    Press, 1970.
Moorsteen, Richard, and Powell, Raymond P. The
    Soviet Capital Stock, 1928-1962. Homewood, Ill.:
    Richard D. Irwin, Inc., 1966.
Nimitz, Nancy. The Structure of Soviet Outlays on
    R&D in 1960 and 1968. Rand, R-1207-DDRE. Santa
    Monica, California, June, 1974.
New Methods of Economic Management in the USSR.
    Moscow: Novosti Press Agency Publishing House,
    1965.
Nove, Alec. An Economic History of the U.S.S.R.
    Baltimore: Penguin Books, 1972.
Ordzhonikidze, S. Itogi razvitiia promyshlennosti
    za 1931 g. i zadachi 1932 g.: doklad i
    zakliuchitel'noe slovo na XVII Vsesoiuznoi
    konferentsii VKP(b). Moscow: Partiinoe
    izdatel'stvo, 1932.
_____. Zavershim rekonstruktsiiu vsego narodnogo
    khoziaistva: rech' na XVII s"ezde VKP (b).
    Moscow: Partiinoe izdatel'stvo, 1934.
Organisation for Economic Co-operation and Develop-
    ment. Directorate for Scientific Affairs.
    Science Policy in the USSR. Paris, 1968.
Osip'ian, A., and Iapidus, M. Industrializatsiia--
    osnova ekonomicheskoi nezavisimosti SSSR.
    Moscow: Moskovskii rabochii, 1928.
Oznobin, N. M.; Rogov, A. I.; and Klinskii, A. I.
    Tekhnicheskii progress i planomernoe razvitie
    narodnogo khoziaistva. Moscow: "Mysl'," 1971.
Reynolds, Lloyd G., ed. The Economics of Technologi-
    cal Progress. Papers presented at a U.S.-U.S.S.R.

206

Symposium, Moscow, June 8-11, 1976. (Available
from Lloyd G. Reynolds, Department of Economics,
Yale University.)

Schroeder, Gertrude E. "Soviet Technology: System
vs. Progress." Problems of Communism, September-
October, 1970, pp. 19-30.

Slama, Jiri, and Vogel, Heinrich. "On the Measure-
ment of Technological Levels for the Soviet
Economy." Forschungsbericht 1974. Munich:
Osteuropa-Institut, 1974.

Smolinski, Leon. "The Scale of Soviet Industrial
Establsihment." Unpublished Ph.D. dissertation,
Columbia University, 1960.

Spechler, Martin C. "The Pattern of Technological
Achievement in the Soviet Enterprise." ACES
Bulletin, XVII (summer, 1975), 63-87.

Spulber, Nicolas, ed. Foundations of Soviet Strategy
for Economic Growth: Selected Soviet Essays,
1924-1930. Bloomington: Indiana University
Press, 1964.

Staritskiy, V. "The Reconstruction of Industrial
Enterprises Under the Conditions of the Scientific and Technical Revolution. Kommunist,
No. 2, January, 1973, pp. 64-75. (Translated
in Joint Publications Research Service. Translations from Kommunist, March 12, 1973.)

Subotskiy, Yu. "The Associations in the Economic
System of Developed Socialism." Kommunist,
No. 13, September, 1973, pp. 52-64. (Translated
by Joint Publications Research Service, October
25, 1973.)

U.S. Central Intelligence Agency. Soviet Economic
Plans for 1976-80: A First Look (ER 76-10471),
August, 1976.
_____. The Soviet Economy: Performance in 1975
and Prospects for 1976. (ER 76-10296), May,
1976.

U.S. Congress. Joint Economic Committee. East
European Economies Post-Helsinki. Joint
Committee Print. Washington, D.C.: Government
Printing Office, August 25, 1977.
_____. Soviet Economic Prospects for the Seven-
ties. Joint Committee Print. Washington, D.C.:
Government Printing Office, June 27, 1973.
_____. Soviet Economy in a New Perspective. Joint
Committee Print. Washington, D.C.: Government
Printing Office, October 14, 1976.

U.S. Department of Commerce. Foreign Demographic
Analysis Division. Sources of Financing the
Stages of the Research, Development and Innova-
tion Cycle in the U.S.S.R., by Louvan E. Nolting.
Foreign Economic Reports, No. 3. September 1973.

U.S. National Science Foundation. Office of Science
    Information Service. The U.S.S.R. Scientific
    and Technical Information System: A U.S. View.
    Report of the U.S. participants in the U.S./
    U.S.S.R. Symposium on Scientific and Technical
    Information, Moscow, June 18-30, 1973. Washing-
    ton, D.C., October 1973. (Distributed by the
    National Technical Information Service.)
Wilber, Charles K. The Soviet Model and Under-
    developed Countries. Chapel Hill: The Univer-
    sity of North Carolina Press, 1969.
Wilczynski, Jozef. Technology in Comecon: Accelera-
    tion of Technological Progress Through Economic
    Planning and the Market. New York: Praeger
    Publishers, 1974.
Zaleski, Eugene. Planning for Economic Growth in
    the Soviet Union, 1918-1932. Translated and
    edited by Marie-Christine MacAndrew and
    G. Warren Nutter. Chapel Hill: The University
    of North Carolina Press, 1962.

Soviet Foreign Economic and Technological Relations

Adler-Karlsson, Gunnar. Western Economic Warfare,
    1947-1967: A Case Study in Foreign Economic
    Policy. Stockholm: Almqvist & Wiksell, 1968.
Artem'ev, I. E., and Sheidina, I. L. "Nauchno-
    tekhnicheskie sviazi: pervye itogi." SShA:
    Ekonomika, politika, ideologiia, May, 1977.
Baykov, Alexander. Soviet Foreign Trade. Princeton:
    Princeton University Press, 1946.
Berliner, Joseph S. "Soviet Foreign Economic Compe-
    tition." Readings on the Soviet Economy.
    Edited by Franklyn D. Holzman. Chicago: Rand
    McNally, 1962.
Bogomolov, O. "O vneshneekonomicheskikh sviaziakh
    SSSR." Kommunist. March, 1974.
Boltho, Andrea. Foreign Trade Criteria in Socialist
    Economies. Cambridge: The University Press,
    1971.
Boyeff, Ivan V. "The Soviet State Monopoly of
    Foreign Trade." The Soviet Union and World
    Problems. Edited by Samuel N. Harper. Chicago:
    University of Chicago Press, 1935.
Branscomb, Lewis M. Science, Technology and Detente.
    Program of Policy Studies in Science and Tech-
    nology, The George Washington University.
    Occasional Paper No. 17. Washington, D.C.,
    March, 1975.

Bron, Saul G. *Soviet Economic Development and American Business*. New York: Horace Liveright, 1930.

Brown, Alan A., and Neuberger, Egon. *International Trade and Central Planning: An Analysis of Interactions*. Berkeley: University of California Press, 1968.

Brzak, V., and Marsikova, D. "New Methods of Management and Organization of Foreign Trade in Socialist Countries (A Comparative Analysis)." *Soviet and Eastern European Foreign Trade*, VI (Fall-Winter, 1970), 214-67.

Budish, J. M., and Shipman, S. S. *Soviet Foreign Trade: Menace or Promise*. New York: Horace Liveright, Inc., 1931.

Business International, S. A. *Doing Business With the U.S.S.R.* Geneva, 1971.

Campbell, Robert W., and Marer, Paul, eds. *East-West Trade and Technology Transfer: An Agenda of Research Needs*. Proceedings of a Conference. International Development Research Center, Bloomington, Indiana, 1974.

Carr, Edward Hallett, and Davies, R. W. *Foundation of a Planned Economy*. New York: The MacMillan Company, 1969.

Cherviakov, Pavel A. *Organizatsiia i tekhnika vneshnei torgovli SSSR*. Moscow: Vneshtorgizdat, 1958.

Dohan, Michael R. "The Economic Origins of Soviet Autarky, 1927/28-1934." *Slavic Review*, LXV (December, 1976), 603-35.

_____, and Hewett, Edward. *Two Studies in Soviet Terms of Trade 1918-1970*. Bloomington, Indiana: International Development Research Center, 1973.

Dyck, Harvey L. *Weimar Germany and Soviet Russia, 1926-1933: A Study in Diplomatic Instability*. New York: Columbia University Press, 1966.

Dzhibladze, Dmitrii Nestorovich. *Kontsessionnye predpriiatiia v Zakavkaz'e 1926-1929 gg.* Tbilisi: Izdatel'stvo "Sabchota Sakartvelo," 1973.

Eventov, Lev Iakovlevich. *Inostrannye kapitaly v russkoi promyshlennosti*. Moscow: Sotsial'no-ekonomicheskoe izdatel'stvo, 1931.

Fomin, B. S. *Ekonometricheskie teorii i modeli mezhdunarodnykh ekonomicheskikh otnoshenii*. Moscow: Izdatel'stvo "Mysl'," 1970.

Fokin, D. F., ed. *Vneshniaia torgovlia SSSR (1946-1963 gg.)*. Moscow: Izdatel'stvo "mezhdunarodnye otnosheniia," 1964.

Frumkin, A. B. *Kritika sovremennykh burzhuaznykh teorii mezhdunarodnykh ekonomicheskikh otnoshenii*. Moscow: Vneshtorgizdat, 1964.

Frumkin, A. B. "O nekotorykh burzhuaznykh vzgliadakh
    na sovetskuiu torgovlia." Vneshniaia torgovlia,
    October, 1974, p. 49.
Gerschenkron, Alexander. Economic Relations with
    the U.S.S.R. New York: The Committee on
    International Economic Policy and the Carnegie
    Endowment for International Peace, 1945.
Giffin, James Henry. The Legal and Practical Aspects
    of Trade with the Soviet Union. Revised ed.
    New York: Praeger Publishers, 1971.
Ginzburg, Iosif Samoilovich. Vneshniaia torgovlia
    SSSR. Moscow: Gosudarstvennoe sotsial'no-
    ekonomicheskoe izdatel'stvo, 1937.
Goldman, Marshall I. Detente and Dollars: Doing
    Business with the Soviets. New York: Basic
    Books, Inc., 1975.
Gorbunov, Rem Grigor'evich. Sovetsko-Amerikanskie
    torgovye otnosheniia. Moscow: Vneshtorgizdat,
    1961.
Gorodisskiy, M. I. Licenses in U.S.S.R. Foreign
    Trade. Translated by the National Technical
    Information Service. Moscow: Mezhdunarodnye
    otnosheniia, 1972.
Grinko, G. T. The Five-Year Plan of the Soviet
    Union, A Political Interpretation. New York:
    International Publishers, 1930.
Grub, Phillip, and Holbik, Karel, eds. American-
    East European Trade: Controversy, Progress,
    Prospects. Washington, D.C.: The National
    Press, Inc., 1969.
Gvishiani, A. "Nauchno-tekhnicheskaia revoliutsiia
    i ekonomicheskoe sotrudnichestvo." Vneshniaia
    torgovlia, No. 12, 1973, pp. 2-5.
Hanson, Philip. External Influences on the Soviet
    Economy Since the Mid-1950's: The Import of
    Western Technology. Center for Russian and
    East European Studies, University of Birmingham.
    Discussion Paper, No. 7. Birmingham, England,
    n.d.
_____. U.S.S.R.: Foreign Trade Implications of
    the 1976-80 Plan. EIU Special Report No. 36.
    London: The Economist Intelligence Unit Ltd.,
    October 1976.
Hardt, John P., ed. Tariff, Legal and Credit Con-
    straints on East-West Commercial Relations.
    Institute of Soviet and East European Studies,
    Carleton University, Ottawa, Canada. East-West
    Commercial Relations Series, Special Study 1,
    May 1975.
Harvey, Mose L.; Goure, Leon; and Prokofieff, Vladimir.
    Science and Technology as an Instrument of Soviet

Policy. Monographs in International Affairs.
Miami: Center for Advanced International
Studies, University of Miami, 1972.
Hayden, Eric W. Technology Transfer to Eastern
Europe: U.S. Corporate Experience. New York:
Praeger Publishers, 1976.
Hewett, Edward A. "The Economics of East European
Technology Imports from the West." American
Economic Review, IV (May, 1975), 377-82.
Heymann, Hans. We Can Do Business With Russia.
Chicago: Ziff Davis Publishing Company, 1945.
Holzman, Franklyn D. Foreign Trade Under Central
Planning. Cambridge, Mass.: Harvard University
Press, 1974.
_____. International Trade Under Communism--
Politics and Economics. New York: Basic Books,
Inc., Publishers, 1976.
Ivanov, I. "Foreign Trade Factors in the USSR's
Economic Growth and Some Perspectives for the
U.S.-Soviet Economic Cooperation." Report
presented to Conference on U.S.-U.S.S.R.: Prob-
lems and Opportunities. Sponsored by Stanford
Research Institute and Institute of World
Economy and International Relations. Arlington,
Va., April 17-19, 1973.
Kapelinskii, Iu. N. Torgovlia SSSR s kapitalisti-
cheskimi stranami posle vtoroi mirovoi voiny.
Moscow: Izdatel'stvo "Meshdunarodnye
otnosheniia," 1970.
Kas'ianenko, V. I. Bor'ba trudiashchikhsia SSSR
za tekhnicheskuiu nezavisimost' promyshlennosti
(1926-1932 gg.). Moscow: Izdatel'stvo VPSh
and AON, TsK KPSS, 1960.
_____. How Soviet Economy Won Technical Inde-
pendence. Translated by Don Danemanis. Moscow:
Progress Publishers, 1966.
_____. Kak byla zavoevana tekhniko-ekonomicheskaia
samstoiatel'nost' SSSR. Moscow: Izdatel'stvo
sotsialno-ekonomicheskoi literatury, "Mysl',"
1964.
_____. Zavoevanie ekonomicheskoi nezavisimosti
SSSR (1917-1940 gg.) Moscow: Politicheskaia
literatura, 1972.
Kaufman, M. "Itogi i perspektivy vneshnei torgovli."
Planovoe khoziaistvo, April, 1929.
Keller, Werner. East Minus West Equals Zero,
1862-1962. Translated by Constantine Fitzgibbon.
New York: G. P. Putnam's Sons, 1962.
Kindleberger, Charles P. Foreign Trade and the
National Economy. New Haven: Yale University
Press, 1962.

Kiser, John W. III.   "Technology is Not a One-Way
    Street." Foreign Policy, summer, 1976, pp.
    131-148.
Knickerbocker, Hubert R. Fighting the Red Trade
    Menace. New York: Dodd, Mead and Company,
    1931.
Kolomenskii, A. Kak my ispol'zuem zagranichnuiu
    tekhniku. Moscow: Gosudarstvennoe izdatel'stvo,
    1930.
Kosnik, Joseph T. Natural Gas Imports from the
    Soviet Union. New York: Praeger Publishers,
    1975.
Kovan, I. "Leninskii printsip vneshneekonomicheskikh
    otnoshenii sovetskogo gosudarstva." Vneshniaia
    torgovlia, No. 4., 1973.
Krasin, Leonid B. Voprosy vneshnei torgovli.
    Edited by Iu. V. Goldstein and M. Iu. Kaufman.
    2d ed. Moscow: Gosudarstvennoe izdatel'stvo,
    1970.
Kretschmar, Robert S., Jr. and Foor, Robin. The
    Potential for Joint Ventures in Eastern Europe.
    New York: Praeger Publishers, 1972.
Kumykin, P. N. 50 let sovetskoi vneshnei torgovli.
    Moscow: Izdatel'stvo "Mezhdunarodnye otnosheniia,"
    1967.
Kuzbasov, G. A. Rabota profsoiuzov na kontsessionnykh
    predpriiatiiakh. Moscow: Knigoizdatel'stvo,
    VTsSPS, 1929.
Lauter, Geza P., and Dickie, Paul M. Multinational
    Corporations and East European Socialist
    Economies. New York: Praeger Publishers, 1975.
Lenin, Vladimir Il'ich. O vneshneekonomicheskikh
    sviaziakh sovetskogo gosudarstva. Moscow:
    Izdatel'stvo politicheskoi literatury, 1974.
Levine, Herbert S. "An American View of Economic
    Relations with the U.S.S.R." U.S.A.-U.S.S.R.
    Agenda for Communications. Philadelphia,
    American Academy of Political and Social
    Science, 1974. Annals. July, 1974, pp. 1-17.
    _____; Movit, Charles H.; Earle, M. Mark, Jr.:
    and Lieberman, Anne R. Transfer of U.S. Tech-
    nology to the Soviet Union: Impact on U.S.
    Commercial Interests. Prepared for the Depart-
    ment of State. Stanford Research Institute.
    Strategic Studies Center. SRI Project 3543.
    February, 1976.
McMillan, Carl H. Changing Perspectives in East-
    West Commerce. Lexington, Mass.: Lexington
    Books, 1974.
Maksimova, M. M. SSSR i mezhdunarodnoe ekonomicheskoe
    sotrudnichestvo. Moscow: Izdatel'stvo "Mysl',"
    1977.

Manevich, E. "Problemy vosproizvodstva rabochei
    sily i puti uluchsheniia ispol'zovaniia trudovykh
    resursov v SSSR." Voprosy ekonomiki, No. 10,
    1969.
Mansfield, Edwin. "International Technology Transfer:
    Forms, Resource Requirements, and Policies."
    American Economic Review, LV (May, 1975), 372-6.
Mishustin, Dmitrii Dmitrievich. Sotsialisticheskaia
    monopoliia vneshnei torgovli SSSR. Moscow:
    Izdatel'stvo Mezhdunarodnaia kniga, 1938.
_____. ed. Torgovve otnoshenie s kapitalisti-
    cheskimi stranami. Moscow: Mezhdunarodnaia
    kniga, 1938.
_____. Vneshniaia torgovlia i industrializatsiia
    SSSR. Moscow: Mezhdunarodnaia kniga, 1938.
_____. ed. Vneshniaia torgovlia SSSR. 3d ed.
    Moscow: Mezhdunarodnaia kniga, 1941.
Nagorski, Zygmunt, Jr. The Psychology of East-West
    Trade: Illusions and Opportunities. New York:
    Mason and Lipscomb Publishers, 1974.
NATO. Directorate of Economic Affairs. East-West
    Technological Co-Operation: Main Findings of
    a Colloquium held 17th-19th March, 1976.
    Brussels.
Ogarev, V. Iu. "Novye formy ekonomicheskogo sotrud-
    nichestva i sovetsko-amerikanskie otnosheniia."
    SShA: ekonomika, politika, ideologiia.
    February, 1976, pp. 121-27.
Osipov, A. O vosstanovlenii i razvitii mezhdunarodnykh
    ekonomicheskikh sviazei. Moscow: Akademiia
    nauk SSSR, 1952.
Papichev. N. "Regulirovanie pokupok litsenzii i
    nou-khau." Vneshniaia torgovlia, October, 1975,
    pp. 46-50.
Patolichev, Nikolai. USSR Foreign Trade: Past,
    Present and Future. Moscow: Novosti Press
    Agency Publishing House, n.d.
Pavlov, K. P. Rol' gosudarstvennoi monopolii
    vneshnei torgovli v postroenii sotsializma
    v SSSR, 1918-1937. Moscow: Izdatel'stvo
    sotsial'no-ekonomicheskoi literatury, 1960.
Peterson, Peter G. U.S.-Soviet Commercial Relation-
    ships in a New Era. Washington, D.C.: Depart-
    ment of Commerce, August, 1972.
Pisar, Samuel. Coexistence and Commerce: Guidelines
    for Transactions Between East and West. New
    York: McGraw Hill, 1970.
Pozniakov, Vladimir Sergeevich. Gosudarstvennaia
    monopoliia vneshnei torgovli v SSSR. Moscow:
    "Mezhdunarodnye otnosheniia," 1969.

Pryor, Frederick L. The Communist Foreign Trade
    System. Cambridge, Mass.: The M.I.T. Press,
    1963.
Quigley, John. The Soviet Foreign Trade Monopoly:
    Institutions and Laws. n.p.: The Ohio State
    University Press, 1974.
Robinson, H. E. International Business with the
    USSR. Menlo Park, Calif.: Stanford Research
    Institute, 1974.
Rosefielde, Steven. Soviet International Trade in
    Heckscher-Ohlin Perspective: An Input Output
    Study. Lexington, Mass.: Lexington Books,
    1973.
Rozengol'ts, Arkadii Pavlovich. Vneshniaia torgovlia
    i bor'ba za tekhniko-ekonomicheskuiu nezavisimost'
    SSSR. Moscow: Partizdat Tsk VKP(b), 1935.
Rushing, F. W., and Lieberman, Anne. Impact of U.S.
    Foreign Trade and Investment from Commercial
    Transfers of Advanced Technology to the Soviet
    Union and Eastern Europe. Stanford Research
    Institute, Strategic Studies Center, Project 3543,
    1975.
Savelova, I. "Promyshlennoe kooperirovanie mezhdu
    Vostokom i Zapadom." Vneshniaia torgovlia,
    April, 1977, pp. 20-31.
Savost'ianov, V. "Otsenka importnykh mashin i
    oborudovaniia." Planovoe Khoziaistvo, No. 3,
    1975, pp. 78-86.
Schmitt, Matthias. "East-West Cooperation Through
    Coproduction." Aussenpolitik, No. 2, 1973.
    (Translated in Soviet and Eastern European
    Foreign Trade, X (Spring, 1974), 80-98.
Seleznyov, G. Trade: A Key to Peace and Progress.
    Moscow: Progress Publishers, 1966.
Shatkhan, A. S. Vneshniaia torgovlia v 5-letke.
    Moscow: Gosudarstvennoe izdatel'stvo, 1930.
Shmelev, N. P., ed. Ekonomicheskie sviazi vostok-
    zapad: problemy i vozmozhnosti. Moscow:
    Izdatel'stvo "Mysl'," 1976.
_____. "Mirnoe sosushchestvovanie i ekonomicheskoe
    sotrudnichestvo." Mirovaia ekonomika i
    mezhdunarodnoe otnosheniia. April, 1976,
    pp. 26-36.
_____. "Promyshlennoe i nauchno-tekhnicheskoe
    sotrudnichestvo Evropeiskikh, stran." Voprosy
    ekonomiki, June, 1977, pp. 79-89.
_____. "Scope for Industrial, Scientific and
    Technical Cooperation between East and West."
    Paper presented at the International Economic
    Association Conference, Dresden, German Demo-
    cratic Republic, July, 1976.

Simmons, Michael. "Western Technology and the Soviet Economy." The World Today, XXXI (April, 1975), 166-72.

Skvortsov-Stepanov, Ivan Ivanovich. Ob innostrannykh kontsessiiakh. Moscow: Gosudarstvennoe izdatel'stvo, 1920.

Smeliakov, N. N. "Business Meetings: Comments by the Deputy Minister of Foreign Trade." Novyi Mir, December, 1973, pp. 207-239. (Translated by Joint Publications Research Service, 61148. Translations on USSR Trade and Services, No. 652, February 5, 1974, pp. 1-53.)

_____. S chego nachinaetsia rodina. Moscow: Izdatel'stvo politicheskoi literatury, 1975.

Smith, Glen Alden. Soviet Foreign Trade: Organization, Operations and Policy, 1918-1971. New York: Praeger, 1973.

Starr, Robert, ed. East-West Business Transactions. New York: Praeger, 1974.

Stowell, Christopher E. Soviet Industrial Import Priorities: With Marketing Considerations for Exporting to the USSR. New York: Praeger Publishers, 1975.

Sushkov, V. N. "Dolgosrochnoe torgovo-promyshlennoe sotrudnichestvo SSSR s razvitymi kapitalisticheskimi stranami na kompensatsionnoi osnoz." Vneshniaia torgovlia, May, 1977, pp. 17-22.

_____. "O torgovo-ekonomicheskom sotrudnichestve s kapitalisticheskimi stranami v stroitel'stvo v SSSR krupnykh promyshlennykh ob"ektov." Vneshniaia torgovlia, February, 1976, pp. 8-11.

Sutton, Anthony C. Western Technology and Soviet Economic Development. Volume I: 1917-1930. Stanford: Hoover Institution Press, 1968. Volume II: 1930-1945. Stanford: Hoover Institution Press, 1971. Volume III: 1945-1964. Stanford: Hoover Institution Press, 1973.

"Technology Exchange with the USSR." Research Management, XVII (July, 1974), 7-20.

Thomas, John R. and Ursula M. Kruse-Vaucienne. Soviet Science and Technology: Domestic and Foreign Perspectives. Based on a workshop held at Airlie House, Virginia on November 18-21, 1976. Washington, D.C.: The George Washington University, 1977.

Timofeyev, V. "Leninist Principles Underlying the Structure and Management of Foreign Trade." Foreign Trade, December, 1969, pp. 2-9.

Tsaguriia, M. Osvoenie novykh predpriiatii i novoi tekhniki v tiazheloi promyshlennosti. Moscow: Ob"edinennoe nauchno-tekhnicheskoe izdatel'stvo, 1934.

USSR. Ministerstvo vneshnei torgovli. <u>Vneshniaia</u>
<u>torgovlia SSSR: statisticheskii sbornik,</u>
<u>1918-1966</u>. Moscow: Izdatel'stvo "Mezhdunarodnye
otnosheniia," 1967.
_____. <u>Vneshniaia torgovlia za   god, statisti-</u>
cheskii obzor. Moscow: Vneshtorgizdat, 1960.
_____. <u>Vneshniaia torgovlia SSSR za 1918-1940 gg.:</u>
<u>statisticheskii obzor</u>. Moscow: Vneshtorgizdat,
1960.
_____. Tsentral'noe statisticheskoe upravlenie.
<u>Narodnoe khoziaistvo SSSR v   g.: statisti-</u>
<u>cheskii ezhegodnik</u>. Moscow: Izdatel'stvo
"Statistika."
_____. Vsesoiuznaia torgovaia palata. <u>Sovetskie</u>
<u>vneshnetorgovye organizatsii</u>. Moscow:
Vneshtorgizdat, 1970.
United Nations. Economic Commission for Europe.
<u>Analytical Report on Industrial Cooperation</u>
<u>among ECE Countries</u>. (E/ECE/844/Rev. 1)
Geneva, 1973.
_____. Industrial Development Organization.
<u>Business Organization and the Transfer of Tech-</u>
<u>nology: Experience of the Soviet Union</u>, by
Alexander Woroniak. Ad-hoc Meeting of Experts
on the Role of Advanced Skills and Technologies
in Industrial Development. New York, May 22-29,
1967.
_____. Institute for Training and Research.
<u>Soviet Experience in Transfer of Technology to</u>
<u>Industrially Less Developed Countries</u>, by
A. N. Bykov, M. P. Strepetova and A. V. Letenko.
UNITAR Research Reports, No. 15. New York, 1973.
U.S. Central Intelligence Agency. <u>Soviet Commercial</u>
<u>Operations in the West</u>. (ER 77-10486).
Washington, D.C., September, 1977.
U.S. Congress. House. Committee on Foreign Affairs.
Subcommittee on National Security Policy and
Scientific Developments. <u>U.S.-Soviet Commercial</u>
<u>Relations: the Interplay of Economics, Tech-</u>
<u>nology Transfer and Diplomacy</u>, by John P. Hardt
and George D. Holliday. Committee Print.
Washington, D.C.: Government Printing Office,
June 10, 1973.
_____. Committee on International Relations.
Subcommittee on International Security and
Scientific Affairs. <u>Technology Transfer and</u>
<u>Scientific Cooperation Between the United States</u>
<u>and the Soviet Union: A Review</u>, by the Con-
gressional Research Service, Library of Congress.
Committee Print. Washington, D.C.: Government
Printing Office, May 26, 1977.

U.S. Congress. House. Committee on Science and
Astronautics. The Technology Balance: U.S.-
U.S.S.R. Advanced Technology Transfer. Hearings
before the Subcommittee on International Coop-
eration in Science and Space. 93d Cong., 1st
sess. December 4-6, 1973. Washington, D.C.:
Government Printing Office, 1974.
_____. Committee on Ways and Means. Soviet
Imports of Manufactured Goods from the Industrial
West: An Econometric Forecast. Special Report
to the Congress and the East-West Foreign
Trade Board by the U.S. International Trade
Commission. Committee Print. Washington, D.C.:
Government Printing Office, 1976.
_____. Senate. Committee on Foreign Relations.
A Background Study on East-West Trade. Committee
Print. Washington, D.C.: Government Printing
Office, 1965.
_____. Committee on Foreign Relations. Subcommit-
tee on Multinational Corporations. Western
Investment in Communist Economics. A Selected
Survey on Economic Interdependence, by John P.
Hardt, George D. Holliday and Young C. Kim.
Committee Print. Washington, D.C.: Government
Printing Office, August 5, 1974.
U.S. Department of Commerce. US/USSR Technology
Licensing Prospects, 1973. Summary Report of
U.S. Delegation Visit to U.S.S.R. for Study of
Soviet Management and Licensing Practices.
September, 1973.
_____. Proceedings of the East-West Technological
Trade Symposium. Washington, D.C., November 19,
1975. (National Technical Information Service
publication no. PB-251-383.
_____. Bureau of East-West Trade. "Impact of
Compensation Agreements on Soviet Exports
Through 1980." Unpublished paper, January 18,
1977.
Vaganov, B. S. Organizatsiia i tekhnika vneshnei
torgovli SSSR i drugikh sotsialisticheskikh
stran. Moscow: Izdatel'stvo IMO, 1963.
Vainshtein, V. and Takhnenko, R. "Kompensatsionnye
soglasheniia i voprosy effektivnosti."
Mirovaia ekonomika i mezhdunarodnye otnosheniia,
May, 1974, pp. 95-192.
Vishnevskii, Ie. S., and Cherkasov, N. A. "Eksport
i rentabil'nost' proizvodstva. Reforma stavit
problemy. Edited by N. K. Szaanovich. Moscow:
Izdatel'stvo "Ekonomika," 1968.
Voinov, A. "Dolgosrochnoe ekonomicheskoe sotrudnichestvo sotsialisticheskikh i promyshlenno

217

razvitykh kapitalisticheskikh stran." Planovoe
khoziaistvo, May, 1974, pp. 78-87.
Volynets-Russet, E. Ia. Planirovanie i raschet
effektivnosti priobreteniia litsenzii. Moscow:
"Ekonomika," 1973.
Voronov, K. G., and Pavlov, K. A. Organizatsiia i
tekhnika vneshnei torgovli. Moscow:
Mezhdunarodnye otnosheniia, 1970.
Wasowski, Stanislaw, ed. East-West Trade and the
Technology Gap: A Political and Economic
Appraisal. New York: Praeger Publishers, 1970.
Watstein, Joseph. "The Role of Foreign Trade of
Financing Soviet Modernization. American
Journal of Economics and Sociology, July, 1970,
pp. 305-319.
_____. "Soviet Economic Concessions: The Agony
and the Promise." ACES Bulletin, XVI (Spring,
1974).
White, Edward P. U.S./U.S.S.R. Technology and
Patents: Sale and License Prospects. n.p.:
Licensing Executives Society (U.S.A.), Inc.,
1974.
Wilczynski, Jozef. The Economics and Politics of
East-West Trade. New York: Frederick A.
Praeger, Publishers, 1969.
_____. Joint East-West Ventures and Rights of
Ownership. Institute of Soviet and East
European Studies, Carleton University. East-
West Commercial Relations Series. Working
Paper no. 6. Ottawa, Canada, October, 1975.
_____. The Multinationals and East-West Rela-
tions. Boulder, Colorado: Westview Press, 1976.
Wiles, P. J. D. Communist International Economics.
New York: Frederick A. Praeger, Publishers, 1969.
Wolf, Thomas A. U.S. East-West Trade Policy:
Economic Warfare Versus Economic Welfare.
Lexington, Mass.: Lexington Books, 1973.
Wolynski, Alexander. Western Economic Aid to the
U.S.S.R. The Institute for the Study of
Conflict. Conflict Studies Special Report,
no. 72. London: The Eastern Press, Ltd., 1976.
Zatsarinskii, A. P., ed. Ekonomicheskie otnosheniia
SSSR s zarubezhnymi stranami 1917-1967.
Moscow: Mezhdunarodnye otnosheniia, 1967.
Zav'ialov, P. S. Nauchno-tekhnicheskaia revoliutsiia
i mezhdunarodnaia spetsializatsiia proizvodstva
pri kapitalisme. Moscow: Izdatel'stvo "Mysl',"
1974.

Soviet Automotive Industry

Aleshina, Polina, et al. Gor'kovskii avtomobil'nyi,
    ocherk istorii zavoda. Moscow, Profizdat. 1964.
Amtorg Trading Corporation. Economic Review of the
    Soviet Union, July 1, and November 15, 1929.
Arbatov, G. "Proektirovanie organizatsii krupnykh
    proizvodstevenno-khoziaistvennykh kompleksov
    i upravleniia imi." Planovoe khoziaistvo,
    May, 1975, pp. 18-27.
Barry, Donald D. "Russians and Their Cars." Survey,
    October, 1965, pp. 98-110.
Barun, V. N. KamAZ-novoe semeistvo avtomobilei i
    avtopoezdov. Novoe v zhizni, nauke, tekhnike,
    No. 9, 1975. Seriia transport. Moscow:
    Izdatel'stvo "Znanie," 1975.
Batyr na Kame: ocherki, stat'i, interv'iu, reportazhi,
    statistika, fotodokumenty o stanovlenii Kamskogo
    Avtomobil'nogo kompleksa. God 1971. Kasan':
    Tatarskoe Knizhnoe izdatel'stvo, 1972.
Baxter, William P. "The Soviet Passenger Car Industry."
    Survey, IXX (summer, 1973), 218-40.
Beliaev, R. K. KamAZ: Formirovanie trudovogo
    kollektiva. Moscow: Profizdat, 1975.
"Bendix Breaks Ground in Trade with Russia." Business
    Week, January 31, 1977.
Bogatko, S. A. KamAZ--zvezda pervoi velichiny.
    Moscow: Stroiizdat, 1975.
Buffa, V. "Economic and Commercial Cooperation
    Between East and West: Joint Ventures, Coop-
    eration Agreements and other Forms of Commercial
    Relations." Speech delivered in New York on
    November 3, 1973.
Carver, Walter L. "Amo and Nizhni-Novgorod Plants
    Lead Soviet Vehicle Plans." Automotive Indus-
    tries, LXVI (March 5, 1932), 375-78.
_____. "Tractor is King in Soviet Russia, Lead-
    ing Huge Automotive Plans." Automotive Indus-
    tries, LXVI (March 5, 1932), 375-78.
"The Challenge of Soviet Industry." Automotive
    Industries, CXVII (January 1, 1958), 48-108.
Chase World Information Corporation. KamAZ, the
    Billion Dollar Beginning. New York, 1974.
Chudakov, Evgenii Alekseevich. Dostizheniia
    otechestvennoi tekhniki v mashinostroenii.
    Moscow: Izdatel'stvo "Znanie," 1951.
_____. "Problemy avtotransporta." Sotsialisti-
    cheskaia rekonstruktsiia i nauka, No. 2-3,
    1931, pp. 140-68.
_____. Razvitie avtomobilestroeniia v SSSR.
    Moscow: Gosplanizdat, 1948.

219

Chudakov, Evgenii Alekseevich. "Razvitie dinamicheskikh kachestv avtomobilia." <u>Sotsialisti-
cheskaia rekonstruktsiia i nauka</u>, No. 3, 1936,
pp. 28-91.
Churbanov, V., and Franiuk, V. <u>Utro KamAZa</u>.
Moscow: Molodaia gvardiia, 1974.
Counts, George S. <u>A Ford Crosses Soviet Russia</u>.
Boston: The Stratford Company, 1930.
Dalrymple, Dana G. "The American Tractor Comes
to Soviet Agriculture: The Transfer of Tech-
nology." <u>Technology and Culture</u>, V (spring,
1964), 191-214.
The Economist Intelligence Unit, Ltd. <u>Rubber and
the Automotive Industry in the USSR</u>. EIU
Special Report No. 28, London, December, 1976.
Edwards, Imogene U. "Automotive Trends in the
U.S.S.R." <u>Soviet Economic Prospects for the
Seventies</u>. U.S. Congress. Joint Economic
Committee. Washington, D.C.: Government
Printing Office, June 27, 1973, pp. 291-314.
_____. "The Passenger Car Industries of Eastern
Europe." <u>Economic Developments in Countries
of Eastern Europe</u>. U.S. Congress. Joint
Economic Committee on Foreign Economic Policy.
Joint Committee Print. Washington, D.C.:
Government Printing Office, 1970, pp. 316-328.
_____, and Fraser, Robert. "The Internationali-
zation of the East European Automotive Indus-
tries." <u>East-European Economies Post-Helsinki</u>.
U.S. Congress. Joint Economic Committee. Joint
Committee Print. Washington, D.C.: Government
Printing Office, August 25, 1977, pp. 396-419.
Ford, Henry. "Why I Am Helping Russian Industry."
Interview with William A. McGarry. <u>Nation's
Business</u>, June, 1930, pp. 20-23.
Fursov, V. C.; Katsura, P. M.; and Perevalov, Iu. N.
<u>Vnutrizavodskoi khozraschet na Volzhskom
Avtomobil'nom</u>. Moscow: "Mashinostroenie,"
1976.
Gicquiau, Herve, <u>et al</u>. "L'industrie Automobile en
URSS et en Europe Orientale." <u>Le Courier des
Pays de l'Est</u>, January, 1976, No. 192, pp. E3-
E53; Part II, March, 1977, No. 205, pp. 3-27.
Globokar, Tatjana. <u>Motorisierung in den osteuro-
paischen Landern</u>. Deutsches Institut fur
Wirtschaftsforschung, Institut fur Konjunktur-
forschung, Sonderhefte, No. 84. Berlin:
Duncker & Humblot, 1969.
Gol'd, B. V. "K voprosu o razvitii perspektivnogo
tipazha Sovetskikh avtobilei. <u>Voprosy
mashinovedeniia: sbornik statei posviashchennyi</u>

Granick, David. "Organization and Technology in
     Soviet Metalworking: Some Conditioning Factors."
     American Economic Review, XLVII, (May, 1957),
     631-642.
Guthart, A. "L'Automobile en R.R.S.S. et les
     principaux itineraraires routiers." Notes et
     Etudes Documentaires, Nos. 3720-3721, September
     25, 1970.
Hindus, Maurice. "Henry Ford Conquers Russia."
     The Outlook, CXXVI (June 29, 1927), 280-83.
Hinks-Edwards, Michael, and Sobral, Manuel. The
     Communist Bloc Automobile Industry: Implica-
     tions for Western Manufacturers. n.p.: Euro
     Economics, 1975.
Hunter, Holland. "The Soviet Transport Sector."
     New Directions in the Soviet Economy. Part
     II-B: Economic Performance. U.S. Congress.
     Joint Economic Committee. Joint Committee
     Print. Washington, D.C.: Government Printing
     Office, 1966, pp. 569-91.
Ikonnikov, Igor' Sergeevich. Avtomobili: proizvodstvo
     i vneshniaia torgovlia kapitalisticheskikh
     stran. Moscow: Vneshtorgizdat, 1962.
Iurkovskii, I. M., and Tolpygin, V. A. Avtomobil'
     KamAZ: ustroistvo, tekhnicheskoe obsluzhivanie,
     ekspluatatsiia. Moscow: Izdatel'stvo DOSAAF,
     1975.
Ivanov, V. N. Tekhnicheskii progress i avtomobili-
     zatsiia. Moscow: Izdatel'stvo "znanie," 1970.
Katsura, P. M. "Ekonomicheskie metody upravleniia
     proizvodstvennym ob"edineniem 'AvtoVaz'."
     Planovoe khoziaistvo, January, 1977, pp. 78-89.
_____, and Mescheriakova, M. N. Novye formy
     organizatsii promyshlennogo proizvodstva
     (opyt VAZa). Moscow: Izdatel'stvo "Ekonomika,"
     1974.
Khromov, P. A., ed. Proizvoditel'nost' truda v
     promyshlennosti SSSR. Moscow: Gosplanizdat,
     1940.
Kosygin, A. N. "Povyshenie nauchnoi obosnovannosti
     planov--vazhneishaia zadacha planovykh organov."
     Planovoe khoziaistvo, April, 1965, pp. 3-10.
Kramer, John M. "Soviet Policy towards the Automo-
     bile." Survey, spring, 1976, pp. 16-35.
Lavrovskii, B. V. Tsifry i fakty za 15 let po
     avtostroeniiu v SSSR. Moscow: Gosudarstvennoe
     aviatsionnoe i avtotraktornoe izdatel'stvo,
     1932.
Lipgart, A. A. Perspektivnyi tipazh avtomobilei i
     dvigatelei dlia proizvodstva v SSSR. Moscow:
     Moskovskii dom nauchno-tekhnicheskoi propagandy
     imeni F. E. Dzerzhinskogo, 1957.

Lipgart, A. A. "Razvitie konstruktsii avtomobilei
zavoda im. V. M. Molotova." Voprosy mashino-
vedeniia: sbornik statei posviashchennyi
shestideciatiletiu Akademika E. A. Chudakova.
Moscow, Institut Mashinovedeniia, Akademiia Nauk
SSSR, 1950.
Matveev, S. "Perspectivy razvitiia avtomobil'noi
promyshlennosti v novom piatiletii." Planovoe
Khoziaistvo, July, 1966.
Mertts, L. et al. "GAZ i 'Ford'." Planovoe
khoziaistvo, No. 7, 1932.
Meyer, Herbert E. "A Plant that Could Change the
Shape of Soviet Industry." Fortune, November,
1974, pp. 148-57, 229-31.
_____. "What It's Like to Do Business with the
Russians." Fortune, May, 1972, pp. 167-9,
234-8.
Mil'ner, B. Z. "On the Organization of Management."
Kommunist, February, 1975, pp. 38-47. Trans-
lated by Joint Publications Research Service,
64452. Translations from Kommunist, No. 3,
February, 1975, pp. 45-57.
_____, ed. Organizatsionnye struktury upravleniia
proizvodstvom. Moscow: Izdatel'stvo "Ekonomika,"
1975.
Nevins, Allan, and Hill, Frank Ernest. Ford:
Expansion and Challenge. Volume 2: 1915-1933.
New York: Charles Scribner's Sons, 1957.
Osinskii, N. "Novyi Ford v Amerikanskoi i nashei
obstanovke." Za rulem, no. 9-10, May, 1932.
Papkovskii, V. "Kakogo tipa legkovye avtomobili
nam nuzhny." Kommunist, XXXVI, no. 14, 1959.
Petrov, G. P. Sovremennye legkovye avtomobili.
Moscow: Izdatel'stvo "Znanie," 1972.
Safrai, Gertruda Efimovna. Finansy avtomobil'nogo
transporta. Moscow: Transport, 1970.
Schaum, Jack H. "Kamaz Foundry--U.S.A. on Display."
Modern Casting, March, 1976, pp. 42-55.
Selifonov, V. Ia. Avtomobil'naia promyshlennost'
SSSR v 1959-1965. Moscow: Nauka i tekhnika,
1959.
Sharyi V. "Piatiletnii plan transporta." Ekonomi-
cheskoe obozrenie, No. 7, July 1929, pp. 81-92.
Shupliakov, Sergei Ivanovich. Avtomobil'nyi trans-
port sotsialisticheskikh stran-chlenov SEV.
Moscow: Transport, 1968.
Smith, Hedrick. "The Russian Auto Market: No Trade-
ins, no Imports, no Options, and You Pay Now,
Drive Later." New York Times Magazine, October
8, 1972, pp. 18-20, 24, 30, 35-36, 38, 40, 42,
44, 45, 50.

Solov'ev, Vladimir Sergeevich. Massovyi sovetskii
    avtomobil'. Moscow: Izdatel'stvo "Znanie,"
    1970.
Sorenson, Charles E. (With Samuel T. Williams).
    My Forty Years With Ford. New York: W. W.
    Norton and Company, Inc., 1956.
Sorokin, M. "Ob avtomobilizatsiia Soiuza."
    Ekonomicheskoe obozrenie, No. 7, July 1929,
    pp. 23-100.
_____. Za avtomobilizatsiiu SSSR. Moscow:
    Moskovskii rabochii, 1928.
Stingel, Donald E. Speech at George Washington
    University, Washington, D.C., February 25,
    1975.
Sushkov, V. N. "Sotrudnichestvo s firmoi 'FIAT'
    rasshiriaetsia." Interview in Vneshniaia
    torgovlia, No. 8, 1966.
Tarasov, Aleksandr Mikhailovich. Avtomobil'naia
    promyshlennost'--narodnomu khoziaistvu.
    Moscow: Mashinostroenie, 1971.
_____, et al., eds. Avtomobilestroenie SSSR.
    Moscow: Nauchno-issledovatel'skii institut
    informatsii Avtomobil'noi promyshlennosti
    NIINavtoprom, 1967.
Troitskii, M. "Na novom etape." Novyi mir,
    January, 1975, pp. 169-79.
U.S. Congress. House. Committee on Banking and
    Currency. Subcommittee on International Trade.
    The Fiat-Soviet Auto Plant and Communist
    Economic Reforms. Committee Print. Washington,
    D.C.: Government Printing Office, 1967.
U.S. Department of Commerce. Bureau of the Census.
    Foreign Manpower Research Office. Manpower
    Utilization in the Soviet Automobile Industry,
    by Barney K. Schwalberg. International Popu-
    lation Reports, Series P-95, No. 53, June,
    1959.
U.S. Department of the Air Force: Air Staff,
    Directorate of Intelligence. Industrial Planning
    in the USSR: the Automotive Industry as a
    Typical Branch of the Category of Machine
    Building. Washington, D.C., February, 1954.
U.S.S.R. Tsentral'noe Upravlenie Mestnogo Transporta
    NKPS. Avtotransport SSSR. Moscow: Transpechat',
    1929.
Vasil'ev, V. M. Sto dnei u Forda. Moscow: Izdatel'stvo
    MGSPS "Trud i Kniga." 1927.
Vavilov, M. V. et al. Avtostroi: analiz organizatsii
    stroitel'stva Gor'kovskogo Avtozavoda im. t.
    Molotova. Moscow: Glavnaia redaktsiia
    stroitel'noi literatury, 1934.

Velikanov, D. P. Razvitie avtomobil'nykh transportnykh
    sredstv v 1959-1965 gg. Moscow: Nauchno-
    tekhnicheskoe izdatel'stvo avtomobil'nogo
    transporta i shosseinykh dorog RSFSR, 1960.
    _____. "Razvitie konstruktsii avtomobilei v
    usloviiakh sotsialisticheskoi ekonomiki Sovetskogo
    Soiuza." Voprosy mashinovedeniia: sbornik
    statei posviashchennyi shestideciatiletiu
    Akademika E. A. Chudakova. Institut Mashino-
    vedeniia, Akademiia nauk SSSR, Moscow, 1950,
    pp. 69-89.
    _____, and Sorokin, B. D. Problemy avtomobilizatsiia.
    Moscow: Izdatel'stvo "Znanie," 1976.
Vlasov, B. V., et al. Ekonomicheskie problemy
    proizvodstva avtomobilei. Moscow: Mashinostroenie,
    1971.
"Volzhskii Avtomobil'nyi Zavod." Ekonomika i
    organizatsiia promyshlennogo proizvodstva,
    January, 1976, pp. 47-220.
Vvedensky, G. A. "The Soviet Passenger Automobile
    Industry." Bulletin of the Institute for the
    Study of the USSR, XVI (June, 1969), 31-35.
Zamozikin, U. A.; Zhilina, L. N.; and Frolova, N. I.
    "Sdvigi v massovom potreblenii i lichnost'.
    Voprosy filosofii, (June, 1969).

Periodicals, Newspapers and
Newsletters Frequently Consulted

A. Western

    The Association for Comparative Economic Studies
        Bulletin
    Automotive Industries
    Business Eastern Europe
    Le Courier des Pays de l'Est (Paris)
    Current Digest of the Soviet Press
    Eastern Europe Report
    Eastwest Markets
    Moscow Narodny Bank. Press Bulletin
    New York Times
    Radio Liberty Research Bulletin
    The Reuter East-West Trade News
    Soviet and Eastern European Foreign Trade
    Soviet Business and Trade
    Washington Post

B. Soviet

    Avtomobil'naia promyshlennost'